Practical Authority

Practical Authority
Agency and Institutional Change in Brazilian Water Politics

Rebecca Neaera Abers

and

Margaret E. Keck

OXFORD
UNIVERSITY PRESS

Oxford University Press is a department of the University of Oxford.
It furthers the University's objective of excellence in research, scholarship,
and education by publishing worldwide.

Oxford   New York
Auckland   Cape Town   Dar es Salaam   Hong Kong   Karachi
Kuala Lumpur   Madrid   Melbourne   Mexico City   Nairobi
New Delhi   Shanghai   Taipei   Toronto

With offices in
Argentina   Austria   Brazil   Chile   Czech Republic   France   Greece
Guatemala   Hungary   Italy   Japan   Poland   Portugal   Singapore
South Korea   Switzerland   Thailand   Turkey   Ukraine   Vietnam

Oxford is a registered trademark of Oxford University Press
in the UK and certain other countries.

Published in the United States of America by
Oxford University Press
198 Madison Avenue, New York, NY 10016

Library of Congress Cataloging-in-Publication Data
Abers, Rebecca.
Practical authority : agency and institutional change in Brazilian
water politics / Rebecca Neaera Abers, Margaret E. Keck.
pages cm
Summary: "New institutions don't come into being by themselves: They have to be organized. On the
basis of research from a decade-long, multi-site study of efforts to transform freshwater management
in Brazil, Practical Authority asks how new institutional arrangements established by law become
operational in practice"—Provided by publisher.
ISBN 978-0-19-998526-5 (hardback)—ISBN 978-0-19-998527-2 (paperback)
1. Water-supply—Brazil—Management.   2. Water-supply—Political aspects—Brazil.
3. Water resources development—Political aspects—Brazil.   4. Hydrology—Brazil.
5. Fresh water—Brazil.   6. Brazil—Politics and government—1985–2002.
I. Keck, Margaret E. II.
Title.
TD241.A1A34 2013
333.9100981—dc23
2013003846

We dedicate this book to our children, Nina, Thomas, Laura, and Melissa

CONTENTS

ACKNOWLEDGMENTS

Writing books, like building institutions, is a slow and messy process that depends on the help of very many people. In this case, their numbers are especially large. The ideas that went into this book began to germinate more than 12 years ago with the creation of the Watermark Project, the idea for which grew out of discussions with Rosa Maria Formiga Johnsson and Gerôncio Albuquerque Rocha and spread to include many more. Dozens of people participated in the project's research, and hundreds more have collaborated. Many of them have shared information and insights, some repeatedly; some have become friends. People involved in and outside of water management reform, in Brazil and elsewhere, have taken an interest in what we were doing and encouraged us to do more. We cannot possibly thank all of them individually, but we are deeply grateful to all of them.

A small group of women who became the core of the Watermark Project during most of its duration were our soul mates and helped to formulate some of the central ideas in this book, especially Rosa Formiga Johnsson, Beate Frank, and Manuela Moreira. Our thinking was also influenced by the many long conversations we had with Maria Carmen Lemos, Vanessa Empinotti, Ricardo Gutiérrez, Rosa Mancini, Rosana Garjulli, Gerôncio Rocha, Wilde Cardoso, Oscar Cordeiro, and Bruno Pagnoccheschi.

Paula Lopes, Karina Jorge, and Nilda Matos provided crucial operational support for the research process, besides doing research themselves. Ana Karine Pereira conducted dozens of interviews for us in the field. Cristina Saliba and Jackson de Toni also conducted interviews. Paula Lopes kindly supplied us with the tapes of her interviews from the Piracicaba basin. Yehonatan Abramson commented on the work and helped us format the manuscript and bibliography. Mimi Abers and Ruy Lucas de Souza helped with figures and the map.

The detailed comments we received from people who read conference papers and chapters have been crucial for honing our ideas and thinking of new and, we hope, better ones. We are grateful to Adrian Gurza Lavalle, Alex Livingston, Alison Post, Anna Gruben, Bill Connolly, Brian Wampler, Chris Ansell, Clovis Henrique de Souza, Erin Chung, Evelina

Dagnino, Frank Fischer, Jan French, Jessica Rich, Kathryn Hochstetler, Kellee Tsai, Ken Conca, Leonardo Avritzer, Lindsay Mayka, Luciana Tatagiba, Marilia Oliveira, Marisa von Bülow, Michael McCarthy, Mike Savage, Patrick Laigneau, Paul Steinberg, Peter Evans, Ricardo Gutiérrez, Richard Katz, Roger Haydon, Ruth Collier, Wendy Wofford, and the anonymous reviewers of our manuscript. Kent Eaton read and commented on the entire manuscript carefully at a crucial moment. For countless thought-provoking comments, we also thank participants in the Berkeley Comparative Politics Seminar, the University of São Paulo Political Science Seminar Program, the Johns Hopkins Political Science Departmental Seminar, the Berkeley Environment Seminar, the closing conference of Berkeley's Green Governance Project, the workshop on "Intimate Ethnographies of the Brazilian State" at Cornell University, the Haller Lecture at the University of Wisconsin, the Bellagio workshop on Rethinking Representation, and conference panels at the Latin American Studies Association (LASA), the American Political Science Association (APSA), the Brazilian Political Science Association (ABCP), and the Brazilian Association for Research on Society and the Environment (ANPPAS).

A great many graduate students, at our own universities and others, in Brazil and in the United States, contributed mightily to the energy and freshness of the discussions of this material, to say nothing of the base of information underpinning it. We thank all of them, collectively.

Abers would like to thank the Political Science Institute at the University of Brasília for giving her a leave in which she could work on this book and the political science department at the University of California, Berkeley, for a warm reception during the same leave. Margaret Keck would like to thank the political science department at Johns Hopkins University for its intellectual heft and heterodoxy, and Mary Otterbein and Lisa Williams for their patience and unfailing administrative support.

Our research depended on a substantial amount of funding for which we are very thankful. Abers received postdoctoral fellowships from the National Science Foundation (Grant 0107314) and from the Coordenação para o Aperfeiçoamento de Pessoal de Ensino Superior (CAPES), Ministry of Education, Brazil. During the initial phase of project formulation, Keck was a fellow at the Woodrow Wilson International Center for Scholars in Washington, D.C., and benefited from the assistance of its staff and the stimulation of its collegial atmosphere. Keck also benefited from a grant from the National Oceanic and Atmospheric Administration (NOAA) shared with Maria Carmen Lemos of the University of Michigan's School of Natural Resources. Abers and Keck together received a research and writing grant from the John D. and Catherine T. MacArthur Foundation

(Grant 04-83053-000-GSS). The Watermark Project received funding from the John D. and Catherine T. MacArthur Foundation, the Johns Hopkins University Center for a Livable Future, and the William and Flora Hewlett Foundation U.S.–Latin American Relations Program (Grant 2002-7539); two grants from the Fundo Setorial de Recursos Hídricos (CTHIDRO), of Brazil's Ministry of Science and Technology (MCT/CNPq); and support from the Luce Green Governance Project at UC, Berkeley. These funds have supported the research of a great many people besides ourselves.

Some friends and colleagues were especially important for encouraging us along the way, holding our hands at difficult moments, and keeping us from giving up, especially Marisa von Bülow and Kathy Hochstetler.

Abers would particularly like to thank her parents, Mimi, Ernest, and Sylvia, for giving her shelter, good food, and ideas during hard moments of writing, and her husband and children, Alberto, Thomas, and Nina, for keeping her heart beating. Keck is grateful to her husband and children, Larry, Melissa, and Laura, for the same and also for pushing us to get this finished. She also thanks her parents and her extended family of siblings and partners, John, David, Terry, Theresa, George, Jason, Anne, Jenny, and Maureen, for being in her life.

Finally, we stand on the shoulders of all the scholars and activists who have given us a bias for hope, starting with Albert Hirschman, who coined the term.

LIST OF ABBREVIATIONS

ABC (or ABCD)   the cluster of industrial cities in the southern suburbs of the Greater São Paulo Metropolitan Region, Santo André, São Bernardo do Campo, São Caetano, Diadema, and others

ABRH   Associação Brasileira de Recursos Hídricos (Brazilian Water Resources Association)

AGEVAP   Associação Pró-Gestão das Águas da Bacia do Rio Paraíba do Sul (Association for the Management of the Waters of the Paraiba do Sul Basin)

ANA   Agência Nacional de Águas (National Water Agency)

ASEP   Agência Reguladora de Serviços Públicos Concedidos (Regulatory Agency for Public Service Concessions), Rio de Janeiro

CBHSF   Comitê de Bacia Hidrográfica do São Francisco (São Francisco River Basin Committee)

CEDAE   Companhia Estadual de Águas e Esgotos (State Water and Sanitation Company), Rio de Janeiro

CEEIBH   Comitê Especial de Estudos Integrados de Bacias Hidrográficas (Special Committee for Integrated Studies of River Basins)

CEIVAP   Comitê de Integração da Bacia Hidrográfica do Paraíba do Sul (Committee for the Integration of the Paraíba do Sul River Basin)

CETESB   Companhia de Tecnologia de Saneamento Ambiental (Environmental Sanitation Technology Company), São Paulo

CNBB   Conferência Nacional dos Bispos do Brasil (Nacional Conference of Brazilian Bishops)

CNPq   Conselho Nacional de Desenvolvimento Científico e Tecnológico (National Council for Scientific and Technological Development)

CNRH	Conselho Nacional de Recursos Hídricos (National Water Resources Council)
CODEVASF	Companhia de Desenvolvimento do Vale do São Francisco (São Francisco Valley Development Company)
COGERH	Companhia de Gestão de Recursos Hídricos (Water Resources Management Company), Ceará
COMUA	Comissão Municipal de Usuário de Água (Municipal Commission of Water Users)
COPPE	Instituto Alberto Luiz Coimbra de Pós-Graduação e Pesquisa de Engenharia (Albert Luiz Coimbra Graduate and Research Institute in Engineering), Federal University of Rio de Janeiro
CORHI	Comitê Coordenador do Plano Estadual de Recursos Hídricos e Sistema Estadual de Gestão de Recursos Hídricos (Coordinating Commission of the State Water Resources Plan and State Water Resources System), São Paulo
CPLA	Coordenadoria de Planejamento Ambiental (Office of Environmental Planning), São Paulo Secretariat of Environment
CVSF	Comissão do Vale do São Francisco (São Francisco Valley Commission)
DAEE	Departamento de Águas e Energia Elétrica (Department of Water and Electrical Energy), São Paulo
DFID	Department for International Development, United Kingdom
DNAEE	Departamento Nacional de Águas e Energia Elétrica (National Department of Water and Electrical Energy), Ministry of Mines and Energy
DNOCS	Departamento Nacional de Obras Contra as Secas (National Department for Public Works against Drought)
DNOS	Departamento Nacional de Obras de Saneamento (National Department of Sanitation Works)
DOU	Departamento de Organização dos Usuários (Department of User Organization) of COGERH
FEHIDRO	Fundo Estadual de Recursos Hídricos (State Water Resources Fund), São Paulo

FUNDAP	Fundação do Desenvolvimento Administrativo (Public Administration Development Foundation), São Paulo
FURB	Fundação Universitária Regional Blumenau (Regional University of Blumenau)
IBAMA	Instituto Brasileiro do Meio Ambiente e dos Recursos Naturais Renováveis, (Brazilian Institute for the Environment and Natural Resources)
IBGE	Instituto Brasileiro de Geografia e Estatística (Brazilian Institute for Geography and Statistics), Census Bureau
IMF	International Monetary Fund
IWRM	Integrated Water Resources Management
JICA	Japanese International Development Agency
MME	Ministério de Minas e Energia (Ministry of Mines and Energy)
MP	Ministério Público (Public Ministry)
PCJ	Piracicaba, Jundaí, Capivari (rivers)
PFL	Partido da Frente Liberal (Liberal Front Party)
PLANASA	Plano Nacional de Saneamento (National Sanitation Plan)
PSDB	Partido da Social Democracia Brasileira (Brazilian Social Democratic Party)
PT	Partido dos Trabalhadores (Workers' Party)
SABESP	Companhia de Saneamento Básico de São Paulo (São Paulo State Basic Sanitation Company)
SRH	Secretaria dos Recursos Hídricos (Secretariat of Water Resources), federal government
SUS	Sistema Único de Saúde (Unified Health System)
TVA	Tennessee Valley Authority

PROLOGUE

When we started the Watermark Project, the idea seemed exciting and simple. Water management—indeed, natural resources management in general—posed a critical issue for both national and international politics over the long term. Brazil was gaining fame for experimentation with new participatory arenas, which had spread like wildfire through its political system. The river basin committees created by new legislation on water management seemed to endorse a style of governance that brought together civil society, the private sector, and government to design and monitor policies in an innovative way. Initially, our project proposed to examine comparatively how these committees changed water policy and especially whether they made it more democratic. By investigating these new arenas, created for similar purposes but under diverse social, economic, institutional, and environmental conditions, we would be able to identify the conditions that explained better outcomes. That sounded straightforward to us at the time. It turned out not to be.

As we implemented our original research design with case studies throughout the country, we came up against three problems. In the first place, the effectiveness of the river basin committees did not result directly from the contextual conditions we had been exploring, such as type of water-related problem, political culture, broader institutional environment, social capital, and economic development. We soon realized that many of the river basins we studied were quite similar in terms of these broad categories but experienced radically different outcomes. It seemed not to be the contexts that explained the differences but rather what the people involved did with the resources those contexts provided.

We concluded that to understand why some of these initiatives got off the ground while others fizzled, we needed not just to explore variation in conditions but also to trace and track the processes themselves. As a whole, we found that committees worked best when their members constructed an interpretation of what they were supposed to be doing that pointed to concrete actions they could take. They were best able to become operational when they pooled existing resources in ways that built capabilities and relationships and when they brought in resources and political support from other organizations. They were also more successful when they were able to influence the actions of other organizations in the complex policy network within which they were located. These processes all involved interacting with the institutions around them yet were not the automatic result of characteristics of that context. Action could not be left out of the equation.

A second challenge for our approach was that our cases were not independent. We had presumed that the spread of river basin committees throughout Brazil could be understood as the diffusion of an institutional design, formulated at some other level of analysis. Studying the different effects of that design would be a matter of case study comparison. We discovered, however, that diffusion and design were inseparable. Setting up the kinds of organizations called for in the new institutional design (especially the committees) had important feedback effects on the design process itself (involving not only passage of state and federal laws but also the production and dissemination of interpretations of what they meant). Activists at the national or state level invested in constructing river basin committees as pilot projects to test ideas. People at the river basin level got involved in the lawmaking process to try to change rules in ways they thought would benefit their organizations. Actors at all levels met regularly at conferences and seminars and visited organizing initiatives in other locations. Even when they were not intentionally making these linkages, connections got made. Experiences in particular river basins became models that others followed. Individuals with experience building networks and capabilities in one river basin committee later went on to work in others or in state and federal government positions. Thus, instead of understanding these as independent cases for observing the implementation of a predefined model, we came to see the committees we had chosen to study as sites in a multilevel, interactive, and nonlinear process of institutional conception and construction.

A third problem with our original approach was that before we could compare committees' impact on water management they had to become operational, something that often took far longer than we ever imagined. We would need to study not just how these new organizations worked but also how (and whether) they became functional organizations at all. Although most would not expect all organizing initiatives to result in formal institutions, an underlying presumption of most institutional theories is that if they exist in law they also exist in reality. Institutions may be strong or weak (Levitsky and Murillo 2005), optimal or suboptimal. But once established in law, new actions are supposed to be carried out and new organizations created. The analyst can then judge whether those actions or organizations resolve problems effectively, change behaviors, are democratic, and so on. Arriving on the scene of Brazilian river basin management in 1999, we expected things to proceed in such a stepwise manner and devised our research methodology accordingly. We built a research team, identified a set of 23 river basins for qualitative baseline studies, gathered relevant demographic and socioeconomic data, operationalized our research questions, trained researchers on how to answer them, and coordinated the production of reports with common titles, subtitles, and sub-subtitles. We describe the research process in detail in appendix 1.

It took us some time before we understood that our original objects of study—functioning river basin committees—were not necessarily there. It was hard to be certain whether formally established committees would actually hold meetings and make decisions, even in those Brazilian states where governments purportedly were promoting them. In many cases, governors signed legislation creating the figure of the river basin committee on paper but did nothing to make them a reality. It seemed that there was an important, often long moment between presumptive establishment and practical existence to which political science approaches to institutions paid little attention. Realizing this, we decided that the process of *becoming* (or not) a functioning policy arena had to be our primary object of study.[1]

In sum, our original approach had to adapt to three sets of challenges: the need to look at what actors actually did to build institutions, their practices and not just the context that conditioned them; the existence of interconnections among cases and between them and the broader institutional change under way; and the importance of examining not just outcomes but also the process of institutional creation. Confronting these problems led us to write a very different book from the one we had imagined. Although we present here parts of the stories of 16 river basin committees that we managed to study more or less systematically over a 12-year period, it is no longer, strictly speaking, a case study comparison. Instead, the study took on a nested quality. In one sense, we do compare the cases, searching for explanations of why some became vibrant spaces associated with practical authority over how public and private actors behaved with respect to water issues in their river basins while others did not. However, our focus shifted from the committees as entities to the processes in which they emerged. At the same time, we explore the broader institutional process within which committee formation occurred. That process, which transpired over

---

1. We are aware that for some of our readers the word *becoming* evokes a cluster of theoretical debates and ontological positions. We have doubtless been influenced by some of this philosophical discussion but are not attempting to participate in it directly. We use the word descriptively, to indicate the relational, dynamic, and indeterminate process that we have watched unfolding.

decades, engaged a diverse collection of public and private actors with varying interests and motivations in struggles over the design of state and national water legislation and about how those laws should be interpreted. At all levels, these struggles involved efforts to reshape ideas, resources, and relationships, generating practices intended to bolster particular components and interpretations of those laws. More broadly still, these struggles participated in ongoing negotiations and skirmishes over the configuration of power in Brazilian federalism, partisan allegiances, new forms of participation, interagency bargaining over jurisdictions, and a wide variety of other matters whose connection to water resources management was not immediately apparent.

Our study drew on multiple sources. Much of the work was done as part of a collaborative research initiative, the Watermark Project, that involved academics, their students from various U.S. and Brazilian universities, and different kinds of water management professionals from throughout Brazil. This group conducted 23 qualitative case studies of river basin organizations in 2001 and a series of follow-up interviews with key informants in 2002 and 2003. In 2004, the project commissioned a survey of 626 members of 18 river basin organizations, and in 2008, a smaller group of project members returned to 15 of those basins for workshops with committee members that increased our understanding of the organizing processes under way. In the context of those activities, project participants and their students wrote 13 master's theses and 9 doctoral dissertations along with many other publications, generating a wealth of information about the inner workings and organizational politics of what became a sample of 16 river basin committees on whose history we had systematic data.[2] We carried out in-depth research ourselves (interviews, document collection, participant observation, etc.) on five of those cases (Paranoá, Velhas, Itajaí, Litoral Norte, and Alto Tietê). We also collected documentation and conducted interviews on the history of designing water laws and traced debates over ideas about water reform at the national level and in some states, especially São Paulo. We interviewed public officials, engineers and other experts, legislators, their aides, and a range of other activists. In addition to 144 formal interviews conducted between 1990 and 2011, we had countless informal conversations with key informants, colleagues, specialists, and friends involved in Brazilian water management. There were numerous occasions for participant observation, such as events and meetings, where we discussed river basin politics with practitioners from state and

---

2. Information in Portuguese about the Watermark Project is available at http://www.furb.br/ipa/marcadagua/index.php?a=c#.

civil society organizations. A detailed description of our methodological choices and challenges is presented in appendix 1. The map on the following page shows the location of the river basins discussed in this book.

As teachers, we often advise our students to make sure that the cases they choose to study in the field are solid enough to let them answer their research questions. Such advice, while good for guaranteeing that dissertations get completed, ultimately biases our knowledge of political processes by encouraging the study of only those phenomena that survived the becoming process. We miss cases of aborted development, where something went wrong, and the policy, program, organization, event, or institution never materialized. These are not exactly cases of failure so much as ones in which the phenomenon never reached the stage where it could fail or succeed. Seeing institutions as processes requires us to examine such cases, despite the difficulties involved. In our research, we did this without expecting to, by including in our study many river basin organizations that had only recently been created and then following them over a 12-year period without knowing what would become of them. Some of them faded out of existence altogether. Others turned into vibrant spaces of decision making and action. They gained what we call in this book *practical authority*.

Institutions are not just on or off; they undergo processes of becoming, which they do not necessarily survive. New institutions have to be organized. Even if legislation endows them with formal authority, that authority has to be made real in practice, through action. Even in highly institutionalized polities, this does not always happen in predictable ways, or even at all. In this book, we argue that institutions come into existence when people act creatively to do the hard organizational work to reconfigure ideas, resources, and relationships, persuading influential others in their environments to engage with them in the practice of doing things differently. By thinking of institutions in this way, we are trying to create a conceptual language for exploring the micro-politics of institution building.

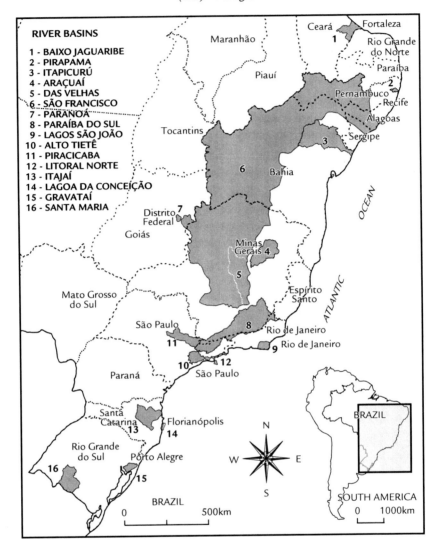

RIVER BASINS

1 - BAIXO JAGUARIBE
2 - PIRAPAMA
3 - ITAPICURÚ
4 - ARAÇUAÍ
5 - DAS VELHAS
6 - SÃO FRANCISCO
7 - PARANOÁ
8 - PARAÍBA DO SUL
9 - LAGOS SÃO JOÃO
10 - ALTO TIETÊ
11 - PIRACICABA
12 - LITORAL NORTE
13 - ITAJAÍ
14 - LAGOA DA CONCEIÇÃO
15 - GRAVATAÍ
16 - SANTA MARIA

Practical Authority

CHAPTER 1

Practical Authority, Institution Building, and Entanglement

Flávio Terra Barth, a rotund, bespectacled, and rather disheveled engineer, seemed remarkably unprepossessing to be the key organizer of São Paulo's water policy reform. Until, that is, he began to talk about planning—a subject that made his eyes sparkle and his body quiver with energy. "This is how we did it. I had a huge sheet of paper like this," he said, arms outstretched, showing a map-sized space on his desk, "and on it I had all the different committees and councils and agencies where water resources management was being discussed. I made sure we had people in each one of those groups. If it turned out that one wasn't going very well, I would deploy someone else to try to energize it." With arrows and arcs, he illustrated the campaign he had orchestrated, drew connections to the allies who had contributed. Pulling open file drawers, he brought out pamphlets and magazines and discussion papers. Each step he outlined represented dozens of meetings and phone calls, trips to Rio, to Brasília, to the interior. He worked with professional organizations, bureaucracies, international agencies, and legislatures in the effort to change water policy. Each move in the planning process involved hard labor, persuasion, logistics, bargaining, time.

Across town from Barth's office, another group of public employees met on Friday afternoons in Stela Goldenstein's garden to strategize about democratizing the water management process. Most were career civil servants, who had risen to positions of influence in their agencies by honing their technical and managerial skills, in the hope of using their positions to bring about change. Goldenstein, a geographer, was head of planning and deputy secretary for São Paulo's environmental secretariat, an institution she had helped design and organize after democratic opposition leader André Franco Montoro won São Paulo's gubernatorial elections in 1982. She and her colleagues did their own mapping of the strategic possibilities for inserting a more environmentalist approach into what they saw to be an endeavor largely dominated by engineers. All of these people were public employees and technical experts; they were also institutional activists.

When people think about Brazilians struggling to change the status quo, most of them would not imagine people like Flávio Barth and Stela Goldenstein. They might picture charismatic politicians, community organizers, labor leaders, or rural activists organizing a land occupation. They might think about environmentalists mobilizing people to form a human chain encircling the polluted Rodrigo de Freitas Lake in Rio or sponsoring a petition in São Paulo to clean up the fetid Tietê River. We could as easily have begun this chapter by describing the picturesque 2003 expedition that members of the Manuelzão Project undertook in Minas Gerais, kayaking the 761 kilometers of the Velhas River to dramatize its progressive degradation, in the best Greenpeace-like traditions of environmental education, athleticism, and showmanship.

Flávio Barth, the civil servants meeting in Goldenstein's garden, and many others were participants in a decades-long effort to promote institutional and policy changes in water resources management. With the proposal that a diverse set of policy areas be integrated in a single system, water management reform became an arena in which a wide variety of differently situated actors, inspired by disparate motivations, worked to change how people understood and made decisions about freshwater resources. It was an attempt to construct a new field of action by realigning and recombining existing institutions and creating others, something that demanded both technical knowledge and political skill. Although it was not at all easy and a great many of their efforts ran into insurmountable obstacles, a surprising number of individuals and the public or private organizations to which they belonged stuck it out for far longer than we had any reason to expect. This kind of slow, laborious effort to enact new policy ideas against obdurate resistance—sometimes unsuccessful, sometimes racking up partial achievements, and often subject to sudden reversals—offers a different vision of political change from the usual assessment of the conditions under which desired changes are more or less likely to occur.

This book is about the kinds of things people actually do when they try to transform institutions. We conceive of such reform efforts as non-zero-sum struggles for what we call *practical authority*, understood as the kind of power-in-practice generated when particular actors (individuals or organizations) develop capabilities and win recognition within a particular policy area, enabling them to influence the behavior of other actors. It is neither a direct function of formal authority nor properly explained in terms of the political legitimacy of the state as a whole. Practical authority over the conduct of policy can shift over time from organization to organization within the state and even into society and can be shared among organizations in complex and changing ways. Our focus here is on the practices that actors invent and deploy when they try to create new sites of practical authority.

We define institutions broadly as "commonly accepted ways of doing things." This loose definition is more useful for our purposes than prevailing definitions in the social sciences, where institutions are usually understood as rules, norms, or procedures that constrain the behavior of individuals. Thinking of institutions as rules or norms makes it difficult to imagine what they were before becoming institutionalized. Posing them as commonly accepted ways of doing things, however, leads us to ask how certain ideas or practices became accepted, to think of institutions as historical products. Defining institutions in this way additionally emphasizes that institutions are not just norms or ideas but also are the actual ways that people act upon the world. New institutions come about through concrete practices that involve not only actions to change ideas and laws but also efforts to transform organizational resources and relationships. By incorporating action and organizations into our concept of institutions, we can recognize the ways in which institutional change reconfigures authority relations in complex political ecologies.

A large literature has grown in recent years about how institutions change over time. Much of it focuses on unintentional processes such as institutional drift or displacement (Streek and Thelen 2005; Mahoney and Thelen 2010) or on how intentional reforms often have unplanned consequences (March and Olsen 1989). This book seeks to contribute to that literature with a focus on the way actors purposefully attempt to change institutions through the design and implementation of new policies, even when the results turn out to be different from those they hoped for. Institution building is a relational *process* that occurs through human action and involves such disparate activities as creating and disseminating ideas, struggling over legal designs, experimenting with new solutions for problems, accumulating organizational and technical capabilities, and building networks of support for the implementation of those ideas and laws. Through such processes, organizational actors learn new capabilities and recognition, on the basis of which they accumulate the practical authority that allows them to influence the actions of others. We intend to show in subsequent chapters that such practices can be studied systematically, even though creative action is, by nature, unpredictable.

A practice-based approach to institutional change prompts us to pay attention to how activists inside and outside the state[1] navigate the complex configurations of organizations and rules in which institutions are embedded and on which they must act if they are to produce change. It

---

1. By recognizing the presence of activism not just in civil society but also in bureaucracies or even the private sector, we follow the lead of other authors, such as Needleman and Needleman (1974), Santoro and McGuire (1997), Keck and Sikkink (1998), Steinberg (2001), and Hochstetler and Keck (2007).

can be especially challenging to create new institutional arrangements in complex environments, where power is distributed according to different logics among multiple, heterogeneous organizations, often with ambiguously shared jurisdictions. This phenomenon, which we call entanglement, increases uncertainty; if on the one hand its inertial force poses a powerful obstacle to action, on the other its juxtapositions may offer unexpected pathways for creative initiative.

ENTANGLEMENT AND INSTITUTIONAL CHANGE: THE PROBLEM OF WATER MANAGEMENT

We explore institution-building practices through a policy window that we believe provides more general insight into the dynamics of agency and institutional change: the construction of new decision-making arenas for governing Brazil's water resources. Freshwater is hard to govern because so many types of actors and interests rely on it. People and animals must have it to drink, and it is often used to dilute domestic sewage, treated or not. It is used to create electric energy and to irrigate crops. Many industries and mining companies use water massively in production or extraction. In some places it is used for navigation, in others for tourism. And of course, water is also part of ecological systems, whose integrity can be put at risk by all of those human uses.

As in many places, Brazil's laws and institutions historically failed to take into account the need to make so many uses compatible with one another and with environmental protection.[2] Different policy sectors (sanitation, industry, agriculture, energy) each had their own rules and programs, often with competing projects for water use. Hydroelectric power generation was privileged over other sectors, seen as fundamental for reaching national development goals. In the 1980s, however, a movement emerged to promote a more holistic approach, a water management "system" that would integrate all of these policy fields. Over the course of two decades, water reform activists negotiated with actors defending a wide range of interests to try to devise a new institutional design. They had to work with various policy sectors at multiple territorial levels, since new legislation would have to be approved in the 26 Brazilian states, in the Federal District and at the national level. By the late 1990s, the basic laws had been passed, but the new way of doing things was still under construction.

Besides realigning existing agencies and attributions, the new legal framework proposed the establishment of several new kinds of decision-making

2. See Conca (2005), Molle and Wester (2009), and Huitema and Meijerink (2009).

organizations. Within state and federal governments, authority over water policy would be transferred to new specialized agencies, which, reformers hoped, would not be captured by any particular economic interest. State and federal level participatory councils would also be created, in which the private sector and civil society would join government actors in formulating the specific rules of the system. More radically, the reformers proposed creating decision-making institutions at the river basin level—a territorial unit that had no precedent in constitutional norms or historical practices. The idea was that by bringing together state, private, and civil society actors, representing all water uses and relevant policy sectors, these *river basin committees* would operationalize the notion of integrated water resources management.

Before the design of the new institutions was finished, people started creating river basin committees. These early experiments influenced further changes in water legislation. By 2011, more than 133 million Brazilians lived within the territorial purview of at least one of them.[3] Yet many committees were unable to carry out the tasks they were assigned by law, either because those responsibilities were vague or because they required the cooperation of other institutions that were unprepared for or even opposed to such changes. Today, some exist only on paper. Others reinvented themselves, finding routes to practical authority without necessarily relying on the formal rules that governed them.[4] Based largely on these experiences, organizers of committees and in other newly created water institutions worked to improve the legal framework more generally, mobilizing for the passage of complementary legislation needed to make portions of the original laws work.

Our main objective in this book is to comprehend the multilevel process through which some of the new organizations created during and after the reform process gained the capabilities and public recognition that allowed them to make decisions with which other organizations and actors would comply. Studying this halting, nonlinear, territorially dispersed, and gradual process of institutional change has forced us to examine what happens on the inside of institution building. It turns out to be exceedingly messy. Constructing institutions involves coming up with new ideas about how people should do things. But the ideational component of institution building is not over at the point where people try to implement ideas or laws.

3. Based on a compilation of data made available by the National Water Agency on the website http://www.cbh.gov.br/ (accessed February 15, 2011).

4. In that the legal reform gave the committees little formal authority, they ended up being similar to the watershed partnerships studied by Sabatier and colleagues in the United States (see Sabatier et al. 2005).

As critics of traditional policy cycle theories have long noticed, the design stage and implementation stage of institution building are iterative and interconnected (Ingram 1977; Sabatier 1986; Thomas and Grindle 1990; Werner and Wegrich 2006; Jenkins-Smith and Sabatier 2003; Hill 2009).

Institution building can also be messy when it requires action at various territorial levels and in multiple arenas: not just the legislature but also within various agencies of the executive branch, governing bodies, and regulatory boards; not just at the federal level but also in the states and municipalities; not just in government but also in private organizations whose cooperation and commitment is necessary. In recent decades, the term *governance* is often employed to express such multilayered, multiactor policy processes.[5] Following Stark (1999) and Ansell (2011, 42), we think of such complex settings as *ecologies*, in which organizations are embedded within histories and places and interconnected with each other.

Creating new institutions under complexity requires creating a space for new organizations and tasks in relation to other organizations; some of these will fail to collaborate and others will actively resist the emergence of new sites of decision making. If the multiplication of actors and arenas fragments political processes, it also means that different sites of decision making overlap and are connected, often in surprising ways. Such overlaps and connections are prevalent in the Brazilian political system, but not particular to it, posing a common policy problem, especially in countries with federal systems and in complex policy sectors. In entangled institutional environments, where actors must work in multiple arenas to get things done, they often discover that neither the passage of new laws nor the approval of policy designs automatically reconfigures decision making. To influence how other actors behave, they must first develop practical authority.

PRACTICAL AUTHORITY

The activation of new institutions depends to a large extent on the ability of new organizations to establish what we call practical authority: the problem-solving capabilities and recognition from key decision makers that allow them to influence public or private behaviors. Practical authority is a provisional and particular attribution that can shift over time from organization

---

5. While this term has sometimes been applied in practice through the belief that putting stakeholders into the same room will produce better and more politically sustainable policies, various authors have suggested that decentered, multilayered policy processes are typically riddled with multidimensional, sometimes invisible power relations (Rose and Miller 1992; Bevir and Rhodes 2010).

to organization. It is not a direct reflection of the general authority relations between state and citizenry, nor does it necessarily affect this sovereign relation. Although organizations sometimes gain the capacity to influence behavior through formal dispensations emanating from state power, they also can, and often do, gain that capacity by other means, such as by garnering social respect, acquiring new technical skills, and taking advantage of private resources. Indeed, as we suggest in this book, state institutions often develop authority less through their formal attributions and more through such relational mechanisms. Nonstate organizations also do so.

Practical authority is a kind of power in which the capabilities to solve problems and recognition by others allows an actor to make decisions that others follow. Our use of *authority* is consistent with its Weberian meaning as the type of power that prompts compliance on the basis of legitimacy (Weber 1968, 212–213),[6] but we do not confine it to the state. Changing institutional arrangements implies modifying the way different kinds of power are accumulated and deployed within and among multiple public and private organizations. A relational approach recognizes that power operates at many different levels and that it is simultaneously ubiquitous and hard to assemble. When we look this way at how actors try to gain power over decisions, agendas, and conduct, our notion of power as the ability of one actor to influence the actions of others is similar to that of authors from Weber (1968, 53) to Lukes (2005). When, however, we see the strikingly uneven territorial and functional distribution of the state's capacity to project power through organization, we are drawing on what Michael Mann calls infrastructural power, a non-zero-sum kind of power whose expansion results in increased power for all parties involved. At the micro level of actors attempting to shift the behavior and capacities of organizations, we also need recourse to something like what John Allen (2008, 1614) refers to as "the power to make a difference in the world." Creating practical authority does not necessarily mean taking power away from other actors; it can be generative, involving the fabrication of capacities to do things that no one was doing before.

The term *authority* is typically used by political philosophers to speak about the establishment of legitimate domination between sovereign and people, and disputes about political authority generally concern the origins of that legitimacy (see, e.g., Arendt 1961). These debates do not address more day-to-day contests within the state and between state and nonstate actors and organizations to control how the powers of the state are to be *used* or to influence how state and nonstate actors should behave

---

6. This discussion of Weber's concept of power and authority draws from Blau (1963).

in particular situations. Nor do they contemplate the competing claims to authority involved when lead organizations in new administrative orders lack the political support to withstand resistance from existing organizations or even the operational capacity to address the problems they are charged with solving. Conflicts and organizing processes such as these— the micro-struggles over decision-making power—are not explained by broader debates about the concept of political authority.

The state, Weber (1968) tells us, is different from other organizations because its monopoly over the legitimate use of violence enables it to do some things that no other organization can. Only the state can (legitimately) use the threat of force to regulate how people or organizations act. Other organizations must find alternative forms of persuasion to influence how private actors act, though they may call upon the state to defend their right to do so. Another capacity rooted in the state's coercive potential is taxation: no other institution can legitimately force people to give money, especially in the absence of a direct exchange. From tax collection we derive another task exclusive to states: deciding how public money should be spent. Since it has been coerced out of the public, spending must also be governed publicly. This means that, even if those funds are transferred to private or nongovernmental organizations, that decision must be approved by a properly authorized state organization.

Institutional reforms are often about redefining which actors and organizations should be able to regulate behavior (with legal backing), raise taxes, and spend public money. This can occur, for example, by transferring decision-making power from one agency to another, by merging agencies, or by creating new oversight agencies. It can occur through decentralization or centralization of decision-making powers. It can also involve reducing or increasing the state's power to do those things altogether, for example, by deregulating the airlines or by creating new environmental controls or even public tariffs, such as user fees for water.

Government agencies do other things that are not exclusive to the state but involve the capacity to get people to do things or to make things happen and in that sense also involve authority. Like other organizations, governments mobilize organizational capabilities and implement projects. They coordinate employees, interact in networks, hold and participate in debates, elaborate plans, generate and use scientific knowledge, occupy offices and buildings, provide services, build roads and hospitals. To get done, these activities do not require a threat of violent coercion or the legitimacy of a state that monopolizes the legitimate use of that threat. They depend instead on capacities that are not exclusive to the state. We can think of the power to influence actions that derives from this kind of capacity as *non-state-exclusive forms of practical authority*.

How do actors, organizations, or rules gain practical authority? The presumption is often that the allocation of authority occurs by decree.[7] A new law determines that, from now on, agency X has the power to do Y and so it shall be. Yet this presumption misses most of the process of institutional construction. Creating and passing a law is a contested process. The actors whose power over decision making could change as a result of a law are likely to try to influence how laws get designed. Once passed, laws do not always state clearly which organization should actually do what. The details—the interpretation of general laws and of the ambiguities in them—often must be worked out through extra-legislative processes. Even when laws are crystal clear, implementing them in ways that endow new arenas with the ability to make binding decisions likely requires the development of organizational and technical capacities among other resources. This is craftwork, sometimes slow and painstaking, involving what Suchman (2011, 8) refers to as a "kind of practical and material intertextuality, a process of assembling together heterogeneous materials into a coherent whole." Assembling these resources occurs through the types of institution-building practices discussed in this book.

We argue that new organizations sometimes get closer to gaining state-exclusive forms of authority by first developing *capabilities* that are not exclusive to the state and do not originally depend on having a monopoly to the legitimate means of violence, that is, formal state power. This may include demonstrating technical competence or scientific knowledge, being able to raise money or receive grants, or simply being able to coordinate multiple organizations in ways that resolve a problem. It also may include less material capabilities, such as the capacity to persuade others that the organization represents relevant interests.[8] It undoubtedly involves enrollment of more people committed to change, who develop a conceptual understanding of its rationale, make a commitment to the new vision, and gain new skills relevant to its realization (Suchman 2011, 10). Sometimes it requires working to reinforce the capability of other organizations in the system to perform the roles assigned to them.

To build practical authority, actors must mobilize not only capabilities but also *recognition*. Latour (1986, 264) argues that the fundamental paradox of power is that it is only meaningful if action is carried out by those

7. Despite the fact that many authors have emphasized the complexity of implementation (see Ingram 1977; Pressman and Wildavsky 1984; Werner and Wegrich 2006; Hill 2009), the presumption that formal laws are implemented still prevails in much of the institutionalist literature.

8. Such claims, as has been shown by recent debates on the representative claims of civil society (Castiglione and Warren 2006; Saward 2006), are not the exclusive prerogative of state legislative or executive organizations.

who do not have it: "a command, if successful, results from the actions of a chain of agents each of whom translates it in accordance with his/her own projects."[9] Practical authority works in the same way: since it is the capacity to influence behaviors, it depends on the recognition of others, who must confirm that such authority exists. Capability and recognition are interdependent. As Daniel Carpenter (2000, 2010) shows, organizations (in his case, bureaucracies) build reputations (a form of recognition) that are based on their ability to resolve problems. Inversely, recognition is often necessary to build capabilities: actors within organizations often sign on to projects or experiments only if they are convinced that leaders have good ideas or that a group has the potential to solve a problem.

Focusing on how organizations gain capabilities and recognition allows us to look inside the process of institutional becoming. In our view, that process cannot be understood without examining actors and the actions they take. Although preexisting conditions (the amount and type of resources available, the existence of powerful interests favorable to change, etc.) may be important parts of the explanation for why some organizations gain practical authority while others do not, they are not sufficient, nor are outcomes necessarily robust. We need to explore processes: what actors do to guarantee that ideas, resources, and relationships are mobilized (and transformed) in ways that produce new capabilities and recognitions.

IDEAS, ACTORS, AND INSTITUTIONAL CHANGE

Our examination of the process of institutional becoming seeks to dialogue with a growing literature on institutional change. When, two decades ago, Sven Steinmo, Kathleen Thelen, and Frank Longstreth (1992) organized a seminal volume on historical institutionalism, they noted, forcefully, that until then neither it nor the predominant rational choice institutionalism had provided good explanations for change. Much of the rational choice literature thought of change as a result of institutional choice, compared by Tsebelis (1990) to long-term investments that decision makers make only after lengthy periods of building up political resources. Historical institutionalists, for the most part, focused on the obstacles to institutional change, a result of positive feedback and path dependency (Thelen and Steinmo 1992).[10]

---

9. See also Haugaard (2003).

Since then, political scientists (especially comparativists) have explored institutional change in three general, not mutually exclusive ways. One approach emphasizes the notion of *critical junctures*: during particular moments in history, contextual changes destabilize existing institutions and make it easier for actors to engage in institutional choice. The central concern of these authors is to understand how choices made at certain historical moments sets institutions on certain paths while others are abandoned. They emphasize moments of abrupt change and their consequences (Mahoney 2001; Collier and Collier 2002; Capoccia and Kelemen 2007). A second approach explains more gradual institutional change by looking at mechanisms of institutional reproduction. Institutions change when glitches occur in those mechanisms or when they get out of sync with their broader contexts (Thelen 1999; Streek and Thelen 2005; Mahoney and Thelen 2010). A key move has been to challenge earlier tendencies in historical institutionalism to presume that institutions reproduce themselves automatically, once set in. Mahoney and Thelen (2010) emphasize that institutions are ambiguous and, to the extent that they distribute power, tend to produce resistance.

These first two approaches discuss actors as agents of change but in ways that place more emphasis on how contexts and conditions influence choices than on the dynamics of choice making itself. The critical junctures view speaks of those moments as less structured periods in history, "characterized by the selection of a particular option... from two or more alternatives" (Mahoney 2001, 6). Rather than focusing on how or why actors make particular choices, studies here tend to look at the antecedent conditions and the nature of the historical moment. Little is said about how the options came to be clearly understood as such. Actors are largely understood as aggregate groups (e.g., the labor movement, the state, liberals) rather than specific people or organizations with distinctive histories.

A more recent discussion by Mahoney and Thelen (2010) makes a strong effort to associate different types of change agents (insurrectionaries, symbionts, subversives, and opportunists) with different kinds of institution-changing action. Although this view draws attention to actors, it still appears to give more causal importance to structural aspects than to the agents themselves, especially when the authors argue that different types of political context and of institutions explain which type of change

---

10. Sociological institutionalism was also overly focused on institutional stability. March and Olsen (1989) challenged the possibility of rational design and emphasized the unintended consequences of attempts to change institutions. Others emphasized isomorphism (Dimaggio and Powell 1991), a mechanism of institutional reproduction that Clegg (2010) argues became reified as scholars began to presume that it would occur almost automatically.

agent is likely to predominate.[11] Even though they acknowledge agency, these approaches still do not ask what actors do when they endeavor to change institutions or what happens when actors behave not as aggregates but according to multiple interpretations, strategies, and interests.

Institutional change at least partially results from action, even if not in the ways that actors expect. A third set of scholars—some of whom identify as *constructivists*—argue that political explanation should explore not just structural conditions or the logic of rational action but also how ideas and cognition influence political action. A central contribution is Blyth's (2001, 2002) study of Swedish economic policy, in which he demonstrates that decision makers frequently made decisions against their own economic interest as a result of the dominant economic ideas of the time. For some authors, the move toward what Hay (2006) dubs *constructivist institutionalism* has meant a greater appreciation of the role of creativity and transformative action in political life: the very fact that institutions are built on ideas means that they are human constructs that can be changed (Schmidt 2008). Still others consider the notion that institutions are stable structures to be misleading: institutions exist only because they are constantly being produced and reproduced by knowledgeable and creative actors (Lund 2006; Berk and Galvan 2009).

While much of the work on how policy ideas influence politics seems to suggest that they are disseminated as unified wholes,[12] our analysis focuses on the contested process through which such ideas are constructed and reconstructed. Studies of institutional diffusion sometimes give the impression that ideas first develop coherence, after which they are transferred, imposed, or copied (DiMaggio and Powell 1991; Molle 2008). But our research suggests that ideational construction continues on during the diffusion process. Indeed, there is no prior, purely cognitive moment in which intellectuals think up a logically coherent policy idea that is then circulated and institutionalized. Instead, policy ideas grow out of a combination of debates among specialists (in which contesting ideas are defended), political struggles (in which ideas that are not specific to the specialist community get into the discussion), and practical experiments in particular locations. This helps explain why institutional designs can end up ambiguous and internally contradictory.

Thus, to explore how institutions change and how the organizations that emerge from such changes gain practical authority, we have to ask

11. Berk and Galvan (2009) make a similar criticism of Streek and Thelen (2005).

12. Exceptions are Sikkink (1991, 245), who notes that policy communities are not necessarily unified groups, and Hajer (2005), who argues that different actors can have entirely different interpretations of similar story lines, which allow them to agree on general ideas even without agreeing on the specifics.

how actors produce not only new ideas but also the resources and relationships necessary to implement them. For some authors in the constructivist school this means studying the social interactions that produce new ideas as well as the ideas themselves. For both Hajer (2005) and Schmidt (2008), these interactions constitute *discourse*, which Hajer (2005, 300) defines as "an ensemble of ideas, concepts and categories through which meaning is given to social and physical phenomena and which is produced and reproduced through an identifiable set of practices." Schmidt (2008, 205) calls it the "interactive processes by which ideas are conveyed." Ideas, as Thomas Risse-Kappen (1996) reminds us, do not float freely; they are carried by people.

In confluence with recently developed concepts in organizational sociology about *institutional work* (Lawrence, Suddaby, and Leca 2009), we argue that explaining how actors contribute to institutional change requires examining the different ways that they intentionally seek to influence institutions, even if they are not successful in doing so. Lawrence, Suddaby, and Leca (2009, 1) refer to institutional work as "the practical actions through which institutions are created, maintained, and disrupted." Like Clegg (2010), the authors note that much of the sociological literature on institutions has oscillated between an overly deterministic conception of automatized institutional reproduction and a heroic notion of the agent—the institutional entrepreneur—who somehow breaks with those structures. They propose a less romantic notion of action, something that occurs often behind the scenes and by multiple actors, not just highly visible heroes. In this book, we call such efforts *institution-building practices*.

By examining how actors engage in institution-building practices, we can bring action into our conception of institutional change without reducing it to a simple choice-making process among homogenized groups. Getting new institutions to function often involves active interchange among a wide variety of actors, who may have very different views of what should be happening. Moments of institutional choice that initiate a path-dependent process are easier to detect retrospectively and may reflect choices by the analyst as much as those of the actors. A path can take a very long time to get set, if it ever does.

AGENCY AND PRACTICES

Our use of the term *practice* intentionally locates our approach to politics within a broad swath of contemporary social thought that, largely inspired by the work of Bourdieu (1977) and Giddens (1984), rejects dichotomies both between structure and agency and between the material and ideal worlds. Breaking with the emphasis on rote socialization in Parsonian sociology, a major theme has been how agents and structures constitute each other in what Giddens calls *structuration*. But, as Sewell (1992) notes, those theories still tend to emphasize the reproduction of structures (now with the active participation of individuals) over agency. Sewell moves toward a theory of transformative agency by building on dual theories of structure present in both Bourdieu and Giddens. The duality lies in that structures are more than just rules or schemas (Giddens) or mental objects (Bourdieu) that people are somehow required to follow. They are also embodied in concrete objects (Bourdieu) or resources (Giddens) that individuals use. Through the use of resources, people enact and thus learn and instantiate schemas. For Bourdieu, individuals almost inexorably reproduce the structures that constrain them through everyday practices, what he calls *habitus*. Sewell, on the other hand—following Giddens—suggests that the notion that structures are dual opens the door to a more flexible notion of agency.

The characteristics of structures and of the structuration process create opportunities for creativity. For Sewell, transformative action is possible because, as Giddens suggests, individuals are knowledgeable: they are capable of creative and reflective thinking about the schemas and resources of their world. Contrary to the totalizing vision of structural reproduction in Bourdieu's approach, Sewell argues that the process through which actors enact structures is imperfect. "Social actors are capable of applying a wide range of different and even incompatible schemas and have access to heterogeneous arrays of resources" (Sewell 1992, 17); they can interpret schemas and resources in a variety of ways and transfer those meanings to other contexts.[13]

Yet even Sewell's approach to agency pays more attention to the characteristics of structures than to what agents actually do. Here, Emirbayer and Mische (1998) help us by distinguishing among three kinds of agency. When actors reproduce existing structures, they engage in *habit*, which is similar to the *habitus* proposed by Bourdieu. Actors are doing something qualitatively different when they use *judgment* to make decisions in situations when no clear rules apply or, alternatively, when they imagine the future, something the authors call *projective agency*, an idea on which Mische (2009) elaborates in later work. This perspective would suggest that actors have different degrees of freedom at different moments and in different situations. The notion of projective agency is inspired by pragmatist understandings of creativity, experience, and experimentation, something Emirbayer and Mische (1998, 987–988) find in the

---

13. This idea is also suggested by Clemens (1993), who shows effectively how the emerging 19th-century women's movement in the United States adopted organizing repertoires from other types of groups.

work of John Dewey (1927, 1933, 1981) and Hans Joas (1996). For Dewey (1981, 69), "Experience in its vital form is experimental, an effort to change the given; it is characterized by projection, by reaching forward into the unknown; connection with the future is its salient trait" (cited in Emirbayer and Mische 1998, 988). Continuing in that vein, Berk and Galvan (2009, 544) argue that transformative agency is more common than habituation: "Action always takes place in relation to prior rules and practices, which serve not as guides or constraints, but as mutable raw material for new action." Focusing on institutional work, Lawrence, Suddaby, and Leca (2009, 9) write that understanding transformative agency requires examining not only how actors create new institutions (or creatively maintain old ones) but also how they actively disrupt and undermine current ways of doing things.

Like structures, we propose, agency is also dual: it melts away if not instantiated in practice; creative capacity might as well not exist if left on the shelf. Here we diverge from authors who understand agency as a quality of mind—as no more than the capacity to think critically and come up with alternative ideas—and who attribute institutional transformation to "the capacity to use reflexive knowledge to transform situations and to engage in learning as a result" (O'Neill, Balsiger, and VanDeveer 2004, 158). This essentially cognitive view of agency, which much of the constructivist literature shares, ignores the material side of structuration. If structures are not just cognitive schemas but also involve material resources, then it seems reasonable to suppose that agency also involves both creating ideas and creating something more material.

By using the term *practice*, we join a tradition that explores the interpenetration of the ideational and material realms.[14] Drawing on the work of Pitkin and Ortner, among others, Wedeen (2002, 720) writes, "Practices are actions or deeds that are repeated over time; they are learned, reproduced, and subject to risks through social interaction [and are] composed both of what the outside observer can see and of the actors' understandings of what they are doing." This approach encourages "an attention to politics, to social asymmetry, historical contingencies, and political domination, key dimensions of both action and structure." According to Breiger (2000, 27), "the 'key argument' of practice is that the material world (the world of action) and the cultural world (the world of symbols) interpenetrate, are built up through the immediate association of each with the other." Our use of the term is similar to that of others who draw from a pragmatist tradition, in which creative actors experiment with solutions to problems, recognizing

---

14. The pantheon that Wagenaar and Cook (2003) invoke in their review of practice theories includes thinkers as diverse as Comte, Aristotle, Bourdieu, Giddens, MacIntyre, Taylor, Lave, and Dewey.

that "what works best in any given situation cannot be known in advance, only in practice" (Allen 2008, 1616; see also Chisholm 1995; Stark 1999; Ansell 2011).

Institution-building practices, as we conceive of them, involve transforming ideas, resources, and relationships in creative ways. *Resources* can be thought of as tools that can be used for action. Such tools include material things, such as office space and computers. But they may also include less material tools, such as knowledge, technical capabilities, organizing capacities, and political support; institutional design ideas can themselves become resources in local political struggles. *Relationships* are connections among people, and clusters of such relationships, sometimes called ties, form networks whose structures sometimes have effects independent of the intentions of any individual (or node) within them.[15] However, as Emirbayer and Goodwin (1994) proposed, network structures have been structured by human action; although relationships do constrain what actors can do, they are also produced by them (see also Padgett and Ansell 1993; Keck and Sikkink 1998; Hochstetler and Keck 2007; Mische 2009; von Bülow 2010).

There are significant conceptual overlaps among ideas, resources, and relationships. Some resources—such as knowledge—are obviously cognitive. Indeed, an idea can function as a resource if it helps people do what they need to do. Ann Swidler (1986) memorably characterized cultures as tool kits. Relationships are also means of gaining access to resources (Lin 2001). A position in a social network is directly associated with social, economic, and political advantages or disadvantages. In this sense, relationships are a kind of resource: they can be used as tools for getting things done. For some network theorists, "a social network is a network of meanings" (White 1992, 65, 67, cited in Emirbayer and Goodwin 1994, 1437). Yet not all resources can be easily understood as kinds of ideas or kinds of relationships. Rather mundane material things, such as a car, can make a tremendous difference to an organizer. The line between relationships and ideas is also unclear. These overlaps are a product not of conceptual inconsistency but of the impossibility of drawing a bright line between the material and the ideational—and, ultimately, the undesirability of doing so.

By focusing on creative practices, our purpose is not to deny the importance of power politics or of structural conditions in processes of institutional change. As already suggested, institutional activism involves struggles for power and authority. Even powerful actors engage and experiment in order to creatively build authority to do things in new ways. The

---

15. See Emirbayer and Goodwin (1994), Podolny and Page (1998), Watts (2004), and Ward, Stovel, and Sachs (2011).

cognitive turn in sociology that inspires much constructivism emphasizes that power struggles and ideational struggles are one and the same. Lukes speaks of the *third face of power*, Bourdieu of *symbolic-violence*, Gramsci of *hegemony*, Foucault of *power-knowledge*. Yet even if all forms of power can be understood as in some way related to how people think, the notion of power should also involve a capacity to influence what people do. After all, institution builders are normally trying to create institutions because they want to change behaviors and not just minds.

We are highlighting the hard work that goes into building new institutions, through actors' laborious efforts to overcome power asymmetries, to creatively use whatever resources and relationships they can find and to try to make new ones. Although that labor has an intellectual component, it should not be understood as just creative thinking or simply a matter of "disseminating" ideas. Groups of actors argue over ideas and negotiate results, sometimes through consensus building but more often by mobilizing and creating resources to support particular interpretations of the way things are or should be.

Including acting on the material world in our conception of creative agency also helps us explain why institutional change does not always occur, even when actors are extremely creative. Having good ideas is not enough if they are not translated into material resources and relationships through which actors can transform ideas into working organizations, concrete activities, and enforceable decisions. Not everyone will agree that the new ideas are good ones. Struggles over ideas often happen on the ground through efforts to rearrange material and nonmaterial resources and relationships in ways that give the proponents of some interpretations more influence or make new ideas practically possible. Even the most creative actors may not be able to do so in the face of powerful opposition.

INSTITUTION-BUILDING PRACTICES AND PRACTICAL AUTHORITY

People modify ideas, resources, and relationships through two broad types of institution-building practices: *engagement* with other actors and *experimentation* with concrete problem solving. When they are successful, these two interrelated activities enhance capabilities and generate recognition by others, contributing to practical authority. Experimentation involves combining and using ideas, resources, and relationships in new ways. Engagement occurs when actors start connecting with other actors in their networks, using those connections to move resources and ideas around.

One way that actors engage others is simply through promoting conversation. The institution builders we studied spent what sometimes seemed like an inordinate amount of time in meetings, seminars, and other arenas of debate. The result was often the emergence of new ways of thinking about problems. Conversations can have transformative effects, as new connections between people may make it possible to resolve (in practice) problems that actors had not even thought of addressing before encountering one another, what Lane and Maxfield (1996) refer to as *generative relationships*. What changes is not just the way people think but also the concrete possibilities for acting. Although ultimately these possibilities must be acted upon if they are not to fade away, promoting and participating in such moments of intersection are themselves explicit moves in a change process.

Engagement usually involves using networks—in our study, often professional associations—to disseminate ideas and to gain access to resources (Lin 2001). Organizational sociologists have long emphasized the role of professional networks in the diffusion of organizational patterns and procedures (Meyer and Rowan 1977; DiMaggio and Powell 1991; Scott et al. 2000; Owen-Smith and Powell 2008). Lin (2001, 165–183) connects idea diffusion through networks directly to institutional transformation, arguing that when networks of individuals promoting alternative ideas can argue their case successfully within professional organizations, the resulting new consensus will then be disseminated throughout the other organizations within their sphere of influence.[16] Yet this is not just a process of building consensus. Actors can use networks to get access to key positions in a bureaucracy (Haas 1992) or to other resources.

Experimentation with new ways of addressing problems is another type of practice employed by those trying to build new institutions. Dewey (1933, 11) described problems as situations in which habitual ways of doing things do not work, and in this sense they push actors to be creative (Ansell 2011, 11). Often such experiments begin as small-scale collaborative efforts involving small numbers of people or a very modest commitment toward goals that are readily achievable. As Ansell and Gash (2008) note, in working toward those goals, bonds are strengthened between individuals, and experience produces new skills and knowledge. When others perceive these efforts as successful, they are more apt to sign on, and participants are more likely to increase their commitment. Such experiments can change existing relationships and resources in ways that make more ambitious ideas, which earlier may have seemed outlandish, appear reasonable.

---

16. Many other authors have similarly thought of networks as channels for sharing or disseminating ideas, meanings, or frames. See, for example, Haas (1992), Sabatier and Jenkins-Smith (1993), Keck and Sikkink (1998), and Bevir and Richards (2009).

Experimentation and engagement are deeply interrelated. Experimentation generally relies on networks for backup and support. Organizers may promote collaborative problem-solving efforts through local networks, or they may use (or create) connections to more distant sources of support. This is sort of like plugging into an electrical power grid—drawing energy generated elsewhere into your household. It can involve getting funding for a project, a favorable decision from a higher authority, an act of support by a connected institution.

Such practices as conducting policy experiments, building networks, discussing ideas, and pooling resources have transformative potential. New capabilities thus gained may make it possible to act in new ways, because organizations gain the skills or technology, for example, to enforce particular interpretations of the law or to engage with actors whose support is necessary. To gain practical authority, activists in new institutions must work to ensure their organization's strategic location in relation to other organizations, some of which may control important decisions. What that strategic location might be, however, is not always obvious. Gaining the recognition needed to exercise practical authority may require complex negotiations, the development of relationships, pressure politics, demonstrations of capacity, or all of these.

In figure 1.1, we tentatively outline this argument but warn the reader that the intention is not to present a linear causal model; at most, this is a complex and contingent one. Broken lines in some of the arrows represent "if" or "may" statements, not "must" statements. By this, we mean that *if* a process results in certain changes, there may be movement toward building practical authority, but it is perfectly possible that practices lead to other outcomes, given the large number of other actors and materials present in a complex environment. Thus, if institution-building practices lead to the transformation of ideas, resources, and relationships, then it may be possible to construct capabilities and recognition; of course, it is also possible that practices have negative effects. Insofar as positive associations occur, an organization is likely to advance in building practical authority.

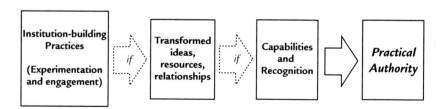

Figure 1.1. The Construction of Practical Authority.

THE PROBLEM OF INSTITUTIONAL ENTANGLEMENT

Brazil's political system has developed over the last century into a complex network of overlapping institutions and contradictory political traditions. Up to the 1930s, the federation was held together by patronage relationships between central powers and local bosses in the hinterlands of a huge, largely rural country (Nunes Leal 1948). In the 1930s, the authoritarian, populist, Estado Novo regime, led by Getúlio Vargas, was largely responsible for establishing the basis for rapid industrialization in Brazil, through targeted state investment, social protection for industrial and public service workers, and strict controls on labor organization. Along with all that came efforts to create a strong, technically competent national state. After the Estado Novo, there followed a period of competitive electoral politics and increased decentralization. Then, in 1964, a military coup initiated two decades of more authoritarianism and centralism, guided by an ideology of national security, highly interventionist economic policies, close ties between government and the private sector, and violent repression of popular organizing. In the late 1970s, that regime began to falter. To maintain popularity, the government improved public services and reduced violence against the free press and civic associations. The response was an upsurge of civic and union organizing and, starting in the 1980s, new political parties. With democratic elections now occurring normally, the 1990s were dominated by experiments in state reform, ranging from privatization to various forms of administrative reform to experiments, especially at the local level, in direct citizen participation.

As each of these mobilizations to change Brazil left its mark, traces of earlier ones remained, often quite conspicuously. The various reform projects of the last century that sought to eliminate vices by creating new institutions rarely attracted coalitions sufficiently powerful to entirely get rid of the old ones. To get things done in this context, both state and societal actors have had to learn a particular grammar for negotiating complexity. As we show in the next chapter, one result of partial reforms is the proliferation of organizations with overlapping responsibilities, some of which have little authority. In environmental resource management alone in Brazil, most state governments today have a water agency, an environmental licensing agency (which may or may not be the same as the agency responsible for forest management or protected areas), a secretariat of environmental policy (supposedly intended to make policies that the aforementioned agencies should implement), a water supply and sanitation company (possibly state-owned), a state water council, and a state environmental council. Municipal governments also often have environmental councils and environmental agencies. The Ministério Público (Public Ministry)—the agency responsible for promoting class action suits in the public interest—has an environmental department that brings suit against other public agencies for dereliction of responsibilities and negotiates *conduct adjustment agreements* in disputes involving private or public actors. The division of labor among these different agencies and organizations is far from clear.

This kind of institutional entanglement is not unique to Brazil and is particularly characteristic of federalist arrangements. In the United States, federalism famously produces struggles for authority among and within different levels of government, resulting in a variegated pattern that Grodzins (1966) describes as more like a marble cake than a layer cake (see also Ostrom, Bish, and Ostrom 1988). Studies of environmental management very often examine complex interactions among multiple governmental and nongovernmental organizations (Jenkins-Smith and Sabatier 2003; Evans 2002; Montpetit 2002; Jordan, Wurzel, and Zito 2005). Similar overlaps occur in other fields: employment policy influences health policy; transportation policy affects work policy; and so on. The prevalence of such interconnections means that problem solving in a complex environment can be frustrated by the actions of others in unexpected ways. In recent decades, social scientists have increasingly spoken of complexity to evoke conditions in which power is decentered, hierarchy may not be the dominant form of organization, organizations are heterogeneous and multivalent (Dooley 1997; Stark 1999; Axelrod and Cohen 2001), and governance occurs at least partly through policy networks.[17] The notion of *entanglement* suggests that overlapping administrative jurisdictions layered upon ambiguous functional divisions of labor may produce competition for, confusion about, or even gaps in political authority. Although the resulting uncertainty very likely creates more obstacles than opportunities, every once in a while, an organization or an actor can use the muddle to find alternative routes to get something done.

Conceiving of the environment within which these processes occur as an organizational ecology (Stark 1999; Ansell 2011) highlights the complex interdependence of the multitude of organizations and institutional logics that may coexist within a policy space (see also Rhodes 1997; Ansell 2000). From an institutional standpoint, it resembles the *regime complex* concept that Raustiala and Victor (2004, 279, 305) introduce in an international context, describing "an array of partially overlapping and nonhierarchical institutions governing a particular issue area," with "the presence of divergent rules and norms" and with the notable absence of some of

---

17. For reviews of the policy network literature, see Börzel 1998; Bevir and Richards 2009; and Rhodes 1997, 2006. For a review of the governance literature, see Ansell and Gash 2008.

the key building blocks necessary to ensure collaboration. Institutional interactions within domestic politics also can operate in this way. In highly complex environments, with lots of overlap and redundancy and varying organizational capabilities, institutions may operate through linkages and resource exchanges that are not part of any formal institutional design. Personal networks may facilitate negotiations among formally separated authorities, sometimes via meandering pathways that wind outside of a particular policy field or even outside of government altogether. Sometimes linkages are embodied in particular individuals who move from one situation to another within a policy arena, transiting from nonprofit to state to private-sector jobs. This kind of mobility, especially among professionals, is extremely common in Brazil, as in many other places.

Entanglement likely provides more opportunities for creative venue shifting and institutional innovation than more uniform, clearly hierarchical institutional settings. The palate of existing rules, regulations, and forms of interaction is colorful, allowing room for interpretation and bricolage (Douglas 1986; Clemens 1993; Cleaver 2002; Lund 2006). On the other hand, it can be harder to transform those innovations into long-lasting practices, since resources are dispersed and hierarchies contested. Decisions must be constantly renegotiated among the organizations and actors that compete for influence. Under these conditions, institutions can undergo extremely long processes of change, during which it remains unclear what path they are taking. Many such efforts stall, leaving institutional shadows—underfunded, understaffed organizations that continue to exist and maintain some resources and authority. Those incomplete paths fill up the institutional space, like the many branches in a tree, some of which never manage to bear fruit. The image of crisscrossing tree branches contrasts with the traditional notions of path dependence, in which it is presumed that the branches never meet after growing out from the trunk (Pierson 2000, 252–253). In the entangled system we study, there are many opportunities to jump from one branch to another or to leap onto and cultivate older paths whose sequences have been interrupted.

BUILDING PRACTICAL AUTHORITY IN ENTANGLED SETTINGS

The proposals for institutional reform disseminated in the developing world in the 1980s and 1990s were often portrayed as transfers of power from one kind of organization or actor to another. Privatization would transfer control over parts of the economy from government to market. Decentralization would devolve functions from central to local governing authorities. New participatory arenas proposed to transfer decision-making power from bureaucrats to civil society. The water resource management reform project we studied drew upon all three of these proposals.

The idea of a transfer, however, implies that decision-making authority is both situated and portable. In complex policy arenas such as water management, whose very definition implies high levels of coordination, this may not be the case. Decision-making authority prior to reform may be dispersed; agencies may be differentially (or not at all) endowed with skilled personnel or funding; some nominally responsible organs are captured by private interests; and others suffer from neglect that reflects the absence of anyone's interest. Decision-making processes are often opaque or ad hoc, involving multiple actors located in different parts of the state and sometimes outside of it; in some instances, it is more accurate to talk about nondecisions. Thus, reforms that purport to change how and where decisions are made and the institutional arrangements contributing to them may involve more than a transfer. Besides affecting the distribution of decision-making roles and capabilities, such reforms may imply *creating* new roles and capabilities to make and implement decisions that no one may have been making in the past.

Dealing with entanglement requires certain kinds of institution-building practices. Our language is careful here, because our study has not identified repeated *specific* combinations of activities. The improvisational component of institution-building practices is too strong for that. We do find that actors deal with the challenge of complexity in analogous ways, what we call *routes through entanglement*. In particular, we have identified two routes to building practical authority in complex institutional settings, often taken simultaneously: in the first, actors try to find spaces of action in the interstices of contending power networks, where they can build capabilities and recognition at a small scale; in the second, they bet on nonlinear outcomes by engaging creatively with different arenas and scales of action at the same time.

The first strategy involves, essentially, keeping one's head down, engaging in *practical experimentation at a small scale* where competition for authority is not strong. Starting small, resolving local problems, actors can build networks and capabilities. These actions produce what Ansell and Gash (2008) call *intermediate outcomes* that build trust and organizing capacity for future collaboration. But such initial actions also build external recognition for organizations (vis-à-vis other policy actors, specialists, or even the general public) as effective problem-solving arenas. That recognition can support later efforts at acquiring more formal power.

Some efforts at building capabilities and recognition through experimentation have more success than others. This is in part because such practices take place in a context with strong inertial forces and where political and administrative units as well as private actors wield a multitude of different, potentially relevant power resources. Some institution builders have strong connections with politically powerful actors; this was the case for some of the most active committees in our study. Of course, in a country with regional inequalities as extreme as those in Brazil, the available resources for establishing a new water management system also varied accordingly. In the poorest river basins we studied, mainly in the Northeast of Brazil, organizations relied heavily on outside funders—often the World Bank or other aid agencies—for support that elsewhere in the country often came from local institutions.

Despite such asymmetries—or perhaps because of them—experimenting at the small scale involves a great deal of perseverance by actors who were otherwise disadvantaged politically (March and Olsen 1989, 86). Since power holders tend to resist institutional changes that might put their authority into question, people intent on creating new sites of authority often have to work under the radar in arenas that the more powerful do not consider to be strategic or important for their interests. Most of the more successful cases we examine in this book started off with small, often very local, and sometimes uncontroversial projects. Some of the failures occurred because committees tried to take on powerful opposition forces too early.

An example of how small experiments can build capabilities and recognition is the work of institution builders in the Itajaí River Basin. The Itajaí River Basin Committee began with a seminar to write an emergency flood prevention plan in the wake of a devastating deluge. A federal agency heard about the flood prevention plan and soon after pressured the state government to sign an agreement to implement parts of it. That outcome encouraged participants to keep working together and attracted others, leading to more action: an information system, a reforestation project. The group eventually had enough experience to persuade a major funding agency to support their work, allowing them to scale up even more. Starting small, the Itajaí basin activists not only built confidence among members that their effort was worthwhile but also built capabilities that had not existed before. Even in the face of resistance from the state government to institutional change in water management, that committee gradually developed considerable regional and national credibility, giving it influence (albeit not overriding influence) despite the state's opposition.

Getting even the smallest experiments to work, and certainly going beyond the small scale of action, requires that people find ways to engage with other organizations and sites of decision making in a complex—and dynamic—environment. This involves finding ways to work with and around existing arrangements and sometimes requires working to change elements of the context that currently impede implementation of new policies. Activists we studied did this in three general ways: *bricolage, hedging,* and *shifting scales. Bricolage* as we use it here means appropriating institutional forms and procedures or even "styles of thinking and sanctioned social relations" from other settings and using them in new combinations and new ways (Cleaver 2002, 16; see also Douglas 1986, Clemens 1993; Lund 2006). Bricolage is improvisation but improvisation facilitated by action within multiple, overlapping personal and institutional networks (Sewell 1992; Emirbayer and Mische 1998). It is material action; the bricoleur's tinkering aims to produce facts on the ground, which in turn become resources for further action.

A different strategy for navigating complex contexts is the ubiquitous practice of hedging. Here, institutional organizers work on construction of more than one institutional arena at the same time. They are, proverbially, putting their eggs in more than one basket, under conditions of substantial uncertainty about the future of any given effort.

Scalar boundaries, often presumed to be clearly delimited, are often porous, allowing actors to engage in a politics of scale, framing problems and solutions in particular ways to favor particular courses of action, or attempting to rescale or hierarchically reorder scales of action (Molle 2007, 359). Not all of these are clearly visible: Our understanding of any process is also affected by the scale of our observations, as we zoom in to observe micro-processes or zoom out to try to map the big picture (Nicolini 2009). This calls for an approach that incorporates multiple perspectives.

In *Dynamics of Contention,* McAdam, Tarrow, and Tilly (2001) identify *scale shift* as a key mechanism through which activists strive to bring about political change, both domestically and later (Tarrow 2005) transnationally. In this sense, the term's meaning is similar to the venue shopping strategy that Baumgartner and Jones (1993) identify in policy subsystems or Keck and Sikkink's (1998) boomerang effect. Our study confirms the central importance of individuals and groups that are or can be present at multiple scales and can interact with authorities at multiple levels of government. In design and implementation of the reform process explored here, for example, the interaction between lawmaking at the national level and experimentation with local level pilot projects was important to both. Over the long haul, river basin committees attempting to find a niche within which they could be effective sometimes had to rescale their activities in relation to both the interorganizational context and the scalar dynamics of the river itself (Molle 2007, 359).

This book will explore both ways in which actors navigate entanglement to explain two general types of (interrelated processes): the construction of a legally defined institutional design for water management and the construction of practical authority in river basin committees. These things were happening in a Brazil that was undergoing significant political and economic changes in the 1980s and 1990s, explained in chapter 2. That chapter also explores how a history of diverse institutional reforms in Brazil has produced entanglement. Chapters 3 and 4 explore the complex process of creating and passing reform legislation for water policy in such an entangled setting. This process occurred at multiple levels of government, involved a diverse group of actors in state and society, and proceeded both through preliminary discussions and deliberations that resulted in new water laws (chapter 3) and through experiments with implementation (chapter 4). Freshwater resources in Brazil are in the public domain but can be governed under either state or federal law, depending mainly on whether they cross state lines. These systems are interdependent: although large river systems are generally under federal domain, they may have tributaries that fall within the domain of states. Thus, the legal action required for changing the water management framework engaged multiple agencies in executive branches and legislatures at both state and federal levels.

The political compromises required to get new laws passed left unresolved a great many contentious issues, and implementation efforts starkly revealed legal lacunae. Resolving these problems sometimes required the creative adaptation of institutional rules that had originally been made for other purposes; in the quest for a way to resolve the seemingly intractable jurisdictional problems involved in charging high-volume users for the water resources they used, reformers appropriated a subcontracting mechanism that had been adopted to provide greater flexibility in government funding for nonprofits, facilitating public–private partnerships mainly for social policy. The process by which this occurred, discussed in chapter 4, mobilized powerful industries and other private actors who had remained mainly on the sidelines during the early phases of the reform initiative and involved strategic action simultaneously at river basin, state, and federal levels.

In chapters 5, 6, and 7, we look more closely at the creation and evolution of river basin committees, key components of the new system. As organizations in which major stakeholders were supposed to be represented, they can be viewed as microcosms of the system as a whole. Here the question of scale moves front and center, as does the tremendous variation in the political ecology—the configuration of water problems, political power, interorganizational context and relationships, resources, the variety of time horizons within which actions could be understood, and the availability and commitment of creative organizers—within which the committees were being created.

To make sense of this diversity, we found it necessary to focus more on processes than on the correlation between conditions and outcomes that characterizes most comparative work. This shift in focus, alluded to in the prologue, was necessary in part because we found it impossible to compare constantly shifting outcomes along a common scale of effectiveness. We also found that the organizers we studied frequently attempted to change the conditions that supposedly constrained their actions, for example, by trying to improve the capacity of other institutions to provide committees with information and to implement their proposals. An attempt to compare very different kinds of organizing processes seemed more fruitful, but it implied looking for ways to make sense of processes whose time lines were quite different from the one our research project followed. The formation of river basin committees was a moment in longer and locally distinctive institutional and individual histories; the meanings attached to water and to the advantages and problems it brought were more distinctive still; and the practices appropriate to one situation did not necessarily apply to others, however similar they might appear to be. What, in the end, were we comparing?

The concept of practical authority helps us to identify possible patterns in these interactions without attempting to impose order on their irreducible messiness. It exposes, in fact, a question that we rarely ask in political science: How do new organizations of this kind become institutions at all? With few exceptions, the river basin committees we studied were established as a result of new legislation, with associated formal purposes and responsibilities. Since their performance would depend on their ability to coordinate other organizations not necessarily committed to the enterprise, the list of committees' formal responsibilities often represented an aspiration rather than a viable program. As they tried to make those aspirations real, committee organizers discovered that the means for doing so were not necessarily part of the package and that if they wanted to exercise their assigned functions, they were going to have to either demand or assemble the authority to do so. In a great many of the cases we studied, this process of becoming the institutions they were supposed to be either stalled early or veered off in unexpected directions.

To assemble the practical authority they needed to function, committee activists had to build capabilities and recognition not only for their own organizations but also among other recalcitrant, problematic, or simply missing elements of the broader context within which they had to work. The kinds of activities that the committees we studied engaged in were so varied as to defy categorization: conducting studies, holding meetings, negotiating with authorities to build or stop building infrastructure, fighting legal battles, starting environmental education projects, sponsoring local river cleanup and reforestation initiatives, and many more. This assortment of activities seemed to contribute to practical authority especially when directed at three central tasks: framing ideas about what the committee should do in ways that were adapted to local problems and opportunities, developing the administrative structure of their committees, and finding a viable niche within the broader ecology of interdependent organizations within which they operated.

These efforts were not always successful. Indeed, most cases we examined illustrate the risks to which Latour (1996, 58) refers: "The full difficulty of innovation becomes apparent when we recognize that it brings together, in one place, on a joint undertaking, a number of interested people, a good half of whom are prepared to jump ship, and an array of things, most of which are about to break down." Such efforts require attaching and enabling both human and nonhuman elements of a new project, no trivial task.

There are many reasons that a number of river basin committees failed to acquire practical authority. In some cases, formal committee organization occurred, but the kinds of institution-building practices we describe in this book did not take place: leaders either failed to appear or, more often, did not undertake the kind of experimentation and engagement we describe here. Sometimes this was because, like many scholars of institutions, they expected formal institutions to work automatically and simply followed the official guidelines: holding meetings, discussing plans, proposing water charges and other instruments of water management defined by the laws. When these management tools did not implement themselves, some people became frustrated and stopped participating. Some of them found more propitious venues for addressing their concerns. Others simply waited for the model to begin to work. Often, committees stalled because organizers never found a way to translate their abstract missions into viable projects around which people could mobilize. Yet even where they did transform ideas into practices, their efforts did not always pan out (hence the dotted lines in figure 1.1). Experiments faltered; resources never materialized; networks could not mobilize enough political support to sustain the effort or overcome resistance; participants lost patience with the process.

Our purpose in this book is to understand better what institution builders actually do in entangled institutional settings. Ideas about institutional design do not become institutions by themselves; they materialize as actors adapt the ideas and assemble the resources and relationships that make them real. How this happens varies dramatically. This is because of the inherently improvisational nature of any form of action that involves creativity (Bevir 2006, 287). In this sense, our notion of institution-building practices contrasts sharply with the recently popular concept of best practices in policy debates. Precise combinations of practices are rarely repeated. Identifying different routes through entangled institutional settings may be useful for shedding light on how actors build new institutions, but it does not replace creative thinking.

CHAPTER 2

Entangled Institutions and Layered Reform Narratives

Governing Water Resources in Historical Context

The end of the 20th century was a critical moment in recent Brazilian history, abounding with desire for and experiments with reinventing the nation's political life and at the same time with deep uncertainties about the future. When the reform processes analyzed in this study began in earnest, in the late 1980s, the country was undergoing a transition from authoritarian rule. The departing military regime had seized power in 1964 from an elected civilian government on the proposition that economic growth and defense against communism were more worthy of guarantees than political freedom. After riding high during almost a decade of economic miracle, the regime faced a slowdown in the mid-1970s, combined with demands for the restoration of political and civil rights. By the end of the decade, a new brand of union activism and a variety of other social movements were increasingly visible on the political scene. The regime initiated a slow liberalization—reducing censorship, imprisonment, and torture and allowing some (partially competitive) elections—but held on to power for another decade. The first direct elections for president occurred only in 1989.

Those who believed that democratization would usher in a bright future right away had their hopes quickly dashed. The authoritarian legacy included an unmanageable foreign debt, spiraling inflation, an economy in recession, and a vast reservoir of pending social demands. There was widespread disillusionment with the dominant development model, designed to stimulate economic growth with high-impact projects financed by state spending or low-interest foreign loans. But many of the dramatic new ideas attempted early in the democratic transition—a string of heterodox inflation-fighting measures, for example—failed spectacularly, feeding

Brazilians' long-standing skepticism about radical turnarounds. Brazil was the country of the future—and always would be.

Two new transformation narratives sprouted up out of this generalized pessimism in the late 1980s and 1990s. First, the *democratization narrative* marked the 1988 federal constitution, which reflected broad aspirations for a more just and participatory society. It also fostered greater concern with political and civil rights and transparency and spawned a variety of participatory experiments meant to expand the sphere of self-governance. Second, the *liberalization narrative* justified a dramatic lowering of trade barriers, deregulation, and a corresponding reform of the central state apparatus designed to reduce its economic footprint and streamline its operations. Both narratives differentiated themselves from the developmentalist vision of social and economic reform that had dominated Brazilian politics since the 1930s, in which the state was primarily responsible for transformation. The actors involved in water reform situated themselves in relation to different versions of these new idealized narratives of how to transform Brazil, along with older developmentalist ones, and located their interlocutors within those narratives as well.

Multiple reform ideas translated into the creation of a hodgepodge of partially overlapping institutions throughout Brazilian policy making: privatized companies, new regulatory agencies, participatory councils, and so on. Furthermore, consistent with a process that Streek and Thelen (2005, 22–24) call "layering", these changes occurred without the elimination of older institutions. As a result, institutional activists had to navigate many arenas, according to diverse rules, and to deal with multiple understandings of what changes were desirable. In effect, they had to be institutionally multilingual. This multiplicity allowed for creative institution-building practices by offering a broad palette of institutional ideas with which to work and by creating numerous sites for building relationships and garnering resources. However, the context of institutional entanglement also subverted efforts to routinize innovation by propagating myriad sources of potential opposition to new ways of doing things.

This chapter has five sections. First, we briefly discuss how our understanding of institutional entanglement fits with prevailing theories of the state. Second, we present a basic view of the Brazilian political system that describes the kinds of overlapping tensions that contribute to institutional entanglement and uneven institutional strength. Third, we examine the main reform narratives that have guided institution builders in Brazil over the last century: developmentalism, democratization, and liberalization. We then introduce the reader to the pre-reform history of freshwater policy in Brazil, locating its roots in the developmentalist narrative. Finally, we argue that the reform project for governing rivers reflects not only the democratization and liberalization narratives but also the continuing presence of developmentalist ideas.

NEITHER STRONG NOR WEAK: THE ENTANGLED STATE

The view of the Brazilian state as a tangle of fragmented, inconsistently competent, erratically permeable, and partially interconnected organizations does not fit with most theories of how the state works. Historically, state theorizing has oscillated between society-centric and state-centric views. The former includes both pluralist and Marxist traditions in which the state is seen as little more than a reflection of social forces, lacking in resources or interests of its own. Weberian approaches, on the other hand, have often overemphasized the autonomy of bureaucracies from society.

Moving beyond the divide between state-centric and society-centric views, some authors have explored the complex relations between state and nonstate organizations and actors. One approach sees the state as a strong organization at the center of a social system but one that establishes dense links throughout society. In Michael Mann's (1993) conception, the modern state is a central force that wields what he calls "despotic" power, that is, the capacity to force social actors to obey its decisions, even against their will. But it also can develop what he calls "infrastructural power" through which it builds governing capacity by supporting social organization. The resulting theory rejects a zero-sum conception of state–society relations in which the strength of one depends on the weakness of the other. Similarly, Evans's (1995) notion of "embedded autonomy" suggests that strong states and societies can be complementary. He argues that more effective states are both bureaucratically autonomous (in the sense of being technically competent and professionalized) and maintain close ties to well-organized social groups.

Another approach rejects the notion of the state as having a strong center, emphasizing its internal fragmentation and suggesting that there may be no clear division between state and society at all. In Migdal's (2001) "state in society approach," the state is profoundly permeated by networks. Migdal argues that states project a strong "image" of unity, but actual state practices "batter the image of a coherent, controlling state and neutralize the territorial and public–private boundaries" (Migdal 2001, 19). From a Foucaultian perspective, Rose and Miller (1992, 176) advance the notion of a state immersed in a complex web of social institutions: "To the extent that the modern state 'rules,' it does so on the basis of an elaborate network of relations formed amongst the complex of institutions, organizations and apparatuses that make it up, and between state and non-state institutions."

Although they seem to contradict each other, both the more centered conceptions of Mann (1993) and Evans (1995) and the more decentered views of Migdal (2001) and Rose and Miller (1992) seem to describe aspects of the Brazilian state.[1] Capable bureaucracies exist—especially in the federal government and some states—that have strong ties to social organizations. At the same time, it is easy to identify extremely porous institutions, with almost no professional culture, dominated by patronage politics. The state's capacity to enforce the rule of law is highly uneven, with some government agencies occupied by well-trained professionals and working efficiently, while others are unable to implement policies and programs effectively. Technically trained personnel tend to be concentrated in agencies of the federal government or those of wealthier states such as São Paulo. The vast majority of Brazilian municipalities are dramatically understaffed and underfunded. We very often observe public employees forming strategic networks with one another and with actors in the private sphere to move policy design and decision making forward. Numerous authors have warned against assuming that formal institutions in Latin America are stable or that their decisions are enforced and have contended that institutional weakness produces an environment of uncertainty (O'Donnell 1993, 1999; Weyland 2002a; Helmke and Levitsky 2004; Levitsky and Murillo 2005). The caution they recommend applies to Brazilian politics but not all the time or in all places or policy areas.

The coexistence of dispersed and concentrated powers, of strong and weak parts of the state, and of different patterns of state–society interaction has been produced through a long series of unfinished, contradictory state reform processes. Another result of this history is a great deal of redundancy, overlap, and jurisdictional confusion among Brazilian institutions, a situation we call *entanglement*. This is largely a result of the strength (and not the weakness) of previous institutional reform movements. Past efforts at institutional reform leave traces, even when they were unsuccessful. Organizations created to enact prior institutional changes are rarely abolished when new ones are created and continue to be run by actors who may defend "old" ways of doing things. Pendulum-like reform efforts—such as cycles of centralization and decentralization of the federal system in Brazil—can result in deeply seated tensions within as well as among institutions, making it unclear which actors or organizations have authority.

The result is a complex legacy of unevenly strong, overlapping institutions that interact with one another according to different logics. Understanding institution-building efforts in Brazil (especially those that involve reconfiguring practical authority) requires examining how actors deal with this complexity.

---

1. Evans (1995) notes this dual characteristic of the Brazilian state, as does Martins (1997).

THE FOUNDATIONS OF INSTITUTIONAL COMPLEXITY
IN BRAZIL

Edmar Bacha famously described Brazil of the 1970s as "Belindia": it included both a small, rich country, like Belgium, and a huge, poor country, like India. There was certainly nothing novel about recognizing inequality in Brazil; it has been a continuing theme for a century. Again and again, a relatively small set of elites has succeeded in appropriating both economic benefits and political spoils of development policies, social policies, and stabilization policies. For those elites, any call for rapid inclusion of the vast and presumably ignorant masses amounted to populist demagogy; a gradual expansion of the political and economic pie would eventually prepare larger and larger sectors of the population for full participation in political life. This extended history of exclusion was reinforced by limitations on suffrage and obstacles to the legal acquisition of land (Holston 2008).

Yet it would be simplistic to describe Brazilian politics simply in terms of domination of the weak by the strong, of the masses by the elites, of the periphery by the center, or of society by the state. Instead, political institutions empower multiple and contradictory interests and ideas. The tensions among them provide a part of the entangled terrain in which our story unfolds (and through which the actors in it must navigate).

During the first decades of the 20th century, national politics was tied together through patronage relations with regional and local oligarchies. In the 1930s, the populist-authoritarian regime of Getúlio Vargas transformed the country by initiating the developmentalist model, based on heavy state intervention in the economy and the first social protection policies. Industrialization in the cities and the lack of opportunities in the countryside led to an extraordinarily rapid urbanization process, with the urban population exceeding the rural one for the first time in the 1960s. The country became a major industrial force and, more recently, one of the planet's most important producers of primary goods.

Today, Brazil can no longer be called a newly democratizing country. Since 1985, the country has experienced continuous civilian rule, with regular elections, unproblematic presidential succession even in the one case of presidential impeachment, and consistent constitutional government. Beginning in 1994—when hyperinflation was finally brought under control—there has been a remarkable degree of consistency in macroeconomic and social policy and a palpable improvement in the living situations of a large part of the Brazilian population. In 2010, researchers at the Getúlio Vargas Foundation declared that for the first time more than half of the population was officially in the "middle class" socioeconomic range. Income inequality has also fallen significantly over the last two decades (Neri 2010).

Four central tensions characterize the entangled character of the Brazilian state. One is the tension between the central (national) government and regional (state) and local powers. Brazil has three constitutional levels of government: the Union, or national government; state governments, of which there are 26 plus the Federal District; and municipalities, of which there were 5,565 nationwide in 2011. Each of these federal units has a directly elected executive and legislative branch (unicameral at municipal and state levels and bicameral at the national level). Besides the National Constitution, each state and municipality has a charter. Within each of these levels, directly elected executives rarely command a majority of members of the legislature and must normally assemble a coalition to govern.

Over the centuries, the Brazilian federal system has cycled between more centralized and decentralized power. Vargas's Estado Novo regime of 1937–1945 was one period in which the national government took power from the states. The authoritarian regime of 1964–1985 was another period of centralization. The 1988 constitution, in turn, increased the autonomy of states and municipalities, mandating automatic fiscal transfers from the federal government and granting municipalities the status of autonomous federative units (Abrucio 2005). In the 1990s, Fernando Henrique Cardoso's government tried to assert more federal control over fiscal policies (IPEA 2010). But even during the most centralized periods, regional elites retained a strong influence on national politics. Currently, local, state, and federal governments are required to share power in many policy areas (especially environmental ones), though such mandates rarely specify the mechanisms for power sharing, and there is not a strong presumption of subsidiarity. Struggles between state and federal governments for influence are reproduced in relations between municipalities and state governments.

Regionalism retains a strong influence in the National Congress. The Senate, in which each state has three representatives regardless of population, has significant powers to overturn decisions in the lower house along with exclusive powers of its own. What is more unusual is the extreme malapportionment in the lower chamber, owing to a distinctive "floor and ceiling" rule according to which no state can have fewer than 8 federal deputies or more than 70. The poorer states of the North and Northeast thus enjoy constitutionally mandated overrepresentation in Congress, an instrument they use to oppose the wealthy and populous states of the Southeast.[2]

---

2. Alfred Stepan (2000, 149) classifies Brazil's federal system as the world's most "demos-constraining." In the 2002 elections, for example, it took 280,247 votes to elect a federal deputy in São Paulo, as opposed to only 21,122 votes in Roraima. Data calculated from Tribunal Superior Eleitoral (http://www.tse.gov.br/siee/seire/comum/RelatorioHTML.jsp) and from Chamber of Deputies (http://www.camara.gov.br/internet/Deputado/ultimaeleicao.asp).

A second tension is between a highly fragmented party system—which pre-vents presidential parties from obtaining strong majorities in the legislature—and institutions that otherwise give the executive branch substantial legislative powers. Since the 1980s, Brazil has had a multiparty system, "one of the most fractionalized systems in the world" (Power 2010, 19). Parties normally divide into two coalitions, but because of volatility in party identification on the part of both politicians and publics many small parties sometimes hold the balance in coalition formation and bargain accordingly. Members of state congressional delegations often owe greater allegiance to their governor than to leaders of the political parties to which they belong. Getting legislation through Congress often means satisfying regional interests along with partisan ones (Abrucio 1994). Despite the disorganizing potential of party fragmentation, the execu-tive branch retains substantial control over the legislative agenda and relies on multiple institutional mechanisms besides the distribution of pork for get-ting its legislation passed (Abrucio 1994, 19; Limongi and Figueiredo 1998; Figueiredo and Limongi 2006; Power 2010). The result is that 85 percent of legislation approved between 1985 and 2006 was presented by the executive branch, while individual legislators rarely see their propositions voted into law (Figueiredo and Limongi 2006).

An important consequence of the tension between the centrifugal pull of parties and regions and the centripetal force of executive power is the fragmentation produced within the executive branch itself. Brazilian presi-dents obtain governability in a multiparty system where they rarely have a full majority by sharing executive power. In what some have dubbed *coali-tional presidentialism*, Brazilian presidents act much like prime ministers in parliamentary systems, distributing control over government agencies to members of the party coalition, often in proportion to the distribution of coalition seats in the legislature (Limongi and Figueiredo 1998; Pereira, Power, and Rennó 2008; Power 2010). This set of practices renders the system governable but complicates its administration, insofar as granting substantial autonomy to each government agency means that they work according to diverse and sometimes contradictory logics. The Brazilian federal government, for example, includes an agricultural ministry typically dominated by agribusiness and an agrarian reform ministry dominated by rural social movements.

A third political tension is between personalism and professionalism in the bureaucracy. Since the first Vargas government in the 1930s, the Brazilian state has repeatedly invested in the creation of "insulated" bureau-cracies, assigning high-priority issues to new government agencies staffed with well-paid and well-qualified professionals. Yet the creation of such protected spaces has usually occurred without dismantling preexisting institutions (Sikkink 1991; Geddes 1994). Although the rationale for this is to avoid confronting a bureaucracy resistant to change, the result tends to be the opposite. Continuing to function with reduced authority, displaced agencies seek new attributions or wage bureaucratic warfare to recover old ones. Furthermore, at the same time as pockets of expertise and efficiency were being produced in some parts of the state, less technocratic parts were expanding. Martins (1997, 16–17) depicts state agencies dedicated to social policy as highly permeable, populated by badly trained bureaucrats, patronage hiring, and clientelist behavior:

> A dual pattern was established. The upper echelon of public administration...became the best state bureaucracy in Latin America; in the lower echelons (including agencies responsible for health services and social assistance), clientelistic patterns of personnel recruitment involved favoritism and populist manipulation of public resources. [Our translation]

Personal and professional networks are central components of bureaucratic logic, even in more technocratic parts of the state. Despite the rapid expansion of a meritocratic bureaucracy, the Brazilian federal government has a huge number of nominated positions—nearly 22,000 in 2010. But the majority of these hires (70 percent) come from the pool of permanent public employees who have passed civil servant exams (IPEA 2010, 400). State and municipal governments are even more dependent on political nominees, and some have very few meritocratic positions at all. The prevalence of political appointments—which come with significant salary increases for public servants—inserts an element of political competition into the meritocratic bureaucracy. Personal and professional networks deeply influence who gets high-level jobs—even when the choice is only among the highly qualified. Brazilian economic policy, for example, has been long dominated by technical professionals who studied in certain schools, even at the high school level (Loureiro 1997; Morais 2004). Although at both state and federal levels administrative rearrangements are commonplace, with the creation and dissolution of new ministries, departments, agencies, and other institutions, bureaucratic corps often travel together from one place to another (Schneider 1992). Eduardo Marques argues that within the Brazilian state the *positional power* of individuals in networks is just as important as the institutional power that comes from their location in the bureaucratic hierarchy. Such networks may grow out of professional association, out of simultaneous entry into government service, or out of organizational or partisan allegiance, among other sources. Individuals may seek to move together from one bureaucratic appointment to another. The actions and reach of these networks determine whether decisions, once made, actually take root in the social world (Marques 2000, 52–53).

A fourth, closely related set of tensions has to do with the relations between state and organized civil society and more specifically between democratic participation and other kinds of state–society linkages. Another legacy of the Vargas period was a system of state-managed corporatist relations with both labor and (to a lesser extent) business. Between the 1930s and the 1980s, labor unions were tightly controlled by the Brazilian state, with stark limitations on labor organizing (Rodrigues 1990; Cardoso 1999; Collier and Collier 2002). Union leaders were widely considered to be little more than servants of the government (*pelegos*). Other kinds of associations, such as neighborhood organizations, were often dedicated principally to clientelist favor exchange and vote getting for politicians (Gay 1990). Business associations were freer to organize than labor unions, though scholars have shown that interactions between government and the private sector more often occurred through personal relationships than through organizations (Cardoso 1970; Diniz and Boschi 2000). The interpenetration of technocratic elites—in public administration, the private sector, and the military—was one of the pillars of Guillermo O'Donnell's (1973) explanation for the rise of bureaucratic-authoritarian regimes (see also Stepan 1971). In sum, historically, Brazilians identified proximity between state and society with personalistic favoritism toward business interests on the one hand and the cooptation of civil society by the state on the other.

A dramatic effect of political liberalization in the late 1970s, however, was the emergence of new forms of civic organizing: new trade unionism—resistant to government control—along with grassroots movements in urban neighborhoods and rural settlements, new forms of cultural expression, and a new environmentalism (Keck 1989; Keck 1992; Viola and Goldenberg 1992; Doimo 1995). Democratization also saw the appearance of a new kind of political actor in the professional, social change–oriented nonprofit sector called nongovernmental organizations (NGOs), many of which were intent on rescuing the idea of a public interest from an exclusive identification with the state (Landim 1993; Fernandes 1994). Advocates of social change were not the only ones that organized. Although the opening of the economy to international capital was a blow to the industrial sector (Bresser-Pereira and Diniz 2009), business groups began to build more effective interest associations in the 1990s and 2000s than they had in the past. A number of regional and industry-based organizations actively lobbied government, some favorable to neoliberal policies and others against them (Diniz and Boschi 2003).

The social movement and civil society groups that emerged during the transition took two main tacks. Eschewing a long history of state control, they sought greater autonomy, attempting to create a sphere of initiative outside the state. Instead of waiting for the state to confer rights in the form of privileges to preferred groups, new citizens' organizations "discovered" or created or claimed new rights (Scherer-Warren 1993; Doimo 1995; Dagnino 1998). At the same time, new organizations increasingly got involved in party politics—especially through new leftist parties such as the PT (Workers' Party) that argued for a radical democratization of political life (Keck 1992). Social movement activists lobbied and gathered signatures for popular amendments to the 1988 constitution; fought for new health, social assistance, and environmental legislation; and increasingly took government jobs to promote their causes (Abers and von Bülow 2011).[3] Business groups also joined new participatory arenas for policymaking—such as the industrial policy councils set up by the Cardoso and Luis Inácio Lula da Silva administrations (de Toni 2010) and also in other such organizations, among them the river basin committees discussed here.

These changes challenged the automatic presumption that state–society proximity implied corruption, favoritism, and cooptation. They suggested that close ties between government and private actors could also generate greater accountability of the state to civil society, a deepening of democracy. Over the last two decades, there has been a proliferation not only of new civic groups but also of new formal and informal spaces for state–society interaction. These new relationships add a layer of complexity to the policy process, which now regularly includes exchanges between policy makers and both business and civic groups.

Each of the four tensions just described—between central and regional governments, between executive centralism and party fragmentation, between meritocracy and personalism, and between permeability and participation—contributes to making the rules of political action exceedingly complex in Brazil. There is considerable juxtaposition among them. For example, federalism affects the way presidents build party coalitions in Congress, insofar as state caucuses influence their composition (IPEA 2010, 84). In some cases, the distribution of executive power follows not only party but also regional lines. For example, for much of the last decade, the ministry responsible for regional development has been controlled by northeastern politicians. Personalistic politics also interacts with presidential coalition building to the extent that alliances are secured through the distribution of political appointments (IPEA 2010, 84).

These interconnections mean that efforts to bring about institutional change must operate at multiple levels. To build new sites of political

---

3. Among the procedures governing the drafting process for the 1988 federal constitution was one that provided for citizen-initiated amendments, which, if they garnered a sufficient number of signatures, were considered on the same footing as those proposed by elected constituent assembly members.

authority, institution builders might have to work simultaneously with local, state, and federal governments; they often must draw upon both party ties and connections with the executive; they have to seek out strong technical capabilities where they lie and also build and navigate networks within the bureaucracy; and they must interact not only with state actors but also with a broad array of private organizations that are involved in policy processes. In an area such as water policy, such complexity is multiplied by the number of public and private uses for water (energy, drinking water supply, sanitation, irrigation, industry, navigation, tourist development, etc.), each associated with different public agencies, with their own histories and traditions. If navigating such an entangled environment seems like an impossible task, that is because it often is impossible. The efforts at institution building that we describe in this book are partial, incremental, and often unsuccessful.

Thus, a notable trait of institutional complexity in Brazil is that institutional strength is unevenly distributed. If the second half of the 20th century marked the emergence of a technocratic, interventionist state and of a modern, industrial economy, both trends had limited reach. Government capacity and, especially, qualified personnel were concentrated in the capitals and in only some areas of the bureaucracy. Although Brazil is famous for having an inflated state sector, Santos (2006) demonstrates that, compared with those of rich countries, Brazil's public administration is far from oversized; excessive public hiring has mainly occurred at the lowest levels: janitors, coffee servers, doormen, and so on.

The shortage of well-qualified workers in the bureaucracy reflects a more general problem of the geographical distribution of skilled workers in Brazil, especially outside of the big cities. From the 1930s to the 1960s, the Brazilian state expanded under the developmentalist policies of Getúlio Vargas and his successors. Their high-profile projects involved physical infrastructure such as roads, railroads, hydroelectric power generation plants, and steel-making capacity. Social infrastructure—schools, clinics, teacher training, drainage, and sewers—was left to local and state governments or was simply left out. School enrollments lagged well behind those of neighboring countries until quite recently. The portion of 7- to 14-year-olds in school rose from 62 percent in 1970 to 96 percent in 1998 (Rigotti 2001, 62). However, repetition and dropout rates remain extremely high, meaning that despite being in school, Brazilian children do not learn well (Rigotti 2001; Schwartzman 2010). In 2007, less than 10 percent of students received "minimally acceptable" scores in math and less than 25 percent in Portuguese (Schwartzman 2010, 4). Regional differences are enormous. For example, in the southern and southeastern states of the country, 53 percent of 19-year-olds have finished high school, compared with only 29 percent in the northeastern states (Schwartzman 2010, 6). As a whole, the portion of college-age people in higher education institutions is much lower than in neighboring countries: 16.6 percent compared with 47 percent for Argentina and 34 percent for Chile, to say nothing of 66 percent for Korea (Schwartzman 2010, 174). In general, highly skilled professionals remain "concentrated in a few cities in the country" (Queiroz and Golgher 2008, 41).

This excursus into education issues is relevant for our discussion of the institutional terrain in Brazil, because the uneven distribution of educated people has direct consequences for the state. In most regions of the country, there are simply not enough highly educated professionals around to manage municipal offices or state government outposts. The 1988 constitution led to a dramatic decentralization of public employment in Brazil, which had historically been concentrated in the federal government. By 1999, 42 percent of public employees in the country were in municipal government, and 40 percent worked for state governments (IPEA 2010, 256). The vast majority of these workers, however, are primary and secondary school teachers and health-care workers, most without higher degrees. Technical specialists, on the other hand, cluster in the state capitals and in some states. Although data on the education levels of municipal workers are unavailable, the findings of a 2009 study by the Brazilian census bureau (Instituto Brasileiro de Geografia e Estatística, or IBGE) are illustrative. Despite the near-universal existence of computers and Internet connections in municipal offices, only 51 percent of municipalities had working websites, an indicator of the lack of personnel capable of putting such sites together. The same study also found that 15 percent of Brazilian municipalities had no environmental management programs or policy structure. Only 20 percent of municipalities actually had departments exclusively dedicated to environmental management, while the remainder combined that function with other policy areas. Among municipalities with environmental programs of some kind, half of those agencies were headed by people without a college degree (IBGE 2009).

The distribution of qualified personnel through state government is also extremely unequal. Data on state freshwater management agencies in Brazil are indicative of the more general problem: in 2006, the northeastern states of Bahia and Pernambuco had, respectively, 3 and 24 technical professionals working in water management. The southeastern states of Minas Gerais and São Paulo, on the other hand, employed 234 and 658 such professionals, respectively. The distribution was not only a matter of regional development. While the situation in most states resembled the examples of Bahia and Pernambuco, Ceará state had more than 300 technical workers in a strong water management agency (Moreira 2010, 143). This was the result of a history of federal institution building in the region (Gutiérrez 2006a). Inversely, the well-developed (though largely rural) state of Santa Catarina employed only 11 water management professionals in 2006, a result of years of government resistance to environmentally oriented natural resource policies of any kind (Moreira 2010, 143). These different institutional contexts will have important implications for the capacity of river policy reformers to build new decision-making arenas and policy implementation capabilities in the river basins that reformers hoped would become responsible for a large part of freshwater management.

ENTANGLED REFORM NARRATIVES: DEVELOPMENTALISM, LIBERALISM, AND PARTICIPATORY DEMOCRACY

Competing and changing ideas about how to transform Brazilian society and politics contributed to the emergence of an entangled and uneven institutional ecology. For most of the 20th century, the developmentalist narrative was an account of how resolute, targeted state intervention in the economy was propelling Brazil into the modern, industrial era. This assertion underpinned the concentration of power in the federal executive that occurred during the two authoritarian periods Brazil experienced since 1930. It also occupies one pole of the persistent tensions we have discussed in this chapter: regional forces, party diversity, personalistic politics, and civil society activism all produce frictions with the narrative of the strong, technocratic state.

Developmentalism contributed to the unevenness of state institutions in Brazil, insofar as it favored development in big cities and the South of the country. The core idea was to reinforce the economic sectors with the strongest potential, investing public money in the infrastructure necessary to maximize their growth. Today this would likely be referred to as backing champions. Broader developmental effects would be a function of successful investment in industries with forward and backward linkages; these were not, however, territorially dispersed. In the rural Northeast, and in many of the towns of the interior in the rest of the country, people who stayed put experienced development from a distance, reflected on the screens of televisions that arrived along with electrical hookups (as the portrayal in the movie *Bye Bye Brasil* eloquently shows). People who could move did so.

Developmentalist policies combined a promotion of import substitution as a strategy to build a national industrial complex with social policies aimed at guaranteeing a stable, compliant labor force. The policy package included extensive public investment in infrastructure, protection of developing industries, fiscal incentives to attract foreign investment, and the direct state ownership of productive capacity conceived as fundamental for development or national security. It also involved the expansion of social protections such as minimum wage and social security laws alongside the creation of a corporatist system that put labor unions directly under government control, repressing any autonomous labor organizing.

Technocracy, a belief that traced its origins to a movement within the military in the 1920s, was a central tenet in the developmentalist faith.[4] By the 1960s, technocratic ideas had become integral to the national security doctrine with which the Brazilian military justified its overthrow of civilian government in 1964. However, the notion that government needed insulation from society to work effectively had also gained a following outside the military. In all Brazilian governments since the 1930s, whether democratic or authoritarian, presidents have made the establishment of new autonomous agencies with highly qualified, well-paid professionalized staff a key part of attempting to advance their agendas. These "pockets of efficiency" often coexist with patronage politics throughout the rest of government, and their insulation from competition among political interests tends to be short-lived (Sikkink 1991; Geddes 1994).

The idealization of technocracy coincides with the modern themes in planning and policy discourse that dominated the second half of the 20th century in Brazil. "Modernist planning attempts to overcome the contingency of experience by totalizing it; that is, by fixing the present as a totally conceived plan based on an imagined future" (Caldeira and Holston 2005, 399). The implication is that economic, regional, administrative, organizational, and policy plans cannot be devised without technical knowledge and are thus the product of technocratic bureaucracies. As we will see in this book, the idea that policy making should be protected from "politics" as a domain for the application of "neutral" technical knowledge retains a lot of currency in Brazilian policy circles. Indeed, political struggles over different substantive outcomes are often waged as if they were conflicts over technical issues; a good illustration of this pattern appears in chapter 6 regarding the debate over the São Francisco River transposition.

Developmentalism came under fire in the 1980s from two directions. As in many other countries of the region, foreign bank loans had cushioned the impact in Brazil of the 1973 and 1979 oil shocks. The borrowing bonanza came to a screeching halt when sharp rises in short-term interest rates made servicing the debt impossible, bringing Brazil to the brink of default and

---

4. The so-called *tenentes* (lieutenants) "wanted to force Brazil's emergence as a modern nation and believed it could be achieved in the short run only by a totally uncompromised cadre of non-political technocrats with an unswerving sense of national mission" (Skidmore 1967, 10).

to the first of a series of heavily conditioned International Monetary Fund (IMF) loans in 1982. The recession and rising inflation of the period gave credence to neoliberal pro-market ideas then sweeping the globe, with their pointed condemnation of a bloated and ineffective state sector. At the same time, from the left, social movements and civil society groups also opposed the big and centralized state, synonymous for them with exclusion and authoritarianism. They espoused a more decentralized and participatory democracy. These two distinct narratives of change became the most important political projects in Latin American politics in the 1990s and early 2000s (Dagnino, Olvera, and Panfichi 2006).

The rush to free market reform came later in Brazil than in other Latin American countries and was never fully implemented. The authors of the 1988 constitution included numerous requirements, such as stability for public employees, that reaffirmed the need for a large, interventionist state (Couto 1998). But almost a decade of hyperinflation shifted the political winds. Fernando Henrique Cardoso,[5] sociologist turned politician, became finance minister in 1993 and, on the back of his Real Plan's success in stabilizing the economy, was elected president in 1994. Ironically, given that he was famous as one of the fathers of dependency theory, Cardoso was a forceful exponent of liberalizing reforms. To make them politically viable, however, he had to negotiate with competing interests, a fact that limited their reach and required the massive use of patronage (Couto 1998).[6]

Although Cardoso's government followed the neoliberal prescriptions of privatization, budget cuts, and anti-inflationary monetary policy, Brazil benefited from some relaxation in the economic orthodoxy of international financial institutions; extreme antistatism had by then begun to give way to a call for a leaner and more effective state (Grindle 2000; Melo 2002). To move in this direction, Cardoso named economist Luiz Carlos Bresser-Pereira to head up a new Ministry of Federal Administration and State Reform. Influenced by the "new public management" school, Bresser called for more agile and collaborative forms of policy making (Barzelay 2001). Market and state were not the only alternatives, he believed. Civil society organizations, or the "third sector," offered the promise of providing many public services flexibly, effectively, and in a way more responsive to local

---

5. Cardoso's first foray into electoral politics came when he ran for Senate on the opposition party ticket in 1978; as runner-up to André Franco Montoro, he became the designated alternate, assuming the seat when Montoro was elected governor of São Paulo in 1982.

6. Cardoso won passage of constitutional amendments allowing for deregulation (Couto 1998) but was unable to enact other more unpopular structural reforms to address the fiscal crisis of the state. The sale of government-owned companies created during the developmentalist era ended up paying the bill, while monetary policies, such as extremely high interest rates, served to keep the currency stable (Pinheiro 2000; Weyland 2002b, 239–243).

needs (MARE 1995; Bresser Pereira 2001). Cardoso's main antipoverty program, the Comunidade Solidária, relied extensively on volunteering and partnerships with civil society organizations (Draibe 2003). Along the same lines, other new legislation officially recognized new types of non-profit organizations and authorized the transfer of state revenues to them (Arretche 2000; von Bülow and Abers 2000).

At the same time as the federal government tried out neoliberal ideas, some municipalities embarked on a different set of decentralizing experiments. Many activists who cut their political teeth in the social movements of the 1970s and 1980s had developed a deep antipathy to statism, whether in the authoritarian variant that had taken over much of Latin America during this period or in the version on display in Eastern European communist regimes. Instead, they embraced commitments to ideals of autonomy and radical participatory democracy (Weffort 1984). Mobilizing their forces to influence the constitutional assembly of 1987, social movements won inclusion of planks guaranteeing (at least formally) extensive social rights and mandating participatory approaches to decision making. Some groups then worked for national laws that would give civil society a voice in public policy, starting with health-care reform. Many social movements also supported the Workers' Party (Partido dos Trabalhadores, or PT), founded in 1980 by leaders connected to the new unionism, intellectuals, Catholic base communities, and an array of urban and rural movements dissatisfied both with the mainstream parties and with the orthodox left (Keck 1992). In 1989, the PT won the mayor's offices in 36 municipalities, including the city of São Paulo, and began to experiment with participatory policy making. Although in many cities, these experiments were not very successful (Abers 1996), Porto Alegre's participatory budget policy garnered international renown. It not only incorporated tens of thousands of people from poor neighborhoods into urban decision making but also demonstrated that this could occur without losing votes: the PT governed for four consecutive four-year terms in Porto Alegre. In the 1990s, hundreds of PT municipal administrations and some from other parties adopted similar participatory experiments. The PT gained a name as the party of democratic innovation (Santos 1998; Abers 2000; Avritzer 2002; Avritzer 2009; Baiocci 2005; Wampler 2007).

Efforts to reform health care also transformed the policy landscape by pioneering a model for decision making through participatory councils, subsequently adopted in other policy arenas. In 1990, after years of organizing, a network of popular and professional organizations successfully lobbied to get Congress to pass legislation creating the Unified Health System (Sistema Único de Saúde, or SUS), decentralizing health care and creating participatory councils at all three levels of government to regulate and monitor the system. These councils allocated half their seats to health-care providers, health-care workers, and government and reserved the other half for representatives of the public (through community associations and other groups) (Cortês 1998). The health council model was replicated in such areas as social assistance, child and adolescent policy, education, environment, and eventually (although with a novel territorial jurisdiction) freshwater management. All of them were conceived as national systems with councils at municipal and higher territorial levels in which civil society, private actors, and the state would share responsibility for decision making (Tatagiba 2002; Fuks, Perissinotto, and Souza 2004; Cunha 2007; Avritzer 2009; Avritzer 2010). By the end of the 1990s, one estimate counted almost 40,000 participatory councils throughout the country (IPEA 2005, 128).

These participatory reforms spread so rapidly because at the same time as radical democrats were demanding them, liberal state reformers were discovering civil society as a potential replacement for what they considered an inherently ineffective state (Bresser Pereira 2001; Franco 2001). One way of reducing the size of the federal bureaucracy was by decentralizing power and responsibility for some of its attributions to municipalities. Policy councils were useful mechanisms for guaranteeing transparency (Arretche 2000; Souza 2001). Thus, the main reason that almost all of Brazil's more than 5,500 municipalities created health councils was not social movement activism so much as the Cardoso administration's refusal to transfer federal health funds to municipalities without them.

Dagnino, Olvera, and Panfichi (2006) argue that the proximity between the neoliberal and the participatory democratic "projects" has created a "perverse confluence" (Dagnino, Olvera, and Panfichi, 16) that risks undermining efforts to promote a more radical and inclusive democracy in Latin America. The danger they see is that the liberal narrative depoliticizes concepts used in the democratic one, such as participation, civil society, and citizenship. Liberal programs may draw social movements in with a promise of democratic participation, only to neutralize them by turning them into service providers rather than decision makers. But the reverse is also possible; proximity between the two narratives may also mean that democratic results can grow out of liberal proposals. Even if they were created for other purposes, the existence of tens of thousands of participatory arenas throughout Brazil creates a space where civic groups have had access to the interior of public decision making, an opportunity to transform the state rather than simply to participate in its downsizing (Abers and Keck 2009).

The Brazilian political system has never been fully dominated by any of the three reform narratives discussed here. Instead, they coexist with one another and also with older, less intellectually coherent (but no less powerful) political traditions, such as personalistic politics and regionalism. The immortality of seemingly defunct formulations of political authority was dramatized vividly in 1993, when, by constitutional requirement, Brazil held a national plebiscite to decide whether the political system should be a monarchy or a republic (13 percent voted for monarchy!).

More recently, the presidency of Lula (2003–2010), the one-time trade unionist, founder and longtime leader of the Workers' Party, also illustrated the coexistence of different institutional narratives. Considering the experimentalism of Workers' Party municipal administrations, some expected the Lula government to make promotion of participatory practices more central to his administration than it did (Abers, Serafim and Tatagiba 2011; Moroni and Ciconello 2005; Silva 2009). Early on, Lula's government placed a high priority on maintaining fiscal discipline and reassuring an apprehensive business community that there would be no major shifts in economic policy. Over his two terms in office, however, there was a slow increase in the size of the federal civil service and a return to industrial policies, which some have called part of a "neodevelopmentalist" trend (Ridenti 2008; Boschi 2009). At the same time, real increases in the minimum wage, reproduced in public social security benefits, and an extensive program of conditional cash transfers jointly reduced extreme poverty by a substantial amount.

That such varied ideas could coexist would not be a surprise to followers of water resources policy: since the 1990s, the reform processes that have occurred in that field have been infused with both liberal and participatory ideas, standing alongside a still potent strand of developmentalist thinking. The next section will present this developmentalist legacy before we go on to sketch out the main ideas for institutional reform for water policy formulated in recent decades.

GOVERNING RIVERS FOR THE DEVELOPMENTALIST PROJECT

Brazil is by far the country with the largest endowment of freshwater resources. The Amazon basin alone, 60 percent of which is in Brazilian territory, holds 20 percent of the world's freshwater (Agência Nacional de Águas 2007, 9). Recognizing the exceptional opportunity this bounty offered, developmentalists from the 1930s on saw freshwater resources primarily as a source of energy that could fuel the nation's industrial development. From the late 19th century until the 1940s, hydroelectric energy production was dominated by foreign firms.[7] With Getúlio Vargas's Estado Novo regime,

7. As early as 1907, the federal government sought to increase its control over energy services and brought a water code proposal before the National Congress to that end. But foreign-owned electric companies lobbied against the bill, which never came up for a vote (Formiga Johnsson 1998, 59–63).

the state gained the upper hand, and private investors slowly lost control over the energy sector. The 1934 water code gave the federal government control of water rights concessions, required that water service companies be owned by Brazilian nationals, and mandated government approval of all hydroelectric initiatives (Formiga Johnsson 1998, 61). Over the next three decades, the federal government and some state governments took over some of the private electric companies, especially the electricity generation sector. The proportion of installed generation capacity that was publicly owned grew from only 6.8 percent in 1952 to 54.6 percent in 1965 (Hamaguchi 2002, 533).

Investment in large-scale dams began in the 1940s and peaked in the late 1970s, by which time hydropower produced more than 20 percent of Brazil's total energy supply (compared with 4 percent in the United States—Goldemberg 1978, 159) and almost all of its electrical energy. The first phase of big dam production began with the construction of the Paulo Afonso dam on the São Francisco River in 1949. The prevailing model at the time was the Tennessee Valley Authority in the United States. The idea was to connect dam construction to a broader regional development project, involving energy production, irrigation, navigation, and other activities. The creation of the São Francisco Valley Commission (CVSF) in 1948 inaugurated this approach (Formiga Johnsson 1998, 66).

In the 1960s, however, the government abandoned the regional development vision and focused on hydropower (Formiga Johnsson 1998, 76). In 1960, the government founded the Ministry of Mines and Energy (Ministério de Minas e Energia, or MME). Eletrobras, a giant state enterprise with regional subsidiaries, was created in 1962, with a monopoly on electric energy generation. Within the MME, the government established the National Department of Water and Electrical Energy (DNAEE) to oversee all water-related areas except irrigation and sanitation, the latter a state government responsibility (Formiga Johnsson 1998, 71). After the military took power in 1964, energy production moved farther up as a government priority. In 1966, President General Humberto de Alencar Castelo Branco approved a national energy production plan that included a series of large dams, none of which included provisions for navigation or flood control. Those objectives were declared superfluous, since they did not contribute to energy production. This plan guided federal investment in hydroelectric power for the next decade.

Although the energy sector ignored other uses of freshwater, agencies in charge of other policy areas started to develop their own approaches to the use of freshwater. Most notably, with the support of powerful agricultural interests, the agency governing irrigation policy obtained a presidential decree allowing it to issue water use allocations for agricultural use without going through DNAEE (Pagnoccheschi 2000.). Around the same time, in 1971, the military regime's National Sanitation Plan (PLANASA) imposed federal control on that sector, historically a local responsibility. PLANASA created publicly owned companies at the state government level that took over water supply, sewage collection, and treatment from most municipalities.[8] The plan promoted rapid expansion of water provision alongside the elimination of subsidies and economic efficiency. It was relatively successful in terms of increasing access to drinking water, although sewage collection grew at a much slower rate, and only a tiny percentage of domestic sewage was actually treated (Formiga Johnsson 1998, 100–101). Thus, by the late 1970s, three major policy sectors were making decisions affecting water resources: energy, irrigation, and sanitation. The first two were even issuing water permits—authorizing firms or individuals to use freshwater resources—for the same bodies of water.

By the mid-1970s, this fragmented system began to come under attack. Two factors sparked the revolt. First, in the wake of the oil crisis, international funding for investment in large-scale public works dried up. Policy makers from all sectors began to look for new ways to pay for water infrastructure. On the other hand, conflicts among agencies responsible for water-related activities began to increase. Sanitation and energy policies came into direct conflict in the city of São Paulo because the Billings Reservoir was being used for both purposes. Pollution on a river that fed the dam had become so dramatic that one interviewee referred to it as a "scene from Switzerland, because there was so much white foam, meters of foam which was flowing into the Billings dam to be used for energy production" (Interview 13, Brasília, 2002).[9]

In 1976, the MME signed an agreement with the São Paulo state government to improve sanitation conditions in the Tietê and Cubatão River Basins, in the metropolitan area of São Paulo city.[10] The result was the creation of Brazil's first experiment in integrated water management, the Special Committee for the Upper Tietê River Basin. This early river basin committee included DNAEE, Eletrobras, and state agencies from São Paulo (Barth 1998). The following year, the government created a national version of

8. About one-fourth of Brazil's more than 5,000 municipalities, mostly located in Minas Gerais and São Paulo states, continued managing their own water through local agencies.

9. Those interviewed will be identified by a code number, unless interviewees explicitly agreed to having their names revealed.

10. According to Flavio Barth (1998), one of the mentors of the new water model, there were ulterior motives for this accord. Concessions to the sanitation sector would make the energy production of the Billings–Cubatão dam system less lucrative, which would help convince Light Electricity Services, the foreign-owned electric company that dominated the São Paulo region, to sell to the federal government. Light was indeed nationalized in 1978.

the program, the Special Committee for Integrated Studies of River Basins, CEEIBH. This organization had no formal decision-making power but was instead geared to conducting studies and devising proposals. Under its wing, several river basin committees were created in some of the economically or politically most important river basins in the country.[11] The national presidency of CEEIBH alternated between DNAEE and the brand-new national Secretariat of the Environment, an early recognition that the energy sector could not monopolize decision making (Formiga Johnsson 1998, 258). By the late 1970s, sectors of the Brazilian elite representing interests other than electric energy production had begun to call for a more integrated approach to river policy. The tendency of the developmentalist paradigm to produce concentrated benefits had generated its own opposition.

MIXED MESSAGES: REFORMING FRESHWATER POLICY

The reform in freshwater management institutions that the remainder of this book will analyze was strongly influenced by liberal notions of state reform. Yet ideas about participatory democracy also seeped in, as did a good dose of developmentalism. The two themes that appeared in Brazilian river policy debates in the 1970s—the need for integrated water management and the search for new sources of funding—were also on the international agenda. Like Brazil, most countries faced the growing problems of conflicts among different water uses (energy production, water supply and sanitation, agriculture, industry, transportation, environmental protection, etc.) and of difficulty paying for big infrastructure. Two sources of international inspiration in water are regularly cited: the international movement of water professionals called IWRM (integrated water resources management) and the French water management system, which, although predating IWRM, included many of its key aspects and a particularly creative solution for financing water infrastructure. Internationally, these ideas converged with liberalizing trends promoting market solutions, decentralization, and collaborative governance. In Brazil, however, they were also infiltrated by other narratives.

Four ideas became central to the international IWRM approach: decentralization, market incentives, river basin planning, and participation. The reappraisal of heavy state involvement in water management, combined with the fiscal crisis of the 1980s and 1990s, increased international

11. For example, the huge São Francisco River Basin covering much of the semiarid Northeast of Brazil was extremely important for electric energy production and for navigation into the interior of the country. The Paraíba do Sul River Basin, running through São Paulo, Minas Gerais, and Rio de Janeiro states, covers one of Brazil's most highly industrialized river basins and is also largely responsible for water supply in the city of Rio de Janeiro.

support for the first two concepts. While *decentralization* would reduce the influence of inefficient central bureaucracies, *market incentives* would force firms to incorporate the economic value of water into production costs. International agencies such as the World Bank played a key role in promoting both ideas. In particular, the World Bank pressed hard for the creation of bulk water markets—systems in which water allocations or rights to use water resources could be bought and sold—and also privatization of urban water and sanitation services. The other two central tenets of IWRM were related to making the notion of integration operable. Thinking of water as flowing through *river basins* would help broaden the focus from narrow river channels—the dominant idea in the "pushing rivers around" approach—to include land use and environmental protection policies (Mody 2004). *Participatory arenas* would help neutralize the dominance of particular sectors by including in the decision-making process all relevant water users, increasingly referred to in international agency jargon as stakeholders.[12]

Groups that claim to support IWRM interpret the term *participation* in very different ways. For some of them, participation is about making water policy more socially just by guaranteeing the access of the poor, women, and other disadvantaged groups to decision making; for others, it means bringing actors representing different economic interests to the same table in order to minimize conflict between hydroelectric dams and irrigated agriculture, industry, or the transportation of goods along waterways. As Ken Conca (2005, 158) notes about the IWRM literature: "Exactly what constitutes participation is often described in bland, universalizing, and undifferentiated terms."

Indeed, Conca (2005, 154–157) and Molle (2008) effectively show that the entire conceptual apparatus of IWRM is so loosely defined that a wide variety of different concrete approaches draw on it for legitimacy. Although not all proponents of IWRM thought of themselves as neoliberals, the ideas fit nicely with the liberalizing trends of the 1990s. As an institutional package, IWRM proposed abandoning top-down regulations and state-sponsored development, emulating the market, creating voluntary collaborative governance mechanisms, and valuing participation less as a means to political inclusion than for facilitating negotiations among interests.

Some Brazilian water professionals were active in the IWRM debates and participated in the related conferences,[13] while others were more inspired by the French model of water management. This is not surprising, given the

---

12. See Meijerink and Huitema (2010) for a comparative study of IWRM reform efforts around the world and Rahaman and Varis (2005) for a general evaluation of the IWRM approach. On privatization debates, see Bakker (2010).

13. In 1981, water specialists working in the federal government's National Department of Water and Electric Energy (DNAEE) were sent by the government to participate in the Lisbon International Conference on Water (Gutiérrez 2006a, 87).

number of high-level Brazilian water management specialists who studied in France; several bilateral aid projects put French and Brazilian specialists in frequent contact. Created in 1964, the French water management system has a water pricing mechanism that IWRM proponents admire, despite reservations about the fact that it operates as a fund-raising tool more than as a rationalizing market incentive.[14] There are two key river basin institutions in the French model: basin committees for general decision making and more operational basin agencies. The agencies generate revenues for infrastructure by charging water users—sanitation companies, municipal governments, industries, and so on—for withdrawal, pollution, or other water uses. These three ideas—a decision-making committee, an executive agency (both organized at the river basin level), and a charge on water use—became central components of the institutional design package that Brazilians put together during the 1980s and 1990s.

But the Brazilian model of water management was not a copy of the French model, nor did it incorporate all of the most internationally popular components of IWRM. Brazil's river basin committees had a different composition from those of their French counterparts, including not only government and water users (sanitation companies, irrigators, industries, energy companies, etc.) but also local government and civil society (universities, environmentalists, agricultural labor unions, etc.). This reflected the presence in Brazil of other reform narratives, most notably the participatory one discussed above. While the French committees operated, at least until very recently, mainly as an arena for collective negotiation among market-oriented interests (principally sanitation companies), in Brazil, there is a space reserved in deliberative bodies for groups that are expected to speak on behalf of the public interest, including the protection of the natural environment.

Departing from prevailing IWRM concepts, Brazil also resisted the creation of private water markets. While the World Bank intensely promoted the idea that freshwater use would be more rational if water use permits

---

14. The French system was inspired by the German experience of the Ruhr River Valley. In 1913, a commission was established, the Ruhrverband, made up of 983 water users and polluters that collaborated on the financing of infrastructure (Amaral 1998, 22; Barraqué, 2000, 82). According to Barraqué (2000), the French water charging system is often mistaken for a market mechanism of the Polluter Pays Principle (PPP) type, much lauded by international agencies, in the belief that if users paid the "right" price for access to water resources, they would use them more rationally. Notwithstanding its recent fame as a prime example of PPP, the main purpose of the French water charges is to finance infrastructure and programs. Water users on the agency's administrative council develop five-year investment plans and set the price for water based on division of the costs. "In fact," says Barraqué, "the level of the charges was not raised to reach the incentive level of the PPP, so that the Agences de l'Eau operate in fact under another principle, which could be called solidarity or mutuality."

(to withdraw, pollute, or otherwise use a certain amount of water in a river or lake) could be bought and sold on an open market, the Brazilians stuck with the position that the right to use freshwater could be charged for but not traded. The 1988 constitution placed the ownership of water resources firmly in the hands of the state. Rivers or lakes that cross state or international borders belong to the Union; all others belong to states. Reformers insisted on this point, even emphasizing that new participatory arenas could not have the authority actually to issue water permits, only to create general norms for their allocation. This perpetuation of state authority over the central component of freshwater management, the decision about who will have access to water, was a sign that the developmentalist legacy did not die with the new water model.

Another central element in the Brazilian water model was the idea that written technical plans—at the national, state, and river basin level—were important management instruments. Although Brazilian water reformers meant for the plans to be approved in participatory arenas, the documents themselves did not really reflect a collaborative, voluntaristic notion of participatory management. Instead, they tended to be thoroughly technical, in the modernist tradition of "total planning," part and parcel of developmentalism (Friedmann 1987; Caldeira and Holston 2005). Typical water resources plans include in-depth analysis of economic, environmental, and socioeconomic conditions; prevalent water uses; scenarios for future development; a proposal for what types of uses should be promoted; and a list of needed infrastructure and programs. They are almost always designed by outside consultants, presented to the relevant council or committee, and, perhaps after some discussion, approved. One study demonstrated that in Brazil, they are rarely implemented, largely because they lack legal mechanisms for enforcement (Neves 2004). Except in a few cases, where plans have been designed through more local participatory processes, their existence reflects an ongoing faith that purportedly neutral technical knowledge can resolve political problems.[15]

There are other traces of developmentalist ideas in the institutional design of water management that ultimately prevailed in Brazil. Technical personnel who promoted the new system of water management similarly hoped to insulate it from politics. Many of them conceived of participatory decision-making arenas as nonpolitical, in the sense that they hoped that

---

15. One high-level decision maker who recently attempted to implement a more participatory notion of planning told us that the only way that this could be done was to set the consulting budget very low. The only consultants willing to accept such low fees were specialists in community organizing. Water resources engineers stayed away (Interview 114, São Paulo, 2011).

by bringing all the stakeholders to the table it would be possible to prevent either domination by particular interests or patronage politics.

So if the final institutional design package that actors put together was shaped by liberal ideas about voluntary, collaborative governance and market mechanisms, many individuals involved in the reform overlaid these either with more politicized participatory ideals or with a faith in the state and in technical planning characteristic of developmentalism. The mixed messages woven into the institutional design were the product of the entangled institutional setting within which that design was built. Different reform narratives entered into the framework along with the many different actors and interests that had a chance to influence it over a 30-year period. Among them were progressive engineers and not-so-progressive ones, civil society activists and industrialists, scientists and politicians, and many others. The chapters that follow will explain how this complex and internally contradictory institutional design emerged out of the actions of a multiplicity of people engaged in different kinds of institution-building practices.

CHAPTER 3

Institutional Design in Entangled Settings

How to Make an Unfinished Law

In this chapter, we examine the construction of an institutional design package out of disparate ideas and purposes and the process by which that package was translated into law in both São Paulo state and at the national level. Reformers had to act at both levels, because Brazilian law held that rivers or lakes that crossed state lines should be governed by federal laws, while those fully within a state would be under state domain. Although São Paulo played a pioneering role, efforts to change the system for managing water resources at state and national levels were thoroughly interconnected and involved many of the same actors. They resulted in the passage of laws that laid out in initial form an institutional design for water policy that was copied throughout the country. Power politics and creative action were deeply intertwined in the process of designing the two laws and could not always be distinguished from one another. The outcomes of these struggles depended not just on the prior resources of the actors involved (although those did make a difference) but also on institution-building practices in which they engaged along the way. They were struggles not only over ideas but also around the concrete resources and relationships that lent support to some interpretations and not others.

The water laws that many proponents thought constituted the end of the reform initiative were, in fact, only the first steps in a much longer process that continues to this day. The complexity of the issues and relationships involved explains the lack of closure. Actors backed their preferred approaches to water management reform with commitments to institution-building practices that expanded networks and capabilities in line with their ideas. Those with conflicting ideas either did the same or sought to move issues they cared about into other institutional venues where they thought they could have more influence. The emerging interorganizational field involved numerous sites and energized a variety of actors who had different interests at stake and endorsed different perspectives on what should change and how. Given the complexity of the issues and the multiple valences of the interorganizational process, the incoherence of the initial legislative outcomes should not be surprising.

This chapter has two general purposes. First, we describe some of the different kinds of practices through which pro-reform actors tried to shape the lawmaking processes, focusing on how they went about persuading others that change was necessary and enlisting them to help transform ideas into official policy proposals and draft laws. To this end, they created an assortment of debate venues (working groups, seminars, etc.) in which to argue about how water resources should be managed and in which networks formed in support of particular interpretations. Participants appealed to wider audiences by disseminating information and ideas about water reform to professional cohorts (e.g., the water engineers who were not directly involved in constructing the institution design but who would later be required to implement it). They also reached outside their professional communities. At key moments, different kinds of water experts mobilized personal and political ties in unexpected ways, prompting elected officials to pay attention to particular proposals. Legislators, in turn, made overtures to specialists they thought would share their views about what kinds of new institutions should be established.

Second, like numerous scholars before us, we note that in complex policy processes, both design and implementation are subject to unexpected reversals. The messy process by which multiple, entangled interests shape the legal construction of new institutional fields is not fully captured in the veto player concept, used by policy theorists to explain why major policy legislation is so difficult to pass (Mazmanian and Sabatier 1981; Pressman and Wildavsky 1984; Tsebelis 2002). The recombinant aspects of the enterprise meant that a new legal framework had to garner some level of support from actors in many policy sectors, in the executive and in the legislature, and at the state and federal levels, despite uncertainties about their positions in the new system. Negotiators had to persuade these actors that they would not lose under the new system; doing so provided both incentive and opportunity for actors with varying interests and viewpoints to put their stamp on the legislation. In other words, the problem was not so much an excess of veto players as an excess of influential positions. No single actor was in a position to block passage of a bill, but many could influence its language at one point or another. The laws included contradictory ideas and considerable ambiguity, something that would not be at all surprising to policy scholars (Kolko 1965; Davis 1972; Silbey 1984). The institutional design that evolved out of these incremental, multiple actions was one that no particular actor would likely have espoused initially.

That result was a product neither of learning in a cognitive sense nor of the play of power politics. Instead, interest group politics combined with a politics of technical expertise (Gutiérrez 2006a; Gutiérrez 2009). Specialists committed to specific policy prescriptions used what looked like traditional political strategies to promote them. Actors seeking to gain or hold on to power over decision-making processes had to debate policy goals with engineers. Drafters of new laws often skirted conflicts with imprecise language or by postponing contentious issues for complementary legislation. The entangled nature of Brazilian institutions instilled ambiguity in the legislation, keeping open a multitude of conflicting interpretations of the reform's objectives.

Leaders of this reform process faced the tricky problem of trying to channel multiple negotiations in the same direction. One solution was to lower their expectations for the first stage of institutional reform, settling for legislation that was long on principles but short on enforceable legal instruments. The Brazilian reform legislation was strikingly omissive on the integrated water resources management (IWRM) principle that water management should be linked to environmental management and land use. Lawmakers sought to minimize potential conflicts with the other (mainly municipal) levels of government responsible for these areas by simply avoiding these issues; thus, they established mechanisms for regulating the use of freshwater itself but not for influencing the policies or practices of other actors that generated most of the water problems they were trying to solve. Although narrowing the reform agenda did provide a route through entanglement for the time being, it did so at the cost of cementing links with some actors and interests while sidelining connections with others.[1]

In the following section, we begin by outlining some of the key disputes over reform of freshwater management during this period. We go on to examine how proponents of different positions sought venues in which to promote innovative ideas, both in the state of São Paulo and nationally. We trace this lengthy process from 1983, when the first national-level discussions on a new legal framework began, to 1997, when the federal water law passed. In the interim, debates that shaped the 1991 São Paulo water law influenced the designs both of legislation adopted in other states and of the federal law. In the next chapter, we show how the challenge of implementing key parts of the reform—especially water pricing—led to further

---

1. On foregrounding and backgrounding, see Alexander (2004) and Mische (2009).

regulatory and legal innovation, requiring that supporters mobilize new resources and relationships for a second wave of legislative action and the continued transformation of the institutional design.

CONFLICTING IDEAS ABOUT WATER REFORM

To influence policy and institution-building processes, ideas often need to be versatile. If they are to survive in a world of complexity and multiple interests, they have to seem relevant under a variety of conditions. Hajer (2005) suggests that policy makers are influenced by metaphors (images such as *acid rain* that spark the imagination and stand for broader problems) and story lines (commonsense narratives that connect causes and effects and propose particular solutions). Molle (2008) similarly argues that policy makers are drawn to "nirvana concepts," story lines, and icons (or seminal examples). Nirvana concepts are vague, unreachable, but ideal utopias. Molle uses as an example the way that IWRM has become a nirvana concept in international water debates, as it was in many ways also for Brazilian water reformers. Since most water problems can be interpreted as related to conflicts among different uses—energy versus agriculture, one basin's water needs versus another's, upstream versus downstream uses, environmental protection versus economic production—the omnibus notion of *integration* serves to frame reform processes in many countries. Both Molle and Hajer attribute the effectiveness of such widely disseminated policy concepts and stories to their polyvalence, something that allows them to be "easily hijacked by groups seeking to legitimize their own agenda" (Molle 2008, 33) or, more optimistically, allows actors with different understandings to join forces (Hajer 2005).

In this and the next chapter, we explore the construction of an institutional design package, by which we mean a fairly detailed, though malleable, set of policy instructions that others are meant to implement. In Brazil, institutional activists transformed the vague ideas of IWRM into a relatively specific set of proposals, which, with some variation, were incorporated throughout the country in state and national laws. The package included ideas about the organizational structure of water management, such as what kinds of institutions should be created and what their responsibilities should be, and also ideas about the technical instruments that should be used, such as permits, plans, water charges, and other procedures.

At the center of the institutional design package outlined by the 1997 federal water law and by its predecessors and successors in state laws were four central ideas: (1) that water policy should be geared toward multiple uses and include such policy areas as irrigation, sanitation, energy production, industrial use, and environmental protection (what some call integration); (2) that it should involve all levels of government and relevant private and nonprofit institutions in decision making (what some call participation); (3) that to promote more rational use and to raise money to pay for projects and programs, access to water resources (i.e., the water in rivers, lakes, and other water sources) should be charged for (water pricing, not to be confused with service charges for water and sanitation); and (4) that the river basin should be the basic planning unit within which all of this should occur (what some call decentralization). As discussed at the end of chapter 2, this combination of ideas mixed elements of liberal, democratic, and developmentalist reform ideas.

On the surface, water reformers agreed on those ideas. Digging deeper, however, we soon find that they understood them in very different ways. The legislation created a series of new organizations for water management, including state and federal agencies, state and federal participatory councils, state and interstate river basin committees, and river basin agencies. The roles of these organizations, how they would relate to existing institutions, and the tools they would have for managing water were all points of contention. Five "instruments" for water management ended up becoming part of most laws: a system of permits governing water rights, water resource management plans, charges for high-volume use, water quality classification (setting standards for parts of rivers according to intended use), and information systems. There were, however, disputes over how each of these tools should work. To explore these differences, we focus here on two central reform ideas: river basin planning and participation, both of which were understood as ways to integrate multiple water uses. A third highly contentious water management tool, charging for high-volume use, will be discussed in more detail in chapter 4.

River Basin Planning

Although the principle that planning for water management should be organized around the river basin is widely accepted in the international water policy community (Barrow 1998; Conca 2005; Warner, Wester, and Bolding 2008; Molle and Wester 2009), it contains a multitude of possible meanings. In Brazilian water debates, two areas of contention came to the fore. One was over whether the goal should be to manage the water that flows through rivers and lakes or instead to adopt a broader approach that included environmental and land use management of the whole drainage basin. The former orientation corresponds to the realm of traditional water resources engineering, with its focus on big infrastructure, such as building dams or channeling rivers for flood prevention and water storage. From this perspective, working at the river basin level means involving all of the relevant actors who use water resources—that is, who withdraw, pollute, or conduct other activities on lakes and rivers. The previously divided sectors whose management needed to be integrated were those pertaining to water supply and sanitation, hydroelectric power, and irrigation. Proponents of the second, more holistic vision of water management argue that direct consumers or polluters by no means exhaust the range of people with an interest in how the basin is managed, to say nothing of nonhuman interests and those pertaining to the river's own maintenance. Moreover, many factors affecting the supply or quality of water stem from decisions about how land is used and not from water in isolation.

A second dispute around the river basin concept has to do less with defining the object of river basin planning than with how much direct authority river basin organizations should have over it. Organizing water policy according to the river basin logic makes sense from a technical standpoint, since actions upstream affect downstream users, and the volume of water needed for different activities should not exceed the amount available. Still, in the view of many water specialists in government agencies, there was no reason that authority for planning by river basin should be devolved to entities made up of actors from or working in the river basin in question. Others staunchly espoused a decentralized system. Mayors and engineers in São Paulo's Piracicaba basin, for example, believed that as long as key decisions remained in the hands of bureaucrats in the state capital their region's interests would be systematically sold short.

There were thus competing views of what kinds of new river basin organizations should be included in the institutional design and what their powers should be. Most participants agreed that river basin committees should be spaces where representatives of diverse interests and policy sectors could coordinate and negotiate. But they did not agree on how much decision-making power committees should have or that they should set rates for water charges and decide how the proceeds should be spent. Many people thought that since pricing involved technical questions that affected more general water policy goals, it was properly within the purview of state or federal government. The contrary argument was the pro-decentralization position that river basin organizations should be fully responsible for water pricing, for which purpose they would create their own executive river basin agencies that would make the whole enterprise operational, sending out the bills, receiving the funds, and ensuring implementation of projects.

Participation

Pervading the disputes around the role of river basin organizations were very different conceptions of what *participation* implied. Some of those involved in the debates regarded participation mainly as inclusion; others understood it to mean stakeholder bargaining. For the first group, it linked the redesign of water management institutions to the broader participatory project discussed in chapter 2, amplifying the voices of the poor and of environmentalists and other mainly middle-class civic organizations usually excluded in a policy arena dominated by specialists and powerful interest groups. The opposing position was not an argument against participation but rather one that advocated greater participation primarily by high-volume water users with the power to make a difference in the use and management of water in a basin. The rationale was not so much to make economic interests compatible with environmental and social ones as to facilitate negotiation and collaboration among economic actors.[2]

The discussion of participation paralleled the debate about decentralization in raising questions about what decisions could and should be made by nonspecialists. So, for example, although approving water management master plans, one of the main planning instruments envisioned in the reform, was the prerogative of the basin committees, in almost all cases, they were contracted out to specialists—either consultants or particular state agencies. They were then presented to committee members as a package deal for ratification. A few committee organizers objected to this practice and put together more bottom-up planning processes, generally resulting in more accessible plans that appeared to elicit broader public awareness and commitment.

The water pricing issue was at the same time the most contentious and the one whose operationalization was most likely to be postponed during the legislative process described here. A key principle of this kind of reform is the idea that high-volume water users (industries, drinking water suppliers, sanitation companies, hydroelectric power companies, farmers, etc.) should pay for the right either to withdraw water from rivers, lakes, and other bodies of water or to employ it in any other way that affects the amount and quality available for others (e.g., by discharging pollutants or storing water in reservoirs for electricity generation). Charging for water was intended to

---

2. In two Brazilian states, Paraná and Bahia, water legislation explicitly endorsed this view, by privileging not broader committees (with civil society participation) but more narrow consortia made up only of water users, as the main arenas for decision making at the river basin level. Several years after the first legislation passed, a new law passed in Bahia following the committee model.

provide essential lubrication for the water reform process as a whole and was deemed crucial for making decentralized governance financially viable. Nonetheless, resolving the myriad disputes over who should pay and what they should be paying for was beyond the capacity of the reform networks at this stage. Thus, although water charges were included in the initial water management legislation, their specific rationale and operation were left to be worked out in practice, a process we examine in some depth in chapter 4.

EARLY MOVES TOWARD A NATIONAL LEVEL REFORM (1983–1988)

In most countries, innovative ideas make their way into designs for new policies and institutions through the work of countless working groups, seminars, and task forces, many of whose members come from governmental agencies. These discussions constitute preliminary tests of the strength of contending positions before proposals are transformed into legislation. In complex issue areas, finding the right mix and number of people can be tricky: too many, and nothing emerges; too few, and not enough changes. Putting together a new model for water management presented thorny combination problems. While it was intended to reconfigure the roles and relations of multiple policy sectors (energy, irrigation, sanitation, environment, and more) at various territorial levels (involving municipal, state, and federal agencies) and with little prior agreement on the precise meaning of the key reform proposals, there was no clear formula for deciding who had to be involved. There was a lot of trial and error and a great deal of talk. Much of the 30-year process we describe in this and the next chapter took place in and around meetings. Countless working groups, commissions, and seminars generated policy proposals that were then discussed by other working groups, commissions, and seminars. This rather mundane set of practical activities turned out to be key for building not just agreements around particular visions of water management but also networks of actors willing to defend those agreements at later stages.

In 1983, a group of federal agencies—including the National Department of Water and Electrical Energy (DNAEE)[3] and the national Secretariat of the Environment—organized a high-profile international seminar on water resources management (DNAEE/SEMA 1983; Barth 1998; Formiga Johnsson 1998; Gutiérrez 2006a). The keynote speech, given by Eduardo Yassuda, engineering professor at the University of São

---

3. A part of the national Ministry of Mines and Energy.

Paulo and an intellectual leader on water management since the 1970s (Interview 13, Brasilia 2002), contained most of the key ideas of the future model: planning for multiple uses at the level of river basins, the need for participation, and even the implementation of water charges to help finance the system (Yassuda 1983).

From the beginning, differently situated actors vied to shape the reform by playing a role in specialized debates and by so doing to defend their institutional interests. In this initial phase of designing the water management model, two factors appear central to the way reform ideas were formulated and disseminated. The first was widespread dissatisfaction with the old energy production-centered model, coming from all directions (other ministries, state governments). The second was DNAEE's effort to adapt to the new context in order to retain its institutional influence. To do this, DNAEE drew on new ideas espoused by intellectuals closely connected to international water debates.

The energy sector was the proverbial elephant in the room: everyone else was convinced that its long-standing dominance in the area of freshwater management was an obstacle to a new system based on multiple water uses. According to Formiga Johnsson (1998, 262–263), DNAEE maneuvered carefully to maintain its coordinating role, and its draft proposal for a national water resources management plan espoused all the major components of integrated water management (DCRH 1985), including a section authored by Yassuda that called for broadening participation and also for implantation of water charges (Fracalanza 2006, 4).

The ideational struggle over system design seemed to reiterate an ongoing intersectoral power struggle among government institutions, touted as an argument over how to assign priority to the water needs of different economic sectors. By framing the conflict around water allocation (controlling the access to water in rivers and lakes), participants in the debate were already sidelining a more expansive view of water resources management with attention to ecosystem concerns, a view that would soon thereafter be enshrined in the first of the Dublin Principles.[4]

It was also a dispute over the relative weight of state and federal government authorities. The 1983 seminar sparked a series of follow-up meetings between DNAEE and state government water agencies, which were

---

4. The Dublin Statement on Water and Sustainable Development, issued just prior to the 1992 United Nations Conference on Environment and Development ("Earth Summit") in Rio de Janeiro, states in its first principle: "Since water sustains life, effective management of water resources demands a holistic approach, linking social and economic development with the protection of natural ecosystems." From http://www.wmo.int/pages/prog/hwrp/documents/english/icwedece.html, accessed October 18, 2012.

concerned that the new model would be overly centralized (Interview 7, São Paulo, 1999). Changing the stage made a difference to the performance and played to a (somewhat) different audience. Over time, it helped to stitch together a network of advocates for the reform project as a whole, as some individuals from different states and policy sectors who joined the discussion became committed to transforming ideas into actions.

The six meetings between DNAEE and officials from state agencies governing water resources were important not only for sharing and debating ideas but also for building more horizontal networks among reform-minded public officials in different states. Between October 1984, when 20 people participated in the first meeting in São Paulo, and the last meeting two years later in Porto Alegre, attended by 250, participants gained a much broader sense of the way things were done nationwide and the overall state of the system. As they were cobbling together institutional designs for the system, members of the pro-reform network also sought influence in other arenas, for example, by proposing constitutional provisions to the federal and state constitutional conventions that began in 1987. They hoped in this way to jump-start institutional change even in the absence of strong political support or social consensus. In her pioneering study of this process, Formiga Johnsson (1998, 269) credits the 1988 federal constitution's requirement that a national water resources system be set up with furthering these efforts. A year later, in São Paulo, the state constitution laid out the principles of the new institutional design package in surprising detail. Its chapter on water resources calls for water management for multiple uses, decentralization, participation, cost sharing of major water projects, and water use charges.

DESIGNING THE REFORM PROPOSAL IN SÃO PAULO (1987–1991)

Debates at the federal level were deeply intertwined with those occurring over the same period of time in the state of São Paulo (and also in several other states), and some of the same professional networks were involved in both. Nonetheless, for a variety of reasons, legislative change in São Paulo preceded the new federal law by six years and thus influenced (albeit in different ways) the model's development in other states and at the national level.

It is worth recalling that during the period in which this discussion took place, change was in the air. Institutions were being rethought in many different sectors of Brazilian political and administrative life. Between 1978 and 1982, political expectations became unsettled, and the range for creative organizing expanded. This was notable in São Paulo, where expressions of opposition to continued military rule came from such unexpected places as the business association and the supposedly coopted labor unions in some of Brazil's biggest industries, along with other kinds of social movements. The increasingly audacious, officially sanctioned opposition party began to close in on a legislative majority (Keck 1992, 20–60). New political parties formed. In the 1982 elections, Brazilians directly elected state governors for the first time since 1965, and opposition senator André Franco Montoro was elected governor in São Paulo. These events energized would-be reformers, making them believe that conditions for change were favorable.

The crucial influence of the political conjuncture on discussions of the need for institutional change in water management was by no means a linear process. Democratization had multiple effects. The trajectory of Flávio Barth, the engineer and planner whose dedication to water resource planning made him such a central figure in the reform process in the state, provides a good example. When Waldemar Casadei, Montoro's appointment as head of DAEE (São Paulo's Department of Water and Electrical Energy), began an internal shake-up intended to make the agency's practices less authoritarian, Barth saw it as overly politicized. Deeply troubled by what he deemed "confusion," he took a two-year leave and worked as a private consultant.[5] During that period, he met Carlos Estevam Martins, a political scientist who was head of projects for the state's public administration think tank FUNDAP (Fundação do Desenvolvimento Administrativo, or Public Administration Development Foundation). Martins, knowledgeable about the water sector from having helped to resolve complex dam resettlement conflicts, surprised Barth with the notion that political science could have practical applications. Barth returned to DAEE after his leave was up, and when he was organizing a 1986 seminar on reform of the water resources management system, he called together a wide variety of participants and invited Martins to make comments on the proceedings. Martins's commentary introduced an unconventional strategy: a call to think of the reform enterprise as a political rather than a technical one, suggesting that the process was more important than the product. Although this idea met with considerable resistance from some of his fellow engineers, Barth had become convinced of the need to open up the debate.

---

5. Interview with Flávio Barth, by Margaret Keck, São Paulo, 1999. Although most interviews cited in the text were anonymous, a few were with public authorities who did not require anonymity and are hence cited by name.

Barth remained the political entrepreneur most directly associated with moving the process forward in São Paulo, working closely with Stela Goldenstein and her team from the state's environmental agency, CETESB (Environmental Sanitation Technology Company). In 1987, Barth suggested to the newly named superintendent of DAEE, Paulo Bezerril, that he urge the governor to establish a water resources council that would oversee a major restructuring of the state's water management system.[6] Adeptly seizing an opportunity, Bezerril slipped a proposal for a decree to create such a council to Governor Orestes Quércia just before the latter was to deliver a keynote address at a meeting of the National Association of Sanitation Engineers (ABES), suggesting that it would bring him good publicity among the professional community. On the spur of the moment, the governor agreed, taking the first official step toward creating an integrated water management model for São Paulo state.

Soon after the 1987 decree, the government created a series of commissions and subcommittees to organize the new system and draw up a master plan for water resources management. Barth headed the subcommittee for institutional design. At his behest, DAEE signed a contract with FUNDAP to orchestrate the process, under the leadership of Martins, who was research director at the time. FUNDAP had a reputation for competence and neutrality, enabling it to convoke people with very different perspectives in a fragmented policy field (Interview 4, São Paulo, 1999). Besides summoning the obvious interlocutors from sanitation, environmental protection, and energy agencies, the FUNDAP team brought in other relevant agencies and individuals who had hitherto participated very little in water management debates; these included geographers, planners, architects, public administrators, and social scientists. FUNDAP consultants hoped to highlight the social, environmental, and economic purposes of water management. They viewed institutional design as a political rather than technical process and sought simultaneously to dilute the competition between professional fields (e.g., civil and sanitation engineering) and to avoid identification of the process with any political party (Interview 4, São Paulo, 1999).

The working group produced dozens of policy proposals, studies, and other documents, which they discussed at numerous, often contentious meetings involving as many as 200 professionals. Disagreements among different kinds of water specialists along with involvement of people from other areas meant that putting together a common document was extremely complicated. The coordination problems were monumental. We include in box 3.1 a vivid account by an interviewee who was one of the organizers of these discussions.

6. Ibid.

Box 3.1

A DESCRIPTION OF DEBATES AT THE FUNDAP MEETINGS, SÃO PAULO, 1987–1989

"So we got involved, and coordinated things, and started over, and at the end of each meeting I wanted to cry. Because either someone had talked on and on for three hours or two people had insisted on fighting over a tiny point.... Gradually we got better at it.

"Sometimes we avoided inviting people who were simply impossible...while begging other key people to participate, for the love of God....From the beginning, there was a core group that was technically very good—water resources people from DAEE, specialists in environment from the CPLA [the Environmental Planning Department], some consultants from CETESB [the state environmental management company] and FUNDAP—a group of 10 or 15 people who were technically very competent.

"We wrote documents, reports, proposals, water use policies, other types of policies, conservation and maintenance and financial policies. And then we started to discuss each one of the subpolicies. Each one had a short text and annotations. And people started to see what we were doing and started to work with us.

"The people from CESP, Eletropaulo, CPFL [the electric companies], since they owned the world, would only come now and then or not all, until they began to see that this was beginning to gain some substance. Then they started to come to all the meetings...and then at the point when we had a final document on the policy and the model of the state water resources system, everyone got involved.

"And it was a monumental fight. It was very beneficial, because everyone had the chance to have their say. The final document did not end up as coherent as, for example, the environmental policy...because everyone had an opinion on every comma...but we ended up with something that had a lot of legitimacy."
(Interview 5, São Paulo, 1999)

More important even than the formal report that came out of these meetings (FUNDAP 1989) may have been construction of a broad intra-governmental network that would go on to ensure that the proposal was transformed into law (Amaral 1998, chap. 2, 17–18). Participants identify two groups composed mainly of state technical personnel who kept that process going. By all accounts, the strategist was Barth, who maintained a diagram of strategically relevant groups and events in his office in the planning department of DAEE. The group that met on Friday afternoons in Goldenstein's garden was mainly a network of planners from CETESB and other agencies; its members were striving to keep the new system from being dominated by a narrow focus on the economic uses of water.

Goldenstein maintained regular telephone contact with Barth, and the two groups worked together well.[7]

Network building in São Paulo was accompanied by efforts to amplify the impact of these efforts among members of the specialist community nationally. By broadcasting news of what was going on in the state, Barth in particular was committed not only to getting others involved in institutional design but also to convincing ordinary water engineers to think about the political practices required for institution building. One way to do this was to bring the debate to the national meetings of the Brazilian Water Resources Association (ABRH). Formed in 1977, the association had historically avoided advocacy (Formiga Johnsson 1998, 279). At the 1987 meeting, however, Barth proposed that in the tradition of international water conferences, the ABRH should take a position on water management reform. The 1987 Carta de Salvador (Salvador Statement) was the first of a series of ABRH position statements that became focal points for a shifting consensus. The first two clearly reflected the debate under way in São Paulo. The 1987 statement espoused the basic ideas of IWRM. The 1989 Foz do Iguaçu statement was more specific, reflecting developments over the preceding two years in the discussion of the economic value of water and the need for a system of water pricing.

A second strategy was to revive a long-defunct DAEE professional journal, *Águas e Energia Elétrica*. As coeditor, Barth strove to communicate a more political view of water management than was customary for a magazine whose audience was engineers.[8] The magazine, sent out twice a year to 10,000 readers, explained the reform process, published the ABRH position statements just mentioned, and included regular updates on the progress of the two working groups responsible for designing the system and the water resources plan. The magazine also provided coverage of the pioneering organizing efforts then under way in the Piracicaba basin.

THE ROLE OF THE PIRACICABA CONSORTIUM (1981–1991)

Not far to the northwest of metropolitan São Paulo in the region of Campinas, degradation of the Piracicaba River had already begun to generate public protest in the late 1970s and soon inspired a group of activist engineers to speak out. Their activism eventuated in the creation in 1989

7. Interviews with Flávio Barth, Paulo Bezerril, Carlos Estevam Martins, Stela Goldenstein, and Neuza Marcondes, all of which took place in São Paulo in May 1999, by Margaret Keck.
8. Interview with Flávio Barth, São Paulo, May 1999, by Margaret Keck.

of a new consortium of municipal governments dedicated to seeking solutions for the river basin's problems. The degree of commitment of mayors of the region's principal cities provided the consortium with a strong base from which to gain access to the governor's office and catch the attention of political networks in the state and nationally, besides enhancing collaboration among specialists in the region. For the leaders of this regional process, the deliberations we just described were top-down, overly centered in the state capital, and dominated by state government personnel. Determined to combat such tendencies, the Piracicaba group mobilized its political networks, eventually managing to insert language of its own into the draft bill that went before the São Paulo state assembly. This example helps demonstrate the multiplicity of connections, pathways, practices, and resources that constituted this complex institution-building process.

The Piracicaba River Basin is one of Brazil's most important industrial centers, generating today about 7 percent of its gross national product and with a population of 4.7 million people (Castellano 2007). It is also a center of science and technology, with one of the country's best universities, the State University of Campinas (Unicamp). Yet despite its wealth and intellectual power, by 1989, only 3 percent of the domestic sewage in the watershed was being treated (Castellano 2007, 99). Piracicaba was a national hub of the ethanol industry, another part of the developmentalist state's effort to build energy independence. But along with the highly subsidized ethanol came *vinhoto*, a toxic by-product that was dumped into the river. A waterway once used for fishing and water sports was no longer clean enough to swim in.

The pollution problem was particularly hard to solve because, starting in the 1970s, large volumes of the river's waters were being diverted to the city of São Paulo. The diversion occurred through the Cantareira System, a collection of channels and pumps that diverted 31 cubic meters per second of the Piracicaba River to the capital. That amounted to more than the total consumed by all the donating basin's largest cities combined (Mortatti et al. 2004). When the cities of Piracicaba and Campinas faced drinking-water shortages in the 1980s, an obvious solution would have been to decrease the transfer to the state capital (Moretti and Gontijo 2005; Barbi 2007), but those decisions were under the control of state government.

By the end of the 1970s, municipal governments and local civic groups had joined forces to protest the river's degradation, to the point where one public area of Piracicaba was renamed Ecological Protest Square (Praça do Protesto Ecológico). One particularly notable act of protest involved the erection of a sign that read, "There used to be a river here" (*Por aqui passava um rio*) in an area of dry riverbed (Sebastianes 1992, 1). In 1981, that city's mayor unsuccessfully sued the state water agency, SABESP, seeking compensation for the Cantareira System. Around the same time, members of the Piracicaba Engineers and Architects Association (AEAP) began to confer with the Coordinating Council of Civic Organizations of Piracicaba, an umbrella organization that brought together civic groups in the municipality, about ways of organizing to protect the river. In 1985, organizers (most of whom were engineers working at public agencies) launched the Year 2000 Campaign for Ecological Salvation of the Piracicaba Basin and two years later presented a petition in its name to Governor Quércia that contained a series of 32 demands for institutional and technical improvements. The two broadest were points 18, calling for creation of a pilot program for integrated water management in the Piracicaba basin, and 19, calling for the creation of an intermunicipal consortium; the most contentious was a set of demands regarding payment by SABESP of indemnity or reparations in the form of programs for damage caused by the diversion (Associação dos Engenheiros e Arquitetos de Piracicaba 1987, 9, 12–13).

Barth's team was in contact with the activists in Piracicaba, where DAEE had maintained a consistent presence since 1984 (Castellano 2007, 138). After the State Water Resources Council had declared the situation critical, a task force was formed to come up with programs, chaired by DAEE; it comprised 70 representatives of state secretariats and other organizations (FUNDAP 1994, 11). The pilot project was established by decree in 1988 and was the cover story of an issue of *Águas e Energia Eletrica* (5, no. 13), the DAEE magazine that Barth had revived. Yet although working groups produced numerous documents proposing that the Piracicaba basin receive special attention, the Piracicaba engineers and mayors did not have much influence on the draft bill the government eventually sent to the legislature. Castellano's study of the consortium reveals that its members distrusted the state government and were highly skeptical that it would approve a reform model that gave river basin institutions real decision-making authority over their waters. They wanted a much more radical decentralization.

For the moment, the activists in Piracicaba concentrated on building their own capabilities. One of the state deputies the campaign organizers had contacted, José Machado, was elected mayor of Piracicaba in 1988. In line with the petition presented the year before, he espoused the creation of an intermunicipal consortium to deal with water problems. He and nine other mayors founded the Intermunicipal Consortium of the Piracicaba and Capivari River Basins in October 1989. Although established as a nonprofit association of municipal governments, environmentalists, university professors, and other civic activists attended its meetings from the beginning (Castellano 2007). Funded by member municipalities, the consortium set up a technical office and hired a group of water specialists, who began to study the French water system that the DAEE specialists in the capital claimed to be emulating (Interview 28, Brasília, 2011). Consortium staff visited France and eventually set up an exchange program with the Seine-Normandie water agency (Castellano 2007).

From this interaction, they concluded that the French model provided a mechanism for granting river basin organizations executive control over water management that was absent in the FUNDAP-led debates: the Agence de l'Eau, or Water Agency. While the FUNDAP proposals had presented basins as planning units and basin institutions as decision-making forums, the consortium members called for the creation of executive agencies directly controlled by the river basin committees. What they called basin agencies would have the administrative structure and the funding to implement projects and programs on their own, essentially bypassing state government agencies.

After an unsuccessful attempt to convince participants in the São Paulo debates of this idea, the consortium staff took another tack. After DAEE submitted the bill to the state legislature, the consortium's mayors lobbied the region's state deputies to propose an amendment, adding an article about basin agencies into the law. The engineers at DAEE were taken by surprise and did not have time to challenge the proposal or to amend its wording (Interview 28, Brasília, 2011).

PASSAGE OF THE SÃO PAULO LAW (1991)

Over the course of this reform process, many actors endeavored to move the conversation about water management out of a circumscribed world in which water experts talked only to other water experts and onto a more variegated terrain. The goal was both to build more support for change and to generate new ideas. One result of all this was that the professional and personal networks of participants in the process expanded and in many cases became more diverse. On many occasions, actors made use of their network linkages to circumvent obstacles that they believed would otherwise stall the reform process.

The laborious negotiations that went on in São Paulo crafted a reform proposal, but many other barriers had to be overcome before it became law. The State Water Resources Council had to approve the bill if it was to be put before the legislative assembly by the governor's office, as seemed desirable. Members of the council wanted a hand in the drafting process and made major revisions; even though many were directors of the agencies whose personnel had participated in the various working groups, they did not always feel bound by compromises that others had negotiated in the name of their organizations.

Issues that we thought were consensus ended up being vetoed by the Council.... The Secretary... took out articles that gave more autonomy to river basins and granted more authority to the Secretariat of the Environment. This meant that the proposal to be sent by the executive to the state legislature would lose some of its most innovative elements, the product of months of discussion among groups at the meetings of the network. (Amaral 1998, chap. 3, 3).

Fearing that passage of a weakened version would set back reform for a long time, DAEE's superintendent Paulo Bezzaril set out to preempt that process, quickly taking the original bill to the state assembly himself (apparently without the prior knowledge of his colleagues). He entrusted the bill's sponsorship to a fellow Freemason, a state assemblyman he knew could rally the support of other lodge members (by his report, fully a third of the assemblymen).[9] Another occasion when technical professionals used personal ties to move the process forward occurred in 1991, after São Paulo's legislature finally approved the law (with the Piracicaba group's amendment). Passage was not enactment, and Governor Fleury sat on the legislation. Using a boomerang strategy typical of advocacy networks,[10] Barth convinced a colleague at the Inter-American Development Bank to try to make Fleury's signing the water law a condition for approving the Projeto Tietê, a major river cleanup project. Fleury, eager to showcase the project at the 1992 United Nations Conference on Environment and Development in Rio de Janeiro, signed. Barth and his colleagues then mailed thousands of copies of the legislation to colleagues all over Brazil and switched their attention almost immediately to promoting passage of a federal law as well.

THE DEBATE AROUND THE FEDERAL LAW, STAGE 1 (1990–1994)

At first, the federal debates looked a lot like the São Paulo process, with the creation of working groups and seminars to put together a proposal to be presented by the executive to the legislature. But unlike the case with São Paulo, the executive branch portion of the process moved quickly at the national level. It was in the legislature that negotiations stalled, as political actors with a wide variety of interests vied for a model that would give them the most power. Congressmen took a key role, especially the *relatores*,

---

9. Interview with Paulo Bezzaril, São Paulo, May 1999, by Margaret Keck.

10. Boomerang strategies involve appealing for support to external groups to use their leverage with powerful domestic actors in support of goals that the local activists are not strong enough to accomplish by themselves. See Keck and Sikkink (1998, 13).

or rapporteurs, whose job it was to analyze and consolidate (or sometimes rewrite) the draft of a bill: São Paulo environmentalist Fábio Feldmann was rapporteur on the bill from 1991 to 1994; and Aroldo Cedraz, a northeastern politician from a conservative party, from 1995 to 1997. The major divisions were between defenders of more centralized and more decentralized and participatory arrangements, and, within the federal bureaucracy itself, over which agency would coordinate the new water management system.

As in São Paulo, the national water law began to be discussed in working groups largely made up of experts brought in by the government. DNAEE coordinated the first stage in this process, described earlier. The second stage began in 1990, inspired by the 1988 constitution's requirement that the government create a national water resources management system. This time, a presidential decree handed the task of coming up with a national water law to the Secretariat of Strategic Affairs, a planning agency loosely connected to the armed forces.[11] Unlike in São Paulo, the constitution had put the discussion on a timetable. There was pressure to pass a new water law before the 1992 United Nations Conference on the Environment in Rio de Janeiro, certain to draw international attention to Brazil and its natural resources.

Members of the working group came from various governmental ministries and departments, and specialists from professional associations and the academy took part in the debates. The members soon agreed that the basic structure of the new system should include a national executive agency, a national council, and river basin committees. The main controversy was about the distribution of power within the federal government. Like the working group that had inaugurated debates on national water policy in the mid-1980s, this group also could not agree on which federal agency should be responsible for issuing water use permits.

The government ultimately approved a bill that included many of the *principles* (integration, decentralization, participation, river basin management) and *instruments* (including water pricing) of the new institutional design package discussed in the last chapter but configured them within a centralizing organizational structure. Essentially, this version opted for the status quo: DNAEE would retain the executive secretariat; authority to issue water permits would remain with the agencies that currently had it. A National Water Management Council made up exclusively of federal ministries and state water agencies would have primary responsibility for

---

11. We note that before this working group was set up, two federal deputies had presented their own much simpler draft legislation to create a new water management system; these proposals were subsequently combined with the bill written by the executive, once it had gone before the Congress.

adopting and monitoring a national water resources plan. River basin committees comprising state and federal agencies, municipalities, water users, and user associations would have the power to make decisions related to conflict resolution and emergency planning but could only evaluate river basin plans. The bill disappointed those who thought of water reform primarily in terms of decentralization, participation, and multiple uses.

The story of the bill's six-year march through Congress provides some notion of just how entangled an institutional context those contesting centralization had to navigate. The draft legislation was revised every step of the way, as different actors whose support would be necessary had a chance to influence it. After its introduction in the Chamber of Deputies, the bill was first sent to the Consumer, Environment, and Minorities Commission headed by São Paulo environmentalist deputy Fábio Feldmann, who agreed to be the law's rapporteur. Feldmann organized more than 20 hearings with users, civil society, state, and municipal actors, especially from São Paulo (Interview 21, Brasília). According to one participant, a seminar organized by FUNDAP in 1992 helped convince legislators on the commission that the new system should have three interacting components: basin committees with decision-making power, basin agencies capable of producing information and managing water pricing, and revenues from the pricing system to provide funding (Seminário Técnico 1992).

In addition to meetings of this sort, the commission heard individually from civil society organizations, mayors and municipal consortia, water users, state governments, and legislatures, especially in the southeastern part of Brazil. Feldmann had sent a copy of the original bill out to 1,700 nongovernmental organizations (NGOs) requesting input. Several took issue with the bill's centralizing bent and with the continued ascendancy of the energy sector and demanded that river basin institutions be given a more powerful role. AGAPAN, one of the nation's oldest environmental NGOs, raised questions about the separation of water resources policy from environmental policy. Still, relatively few environmental organizations responded. In an interview in São Paulo in 1993, leading environmentalist João Paulo Capobianco told Keck that most activists felt ill equipped to intervene in water management debates because they were so technical. After these consultations and others with municipal governments and the private sector, Feldmann and his staff drafted a substitute bill dramatically different from the one the executive had introduced. In his justification for the new version, Feldmann claimed that the executive's proposal had reinforced the dominance of electric power interests, defying the emerging consensus among water professionals around integrated management for multiple uses (Feldmann 1994). Feldmann's draft called for a decentralized system, structured from the bottom up, beginning with basin committees and moving to regional committees and then to the national level. It was also the first to fully conceive of a decentralized water pricing system. The river basin committees were made responsible for determining the prices to be charged, and river basin agencies had specific functions allowing them to implement a pricing system. Still, although Feldmann was an expert on environmental policy, the proposal included no clear mechanisms for connecting water policy to environmental management, for example by requiring that water use permits and environmental licensing be conducted together (a reform that has only recently begun to be implemented in some states).

STAGE 2: SETTLING THE POWER DISTRIBUTION WITHIN THE FEDERAL ADMINISTRATION (1995–1997)

In 1995, having lost a bid for reelection, Feldmann left Congress and was replaced as rapporteur by Aroldo Cedraz of the conservative Liberal Front Party (Partido da Frente Liberal, PFL) from Bahia state. Cedraz's party was part of Fernando Henrique Cardoso's government coalition, and a PFL member held the position of minister of the environment. This change had important consequences, the first of which was to greatly reduce the emphasis on decentralization Feldmann had supported. While Feldmann had privileged consultations with people in state and municipal governments and in civil society, Cedraz concentrated on obtaining support within the federal government (Interview 17, Brasília, 2002).

Cedraz fit into a new balance of power in which the energy sector's hold on the reform process was giving way to agricultural interests. According to Barth, supporters of irrigated agriculture in the Northeast ended up being crucial for the law's passage.[12] The minister of the environment, northeasterner Gustavo Krause, apparently accepted the job on the condition that the Secretariat of Water Resources (SRH), responsible for irrigation policy and related infrastructure, be transferred to that ministry (Interview 13, Brasília, 2002). The construction of reservoirs, aqueducts, and other infrastructure allowing for perennial farming in semiarid regions of Brazil's Northeast had long been a major source of political clout for regional politicians (in a historically lucrative scheme referred to as the *industria da seca*, or drought industry). Transferring responsibility for irrigation infrastructure from the Ministry of the Interior to the Ministry of Environment changed the coalitional prospects for the water law. Irrigation interests saw

---

12. Interview with Flávio Barth, São Paulo, May 1999, by Margaret Keck.

their chance to wrest control over the system from DNAEE. They joined environmentalists in the claim that relocating the coordination for water management to that ministry would put water management in the hands of an agency unconnected to any particular economic interest group.

Cedraz was an able negotiator and worked out a deal within the executive branch. He had to appease the sectoral agencies and allay the finance ministry's concern that the Feldmann Draft gave too much control over revenues from user fees to basin committees. The resulting revision to the bill was fairly close to the law that finally passed. Although it maintained the spirit of the previous version, it was much simpler and shorter and left many matters ambiguous. For example, the committees lost enforcement mechanisms when provisions were removed that had imposed sanctions on public authorities that made public investments in violation of the committee-approved river basin plans.

Most important, Cedraz was able to get presidential support for the bill. Institutional reform was high on President Cardoso's political agenda, and his administration was promoting decentralization in a variety of policy areas (Arretche 2000) along with privatization of publicly owned services, especially telecommunications and energy. A law regulating water management seemed a good way to give private investors in the energy sector a sense of security. In 1996, with the approval of the commission he headed and indications of support from federal agencies, Cedraz convinced Cardoso to ask Congress to put the bill on the fast track.[13] New disagreements soon emerged, however, and it took another eight months of interagency negotiation within the federal government to produce a version of the law that could come up for vote. The main sticking points concerned energy, finance, and the locus of control in the system. Energy demanded and won a grace period during which it would not be subject to decisions of the new committees and councils. A majority of seats in the National Water Resources Council were allocated to the organs of the federal government, increasing its power in the system. But the system was put under the control of the Ministry of the Environment, seen at the time as a win for irrigation interests.

Even after both the Chamber of Deputies and the Senate approved this version unanimously, presidential line item vetoes removed additional contentious points. Some of these were meant to further appease the energy sector (Pereira 1997; Interview 17, Brasília, 2002). Others took out stipulations on the mechanics of water pricing, leaving these to be resolved by

---

13. Brazilian law allows the executive to pluck any bill out of its trajectory through the commissions and bring it straight to the Chamber floor for a vote.

complementary legislation. The resulting law proclaimed a new system of decentralized management whose feasibility depended on charging for water but left for later such central issues as establishing how pricing would work, how water agencies would be created, how basin committees would control the allocation of revenues, and what form coordination between state and federal governments would take. Resolving some of these problems, it turned out, involved such profound transformations in administrative practices that they would require further legislative action. In essence, the major contentious issues were left as ambiguous as possible.

Although the energy sector won many concessions, it lost control over the water system as a whole, with the Ministry of Environment now heading up water resources management. At first, this augured a stronger Secretariat of Water Resources, then in charge of a huge irrigation budget. However, soon after the final bill passed, irrigation programs were transferred to the new Ministry of Regional Integration, because other agencies representing high-volume water consumers objected to such close association between policy coordinators and a single sector (Interview 16, Brasília, 2002).

Figure 3.1 is a schematic portrayal of the complex web of interests and power affecting the design of the national law. What becomes clear is that

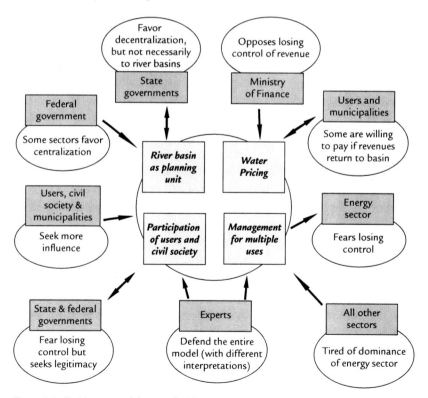

Figure 3.1. Positions around the water legislation.

very few sectors fully supported the entire reform proposal, shown at the center of the figure. Besides water specialists, the institutional design package did not have a natural constituency. Instead, each of its components had both supporters and opponents, and each group did its best to shape the law for its own benefit. During the congressional debates, each group consulted pulled the reform in a different direction. Groups advocating more decentralization to states had the most influence during Feldmann's period as rapporteur; that was also the only period during which civil society groups and the private sector were consulted. After Cedraz took over, the focus changed to working out a deal among federal agencies. Since the legislative process in Brazil grants the federal government the last word, it is not surprising that many decentralizing elements, especially those related to revenue collection and allocation, were ultimately weakened. Still, the fact that principles of river basin management remained in the equation, with power over financial instruments in the hands of river basin organizations, attests to the capacity of water experts in state and federal agencies to promote those ideas through political action. As the figure suggests, these are the only groups that supported the reform in its entirety.

DISENGAGEMENTS

If putting together a new water management system would require finding a route through a tangle of institutions and organizations, each one with a stake in the matter and the resources to make itself heard, it also involved detaching particular issues, organizations, and even entire social groups from the process. One consequential example of such *disengagement* was the absence of environmental and land management instruments in the institutional design. A variety of new organizations—basin committees, basin agencies, state and federal water agencies and councils—were created to confront water problems ranging from pollution to drought to floods. Each one had a series of attributions, connected to the small set of water management instruments the laws defined: water use permits, charges, plans, and so on. These instruments were ultimately intended to facilitate regulating water resource *use*: withdrawing, polluting, or otherwise using the water in river channels, lakes, and groundwater. But the causes of those problems often lay elsewhere. Rivers do not overflow by themselves but often do so because deforestation or some other land use problem has reduced the percolation of water throughout a river basin. Water quality is degraded not only by sewage but also by the expansion of housing settlements.

The separation of water policy from land and environmental management meant that water use permits became, in effect, the only strong regulatory instrument in the water management field. Water use permits authorize a firm, a hydroelectric dam, a sanitation company, or a farmer to withdraw, pollute, or otherwise use water contained in rivers, lakes, and groundwater. Since without such an authorization those initiatives may be derailed, permitting can actually regulate private behavior in a very direct way. At the time that water reform began, most states had precarious water rights systems—they lacked information on the activities of firms using water resources and had little capacity to enforce controls. Over time, however, as those capabilities grew, other water management instruments were increasingly connected to water use permitting. Members of river basin committees realized that setting priorities for water allocations had the potential to be the most powerful component of water use plans, which otherwise had little chance of being implemented. Similarly, water prices came to be understood as charges for water use permits. This focus on water resources *use* rather than on a broader notion of water resources *management* restricted the ambitions of water reform ever more narrowly to the river channel, with a shrinking capacity to resolve water problems whose causes lay outside the waterway.[14]

There are several reasons that the water legislation is so omissive vis-à-vis environmental and land use issues. Federalism provides one set of explanations. One interviewee told us that legislators hesitated to meddle in other jurisdictional purviews, in this case municipalities, for fear of provoking political opposition (Interview 34, Brasília, 2010). Many advocates of reform did conceive of water mainly as an economic resource, not as a component of ecosystems, and might have balked at the idea that the environmental sector might gain control over water use permits. However, federal environmental institutions were singularly uninvolved with water questions during this period (Interview 1, Brasília, 1990). Environmental organizations concerned with water pollution were concentrated in large metropolitan areas and focused their attention at either municipal or state levels. Indeed, many of them avoided taking on water issues, which often seemed dauntingly technical, and usually involved very powerful state agencies (but see Keck 2002). The exception—protests over environmental, indigenous, and resettlement questions involving large dams—normally had much more to do with moral witness than with technical argument. Those environmentalists who were technically equipped to address these issues were spread out among state environmental agencies or in universities and, with few exceptions, appear not to have mustered much influence

14. Recently, some states have recognized and begun to address this problem; in Rio de Janeiro, for example, water permitting and environmental licensing have been combined into a single process.

in this process. More dispersed still were activists working on land use issues closely related to water—such as riverbank restoration, protection of creeks or springs, or fighting local waste dumping into waterways. These activities were very local, and until the preparations for the 1992 Earth Summit, most such organizations had little or no contact with those outside their immediate region.

In addition to land use and environmental policy, important social actors were also left out of the process. This became evident in 2004, when the National Council of Brazilian Bishops (CNBB) organized a campaign about water that explicitly took issue with the idea of water pricing. Some 600,000 people signed a petition proposing that the 1997 water law be replaced with a National Water Patrimony Law (*Lei do Patrimônio Hídrico Nacional*).[15] An ecumenical group attracted press attention with a report that censured the National Water Agency, called river basin committees mouthpieces for powerful interests, and contained other sweeping criticisms of the way water policy was going (Defensoria da Água 2004).

Water management specialists were flabbergasted that the system they defended had been interpreted as a threat to the notion of water as a basic human right. Several wrote letters to church authorities, pointing out technical errors in the report and begging the bishops' council not to forward the report to the United Nations and the Vatican, as press reports announced they would do. The active listserv of the Brazilian Water Resources Association was flooded with shocked messages by water professionals complaining that the campaign participants were misinformed. The main surprise was that the campaign documents failed to understand that the system was already participatory and that water was being recognized as a public good.

The discussion called attention to the fact that a large subset of organized social groups were absent from both the river basin committees and more general debates about water management. The groups were speaking on totally different registers. Large popular organizations, from religious NGOs and pastorals to social movements such as the Movement of People Affected by Dams (MAB), have tended to view river basin committees as bureaucratized spaces dominated by the government agenda and have generally not participated in them. The result has been that their more critical conception of the water management model—despite its impact on public opinion more generally—has had less impact on how the model has been implemented than the other conceptions discussed here (although it likely has diminished public support for the policy).

15. See http://websmed.portoalegre.rs.gov.br/escolas/giudice/abaixo_assinadohidrico. html, accessed September 30, 2010, for the text of the petition.

LEGISLATION WITHOUT RESOLUTION

The São Paulo law was the first in Brazil to identify as core principles that water management should be decentralized, participatory, and integrated, using the river basin as planning unit, and that there should be charges for water use. A number of water management instruments were included in the law, including river basin plans, water permits, and water pricing. The federal law reaffirmed most of these instruments and presented wording that gave more power than the São Paulo law did to river basin committees and their executive arm, the basin agencies.

Both laws lacked clear mechanisms guaranteeing implementation. In particular, they left the operation of the pricing system so vague that additional legislation would be necessary to get it off the ground (the São Paulo law explicitly required the passage of such complementary legislation). Neither law made explicit how river basin agencies would be created or what their status as public institutions would be. In particular, since the territorial boundaries of these new institutions did not coincide with federal, state, or municipal borders—the administrative units provided for in Brazil's constitution—there were unanswered questions about their ability to charge for water or collect public revenues at all. Moreover, ensuring that funds generated would be spent on projects that river basin committees decided to sponsor meant somehow shielding those revenues from the rest of state or federal budgeting processes. At the time, no one knew how to do that. Indeed, one federal budget specialist in the federal government told us that guaranteeing river basin committee control of pricing revenues and the return of funds from water fees to the basin of origin was impossible. The national treasury would not allow another agency to control disbursement of funds so strictly. Thus, although planning, committees, agencies, and water pricing had all made it into legislation, the conceptual map of how these different components would operate in relation to each other remained quite fluid.

This chapter has shown how a wide variety of actors played some part in the long process of designing new water laws, as they attempted to recombine ideas, resources, and organizational missions by adopting new practices. They involved the work of disrupting existing institutions, as when Barth and others were persuaded that to change the way things were done they had to politicize a discussion that had previously been held with small groups of specialist counterparts. The new practices involved a great deal of engagement. They relied heavily on intensive talk and the work of persuasion, rethinking, negotiating, and rewriting. Often they required activating and creating professional, political, and personal networks. Examples ranged from the use of political party ties by the Piracicaba consortium actors to push for the inclusion of agencies in the water law to taking advantage of opportunities for personal intervention, such as when Bezerril suggested the idea of a State Water Resources Council to the São Paulo governor. Publications such as the DAEE magazine and participation in professional congresses and events also helped to build a public for the reform. We can also see even at this early stage how experimentation with different combinations of actions and resources on the ground influenced the broader process of legislative and institutional reform. Consider, for example, the entrepreneurship and autonomous spirit of the Piracicaba group as it proposed new programs and institutions, built a consortium, established collaborative relations with the French water agency, and designed and implemented projects of its own.

The complexity of the task of building a legal framework capable of coordinating among so many economic interests and policy fields at different levels of government certainly helps explain why the laws left so many issues unresolved. The story we have told in this chapter has multiple protagonists. Following the progress of the federal bill as it moved from the executive branch's strategic affairs office to the legislative branch and from the hands of a progressive, environmentalist legislator to those of a member of the conservative governing coalition gives us an idea of how many actors had a chance to leave their stamp on the law. While those in the federal government pushed for a more centralized law, voices from states with more advanced water management systems—most notably, but not only, São Paulo—pressured for a more decentralized system. While the energy sector sought to retain its privileged position, other economic sectors—along with the environmentalists—joined forces in favor of a system favoring multiple uses. The entangled political process of transforming diverging ideas and demands from a variety of sources into a single legal statute ended up producing a notably ambiguous framework, which would have to be improved at later stages. For the moment, organizations with the capabilities and recognition to respond to the new ideas were only embryonic. The laws were on paper, but where the practical authority to carry them out would come from was not yet clear.

The resistance of powerful interests within both the São Paulo and the federal government to changes that would reduce their authority—most notably the energy sector—obviously left its mark on both laws. But understanding the legal framework as no more than a reflection of the classic formula "might makes right" would be a mistake. Although ambiguous and full of loose ends, the new legislation imprinted on future actions a variety of ideas that really were new. By *imprinted*, we mean that, though ambiguous, the wording of the law would influence how people understood the reform process in the future. That wording gives support to a particular interpretation of water reform, one in which river basin committees would have the power to set prices for water and decide how to use revenues and one that proposed the creation of new executive agencies at the river basin level, politically controlled not by state or federal authorities but by the committees themselves. Although translating that interpretation into practice turned out to be much harder than anyone imagined, it did guide much of the process of institution building that we will discuss in the rest of this book.

CHAPTER 4

Practicing Laws

Experiments with Institution Building

In this chapter, we begin to explore what protagonists of the water management reform process did with the ambiguous legal framework that resulted from the multiple entwined processes described in the previous one. The legislation espoused a new approach but left the details to be worked out later. This working-out process involved a mix of experimenting with what could be done under existing legislation, discovering lacunae, negotiating over new rules and initiatives, adapting to different local conditions, and finding ways to get needed additional legislation passed to fill in some of the holes that framers of the first reform laws had left. It is complicated by the sometimes surprising mix of rigidity and flexibility in the Brazilian legal system, in which minute decisions that might in the United States be made in administrative rulings must be voted on by the legislature, often giving rise to a continuous loop of legislation, problem, and revision.

At the center of the institutional design package was the proposal that a new kind of organization—river basin committees—would be responsible for two sets of key decisions: how much high-volume water users should be charged and how the proceeds from those charges should be used. Another new kind of organization, river basin agencies, would be set up to provide technical assistance and help to implement these decisions. Exactly how those organizations would be created and how the funding mechanism would work was far from clear in 1997 when the federal law was enacted. As they experimented with making the new system work in practice, reformers not only discovered insufficiencies in the legislation but also had to adjust many of their own expectations about how the system would work. Pragmatist philosopher John Dewey would have understood this as a process of active learning through experience (Menand 1997, 205–211), in which a problem situation energizes those trying to find solutions, who learn by interacting with the problem and with each other, creating new organizations, mobilizing resources and relationships in new ways, and building capabilities. In the course of the implementation process, different actors moved into the reform coalition, changing the prospects for lawmaking. Their mobilization was responsible for the passage of a second wave of laws in the 2000s that made water pricing viable.

When we explore the interactions between institutional designs and the practical experimentation that takes place as people try to implement them, we follow in the footsteps of distinguished forebears.[1] Pressman and Wildavsky (1984), 40 years ago, wondered how policies get implemented at all, given how highly politicized the implementation process seems to be. They suggested that, as complexity of implementation increased, the likelihood that the original objectives would be maintained decreased accordingly. A number of policy scholars responded by arguing that this kind of adaptation—in which complex networks of local government officials, firms, and nonprofit organizations rewrite the policies handed down from above in order to deal with concrete problems—can be positive.[2] In a study of federal grants-in-aid for state-level water resources planning in the United States, for example, Ingram (1977) maintained that policy implementation is most effective when it allows creative actors the scope to adapt to local circumstances. In the process she studied, the federal government's objectives gradually changed from trying to get state governments to draw up water resource plans whether they wanted to or not to prompting them to increase their capacity to do so. The diversity of bargaining situations (involving multiple actors in both federal and state agencies with different levels and kinds of commitments) guaranteed differentiated processes and outcomes, however much Congress in passing legislation might have stipulated uniformity.

As Werner and Wegrich (2006, 44) point out, "Policies are perpetually reformulated, implemented, evaluated, and adapted. But these processes do not evolve in a pattern of clear-cut sequences; instead, the stages are constantly meshed and entangled in an ongoing process." Our study of

---

1. See Werner and Wegrich (2006) for a recent review of the policy stages concept and Hill (2009) for a discussion of the implementation debate.

2. See review by Sabatier (1986) of the top-down-versus-bottom-up debate on implementation. For an explicitly pragmatist approach but with a focus on enforcement, see Coslovsky, Pires, and Silbey (2012). Some policies purposely promote such creativity (Hill 2009, 198–201). Elmore (1979–1980), for one, suggested that policy design was the partial result of implementation rather than the other way around. Sabatier (1999) was one of the clearest statements of the need to move beyond a stage-based theory of policy analysis. Thomas and Grindle (1990) applied the discussion to policy reforms.

the progress of water policy reform suggests that this kind of intermingled process of policy making, institution building, and negotiating occurs not only before or after laws are passed but also throughout, as different kinds of actors try to enact change both locally and in a broader context. In this chapter we will focus on the way this complex process played out with regard to implementing the principle that high-volume water users should pay a fee for withdrawing, reserving the right to withdraw, or discharging effluents into watercourses. We show how actors developed clearer ideas about what further changes were necessary on the basis of concrete experiences, some of which functioned as small-scale tests that would inform subsequent legislative proposals. Many people who had initially expected the new legislation to lead more or less automatically to the changes they espoused realized that they also had to invest in organization building, both to guarantee the law's implementation and to test ideas and mobilize resources for further legislative action.

Thinking about the way people build institutions as a series of real-time experiments does not imply any judgment about the quality or effectiveness of those institutions. We mainly seek to highlight the fragility and contingency of these processes and the policies they produce. Institutional designs do not become functioning institutions by themselves. In the case study developed in this chapter, we explore the interaction between the practical institution-building efforts of specialists committed to a new conception of water management and the strategies employed by powerful economic actors to make sure that no matter what new system was adopted, their interests would continue to be protected.

We begin the chapter with an account of the decision to establish the National Water Agency (Agência Nacional de Água, ANA), inaugurated in 2000 as a new national-level executive organization to oversee implantation of the new system. We will also briefly introduce the reader to some of the other actors involved in implementing laws, such as state governments and the World Bank. Not long after the creation of ANA, leaders of that new organization decided to invest a large portion of its resources in a policy experiment, the implementation of a water pricing system in a major basin, the Paraíba do Sul. That practical experiment, in turn, reconfigured ideas, resources, and relationships, giving rise to a new network of actors who mobilized and worked strategically to get the complementary legislation needed to make the experiment operationally viable passed at both federal and state levels. The outcome of this process taught the reformers a hard lesson: when the future payers of the user fees played a significant part in setting the rates, the prices they were willing to pay were too low to supply the kind of financing for river basin level water management that they had sought.

CREATING NEW ORGANIZATIONS: THE NATIONAL WATER AGENCY

Soon after passage of the 1997 national water law, the core group of experts that had followed the negotiations since the 1980s—led by Flávio Barth—began to worry about the capacity to implement it, especially in light of its vagueness on key issues. Once again, they would use their political networking capabilities to try to address this. Through the Brazilian Water Resources Association, they organized seminars to assess the issues still pending, including ambiguities regarding federal and state government jurisdiction and what kind of relationship should exist between river basin committees and water agencies. The National Water Resources Council, established in 1998, incorporated many of the resulting proposals as it developed much more explicit rules for administering the system over the next decade. But it did not take them long to realize that rules and regulations were not enough; something had to be done to address the generalized lack of technical capabilities in monitoring, planning, and managing water resource use that plagued the policy field at all levels.

The idea they came up with was to create a new national executive agency, with substantial autonomy—the sort of insulated bureaucracy discussed in chapter 2 that Brazilians have traditionally used to try to make policy work. According to participants we interviewed, this idea emerged at a meeting of water engineers with the World Bank representative in Brasília. The meeting had been requested by Tasso Jereissati, governor of Ceará state (Interview 13, Brasília, 2002; Interview 34, Brasília, 2010). By the late 1990s, Ceará had pioneered a different model of water management, based on the creation of a powerful state water agency. Jereissati also wanted to pursue that idea at the national level. Barth, despite his long history of support for a more decentralized system, declared at this meeting that he had become convinced of the need for a strong federal agency to make the reform work. Three other engineers heavily involved in policy debates at the time were also present. One was Jerson Kelman, a professor at the engineering institute of the Federal University of Rio de Janeiro, who had been a key participant in the Ceará reform and was close to Jereissati. With the exception of the World Bank officer, the Ceará governor, and Barth, who passed away soon after, all of the participants at that meeting eventually served as directors of the agency they imagined that day.

"As soon as the idea came up, it seemed natural, it seemed so obvious," recalled one of the participants at that meeting (Interview 13, Brasília, 2002). Independent regulatory agencies were a new institutional trend, responding to privatization of public services, a central element of President Cardoso's state reform agenda. These agencies were to have nonpartisan oversight boards, in which directors served for staggered terms (in order to prevent the simultaneous turnover of board members from generating policy instability). This format was especially appealing in anticipation of new ministerial and other government appointments at the beginning of Cardoso's second presidential term, raising the possibility that the position of secretary of water resources would go to a political appointment who neither understood nor cared about the new model (Interview 19, Brasília, 2002).[3]

Soon after the meeting at the World Bank office, the group gained Cardoso's endorsement for the agency in a manner reminiscent of Bezerril's suggestion to the São Paulo governor more than a decade before, discussed in chapter 3. Jereissati arranged a meeting with the president in which he and Kelman spelled out the idea just days before the president was to attend a high-profile meeting about privatization of the energy sector. The president agreed that the idea of a regulatory agency for water would give the sector a sense of stability as it was being privatized. In his speech, he placed the proposal in the context of the broader state reform process: "We must transform the state so that it can continue to regulate the interests of the population and encourage actions that we believe will serve the common good. This National Water Agency is a move in this direction" (Agência Nacional de Água 2002, 29).

With presidential support, the lawmaking process went much more quickly this time around. Kelman, hired as a special adviser to the Ministry of the Environment to draft the new law, became a central actor at this point. By July 1999, only a few months later, the draft was already being debated at a seminar of water specialists. Within a year, the law had passed through Congress, and the agency was created. The president appointed its four directors, with Kelman in the lead position as director-president of the new agency.

ANA's origins followed a classic Brazilian pattern, setting up a new insulated bureaucracy alongside (but independent from) a drastically reduced Water Resources Secretariat, both housed in the Ministry of the Environment. At around the same time, the secretariat lost the irrigation portfolio to the Ministry of Agriculture. It retained the executive secretariat of the National Water Resources Council along with responsibility for formulating water policy. Although ANA was formally only an executor, it ended up with the bulk of the funding and technical capacity. Water professionals were divided: some argued that the system needed an agency like ANA to make the water law operational, while others saw it

---

3. It is noteworthy that no mechanisms were included in the law to guarantee that agency directors were nonpartisan, and it was not long before many of the appointments were party nominees who were not technical specialists. One such nominee, approved despite protest from agency staff on the grounds that he was totally unqualified for the job, resigned after being accused in late 2012 of influence peddling.

as recentralization and feared that ANA would replicate the centralizing role that DNAEE had earlier played. This second view was most common among professionals working in state governments, some of whom also supported greater civil society participation in decentralized management. Not surprisingly, much of the staff at the Secretariat of Water Resources regarded ANA as having usurped its role. Thus, after 20 years of institution building, many of the same conflicts were reproduced: tensions between federal and state governments and a new kind of interagency competition.

OTHER ACTORS ON THE STAGE

The implementation of the new water laws would depend not only on the creation of a strong national institution but also on the mobilization of institutional capacity and commitment on the ground, especially in state governments. There was tremendous variation among states with regard to investment in technical aspects of water management. This only partly reflects differences in state capacity and budgets between wealthier and poorer regions of the country.

São Paulo's state agencies have long had the largest concentration of skilled water professionals in Brazil, and the two agencies responsible for water and environmental management had regional offices with well-qualified personnel who managed the executive offices of the new river basin committees. São Paulo was the only state that already had a well-developed permit system in place in the early 2000s. Minas Gerais and a few others built such systems over the next decade, as did the federal government (responsible for issuing permits on federal waters).

Some states, even relatively wealthy ones, resisted becoming involved in water management. In Santa Catarina, conservative governments responsive to agricultural interests interpreted water management as a form of environmental regulation, to which they were generally hostile, at one point changing the name of the state's Secretariat for Sustainable Development to Secretariat of Sustainable Economic Development (Interview 70, Blumenau, 2007). For most of the last decade, that agency had only two or three professional specialists working on water management (Interview 66, Florianópolis, 2007). Efforts to compensate for the state's lack of support had a formative impact on the Itajaí committee, as we will see in more detail in chapter 7.

Whether or not state government agencies invested in water management often resulted from decisions about political projects that had nothing to do with water per se. In Minas Gerais, for example, Governor Aécio Neves (2003–2010) undertook a liberalizing administrative reform of the kind discussed in chapter 2 (Corrêa 2007), one of whose consequences was an overall upgrade of technical capacity for water management. The state water agency hired more specialists, a water resources fund was set up, and a general program of water-related infrastructure improvements began.[4]

Politics also mattered for state governments' attitudes toward specific river basin committees, with partisanship sometimes affecting the role committees were allowed to play. Relations between the PSDB-run São Paulo state government and the Alto Tietê committee (described in the next chapter) took a turn for the worse after the Workers' Party won the São Paulo municipal elections, and the new mayor became the committee president (Interview 30, Brasília, 2011).[5] The previously energized committee was sidelined to the point where the government simply stopped presenting its plans for major water infrastructure projects to the committee for deliberation (Formiga Johnsson and Kemper 2005). In Brasília, an opposition politician's endorsement of a group attempting to establish a Paranoá committee likely intensified the district government's boycott of the endeavor. In other cases, committees gained more influence over infrastructure decisions because government officials believed it would contribute to their electoral success. This happened in Minas Gerais, after committee activists in the Velhas River Basin convinced Governor Neves to make cleaning up the river a priority (see chapter 7).

Some state governments, especially in the Northeast, wanted to invest in water management but did not buy into the decentralized approach expressed, at least in principle, in the national water law. One northeastern state, Ceará, pioneered an alternative approach over the 1990s. There, the choice was to increase the capacity of state-level institutions first, with a strong, new state Water Resources Management Company (Companhia de Gestão de Recursos Hídricos, COGERH) to coordinate studies, do the planning, and implement water charges. COGERH was the first agency in Brazil to charge for water by the amount consumed, but decisions about pricing and use of revenues remained centralized (Formiga Johnsson and Kemper 2008). The agency also developed an alternative model for participatory decision making, discussed further in chapter 5.[6]

4. Luiza Marilac, oral presentation, Água da Gente conference, São Paulo (Watermark Project), August 2008.

5. Partido da Social Democracia Brasileira (Brazilian Social Democratic Party).

6. Another alternative to the committee approach came the state of Paraná, just south of São Paulo. There, anxious to ensure the financial sustainability of the water reform, the designers of the first version of the state's water law attempted to give primacy to a consortium of the largest water users, on the grounds that the latter would be willing to pay for the new system only if they believed it was in their interest to do so. As a state whose politics had long been dominated by private sector interests, Paraná might have been a prime site for this kind of experiment, had the incumbent state administration not lost a crucial election to a more populist opposition candidate, who promptly sent the process back to the drawing board (Gutiérrez 2006a; Ohira, 2010).

Along with a variety of domestic government officials, politicians, political parties, pro-reform administrators, intellectuals, and a few NGOs, external actors also played a role in espousing ideas and funding administrative reform. The World Bank was especially influential, pushing for institutional reform in water management throughout the country, often as part of infrastructure loan projects. In earlier chapters we noted that the bank has promoted IWRM internationally, particularly with regard to the creation of private markets for water rights (which in Brazil would have meant making it possible for users to sell permits). Although this proposal got nowhere in Brazil, the bank did spur federal and state investment in capacity building for water resources management, by making this a component of water supply and sanitation lending.

The World Bank–funded PROÁGUA program provided much of the funding for organization of water users associations and river basin committees in the Northeast. Begun in 1998, PROÁGUA was a $198 million dollar initiative intended to develop the institutional capacity of northeastern state governments to engage in integrated water management and to identify priority infrastructure for improving the lot of the poor in the region. For the bank, the institutional development side of the project was crucial: project failures for which the bank had been severely criticized during the preceding decade had often resulted from a lack of attention to institutional issues. For state governments, the prospect of new infrastructure investments was a powerful carrot; more than a decade of recession and fiscal adjustment had left the coffers bare. Not surprisingly, at a meeting to evaluate the progress of PROÁGUA held in Aracajú, Sergipe, in December 2000, many state officials told us quite openly that they were undertaking institutional reforms only because the World Bank said they had to.[7]

Yet interpreting the World Bank's role as imposing outside ideas on Brazilian reformers would be off the mark. Brazilian government officials who contracted and administered PROÁGUA and other major bank projects often saw them as opportunities to finance the reform effort as they conceived it. Local organization of water users commissions and basin committees in most of the Northeast was promoted and financed by PROÁGUA or other bank lending. However, the institutional changes the bank required were filtered through domestic political processes that affected the form they ultimately took. In Bahia, for example, a World Bank institutional development project funded organization of municipal and intermunicipal water management consortia instead of committees, in

---

7. For that meeting, a progress report was prepared on legal changes and committee organization; see Ministério do Meio Ambiente (2000).

accordance with the state government's policy preferences at the time. In Minas Gerais, a large bank-funded urban sanitation project in metropolitan Belo Horizonte, begun in the early 1990s, required the government to create a basin agency and draw up a water resources plan for the Velhas River Basin. But the state water law that passed shortly after the loan agreement was signed stipulated that river basin committees were to be in charge both of planning and of the agencies, meaning that to abide by the terms of the loan agreement, the state government had first to create the Velhas River Basin committee. The agency took another decade, as we will see in chapter 7. Thus, the bank influenced the adoption of new institutions but did not determine their form.

Another key actor for river basin politics has been the Ministério Público (MP, Public Ministry), an agency similar to a public prosecutor's office responsible for defending the public interest. The MP is a highly professional and semiautonomous agency, known for its zeal for enforcing the law (Arantes 2002). It has offices throughout Brazil specializing in environmental law (Hochstetler and Keck 2007, 51–57; McAllister 2008).[8] It has become involved in river basin conflicts when local actors, often environmental organizations, denounce the government's failure to enforce existing regulations. Faced with the threat of a costly suit, public agencies often respond preemptively and sign on to what are called conduct adjustment agreements. The Lagoa da Conceição committee in Santa Catarina resulted from such a process, after local NGOs got the MP to investigate allegations that the government was not monitoring pollution in an urban lake. In the state of Rio de Janeiro, the MP helped the Lagos São João River Basin Consortium by negotiating a formal agreement with municipal sanitation companies to reduce sewage emissions. Other committees have sought its support to get state agencies to follow through on commitments.

WATER PRICING AND THE PARAÍBA DO SUL EXPERIMENT

The Rationale

A vitally important part of making the new system operational was putting in place a system that charged high-volume users for the water they consumed, polluted, or stored. Water pricing had been the most contentious

---

8. Because the direct translation of this institution's name is not descriptively helpful, it has become conventional in English-language work to retain the original Portuguese when referring to the Ministério Público.

issue in the institutional design, but sources of dispute varied widely. Even this far into the process, the rationale for and necessity of water pricing were far from settled issues. The creation of actual markets in tradable water rights was never seriously contemplated in Brazil, despite the World Bank's efforts to promote them. The idea of state control over natural resources had deep roots in the Brazilian national-developmentalist worldview, and the 1988 constitution clearly established public ownership of water resources (both groundwater and surface water). This position did not waver during the neoliberal 1990s, and the 1997 national water law reaffirmed the principle. However, opposing privatization of water rights did not imply the embrace of the current system, which in most of the country consisted of unregulated open access for those able to abstract water from rivers, lakes, and underground sources.

Brazilian reformers proposed charging users for the right to use specified quantities of public water resources, a procedure that would depend on improved information and permitting systems. Public authorities would issue water use permits in accordance with criteria and priorities established in river basin plans; users would be charged for the amount of water they had permits for, independent of how much they actually used.[9] Besides identifying human and animal consumption as priority uses for water, the law also exempted low-volume water users from permitting and payment requirements. On this much, there was broad agreement. Beyond that, advocates of reform had very different views about the rationale for water charges and the social implications of the scheme, both consequential for the laws' implementation.

Most mainstream water engineers subscribed to one of two proffered justifications for water pricing. One sees the revenues generated as a source of financing for such water-related infrastructure as water and sewage treatment plants, diversion channels, and flood contention dams, all of which tend to be extremely costly. This is often referred to in Brazil as the "cost recovery model" (Azevedo and Asad 2000).[10] The second, more complicated argument sees water charges as a way to internalize the external

9. The idea bears some resemblance to the notion that individuals can be charged for public services, such as electric energy or water supply. Charging for such services evidently puts market pressures into consumer decision making: the wealthier consumers can afford to waste energy, water, gas, and other services the state charges for, while the poor tend to economize. But it is not exactly the same as a market. In the case of water use charges, there is another subtlety: the charge is not for a public service (which a utility had to spend money to provide) but for access to a limited natural (and publicly owned) resource that has historically been free.

10. Internationally, "cost recovery" generally aims to cover costs of operating and maintaining necessary infrastructure and only sometimes (usually in the case of small projects) also to cover construction costs.

costs of water use. As long as an industry or public utility pays nothing for using water inefficiently or for discharging pollutants into a river, there is no incentive for it to stop (Azevedo and Asad 2000, 322). Making water consumption more costly would be an incentive to use it more rationally.

The *cost internalization* or *polluter/user pays principle* approach to water pricing is espoused by most World Bank documents and by a large portion of the mainstream water engineers in Brazil, at least as an ideal, if not a practical option. Numerous scholars and technical specialists have contributed to the seemingly inexhaustible task of determining the right price for promoting rational water use.[11] Should it reflect the value of water as part of a production function? How could such a value be calculated? Or should it instead reflect users' willingness to pay?[12] A further complication is that water is used in different ways by different economic sectors. Should industrial users pay the same rates as agricultural users? The latter use so much more water than the former for every dollar they earn that charging the same could imply either charging virtually nothing to industry or bankrupting the farms. These questions convinced many water specialists to think of pricing as a task for economists. Yet this top-down approach would come into conflict with the more voluntary, collaborative notions of participation held by many reformers. The following account of the implantation of water charges in the Paraíba do Sul basin shows how involving water users in setting the rates and deciding how revenues should be spent was part and parcel of making water charges politically viable.

Water specialists were also divided on a particular innovation in the Brazilian water reform, especially in the 1997 law: river basin committees would decide the prices charged and approve investment plans for the revenues. The idea was inspired by the French system, in which water users share the costs of major investments through a slightly different pricing system (Barraqué 2000). In France, committees made up of water users, public officials, and a small number of civil society organizations negotiate investment plans. The price of water is then calculated so as to raise enough money to pay for those investments. In Brazil, committees, which include a greater proportion of civil society members than in France, would first determine the price they considered appropriate and their members were willing to pay. Investment plans would then be defined on the basis of the

---

11. A review of methodologies can be found in Garrido 2000. Examples of more recent contributions in Brazil are Fontes and Souza (2004) and Silva (2007).

12. The classic solution for coming up with the ideal price is to combine an analysis of the costs for reducing pollution and of "willingness to pay," maximizing the difference between the two so that the greatest relative benefit is associated with the lowest relative cost (Canepa, Pereira, and Lanna 1999).

revenues generated. Influenced by liberalizing reforms of the 1990s, many water reformers believed that even though they had a minority of seats on committees, water users would nonetheless support pricing, because they would understand that the resources generated would ultimately benefit them (Interview 34, Brasília, 2010). To make this idea more convincing, they were able to include in the national law and in many state laws the requirement that the majority of funds generated return to the basin of origin. Not all states followed this route, however. As mentioned above, in Ceará, for example, the reforms of the 1990s produced a centralized system of user fees. Over the course of the 2000s, some water professionals came to doubt the effectiveness of the participatory system of price setting and began to view the idea of a centralized model with more favor.

Outside the mainstream water engineering community, other actors involved in reform had other reasons for supporting or opposing the introduction of water pricing. Many environmentalists and NGO activists supported both the polluter pays principle and the belief that regulation of high-volume users was necessary on grounds of social equity and protection of the public good. Although members of this group were skeptical that such market mechanisms would advance environmental protection, they approved the notion that the proceeds could provide an autonomous funding source for participatory decision-making entities and were in favor of making users pay for the use of public resources for private gain. A good illustration is the statement on the website of São Paulo-based Rede das Águas (Water Network) asserting that the policy would counter the "false idea that there is abundant water in the country and that because this resource is in Nature it belongs to no one." At the same time, these groups (like most representatives of users and of state or municipal governments) insisted that funds had to return to the river basin where they were generated. Here they were expressing a well-founded worry that revenues that flow into the public coffers often do not reemerge and a desire to ensure that revenues be invested in water management instead of becoming part of the common fund (César, Born, and Ribeiro n.d.). This group of arguments combines a preoccupation with the public nature of water with a distrust of the centralized state.

Overt opposition to the idea of water pricing came from outside the specialist community. Leading opponents to the proposal were the Catholic church and potential payers—especially farmers, for different reasons. The National Conference of Brazilian Bishops (CNBB) led the principled opposition, with a 2004 campaign about "Water: Source of Life," one of whose platforms was the claim that water pricing would lead inevitably to acceptance of the idea that water was just one more commodity among many, to be governed by the logic of the market. This corresponded to the official Vatican stance on the issue, as reflected in its statements both at the 3rd World Water Forum in Kyoto in 2003 and in the 2004 Compendium of the Social Doctrine of the Church (Pontifical Council for Justice and Peace 2004, paras. 484–485). Nonetheless, for the Brazilian church, with its history of liberation theology and defense of the rural poor, this became a particularly strong commitment. The campaign's organizers considered pure malarkey the claim that charging for a publicly owned natural resource did not qualify as creating a water market:

> The economic value of water has been the central mechanism applied to manage water resources, now considered scarce. The rationale is simple: if payment is required, water use will be more rational. . . . In the final instance, water is transformed into a commodity among others, ruled by the laws of the market. (CNBB 2004, 14)

Marketizing water would exacerbate social exclusion, reducing access for the poor. But even more broadly, campaigners claimed, "Reducing water to an ordinary commodity takes away from its character as a primary necessity, a fundamental human right, vital and sacred" (CNBB 2004, 15).

Opposition from the agricultural sector was more obviously self-interested, and in many states, it exercised a powerful influence on the new policy's formulation. According to the Food and Agriculture Organization, in 1996, agricultural uses claimed 61 percent of water withdrawals in Brazil.[13] Although farmers were certainly not the only private sector actors who opposed water charges, nationwide they were the most vociferous opponents. For example, in 2002, before the Santa Catarina state government had even broached the issue, the Itajaí River Basin Committee invited farmers from the region to an exploratory meeting intended to discuss the possibility of water charges. They were met by "caravans of farmers from all parts of the basin…prepared to stand firm against any proposal to charge user fees for water, armed with a petition, protest speeches, slogans and chants and everything else" (Liberato 2004, 214). In the face of such a strong reaction, the committee decided to postpone the discussion of water charges until the political climate changed. In neighboring Paraná, the 1999 water law passed the state assembly only after last-minute negotiations explicitly exempted the agricultural sector from having to pay for the water it used (Ohira 2010).[14]

---

13. http://www.fao.org/nr/water/aquastat/countries_regions/BRA/index.stm, accessed March 27, 2013.

14. According to Ohira, proponents of the law decided not to resist demands for the exemption because large-scale irrigation is a rare practice in the state, and most of the farmers there would likely be exempted from having to pay in any case.

Although this kind of interest-based opposition seems very different from the appeals to technical rationality, social equity, or human dignity previously discussed, all of these different positions reflect assumptions about how states and markets behave and beliefs about the state's proper role in economy and society. Distrust of the state permeates the discourse of all actors in the story—it is too big, opaque, inefficient, misguided, or undemocratic. Yet both private users and civil society organizations still considered the provision of large-scale public infrastructure to be the state's job—at least in the absence of obvious alternatives. This reflects the Brazilian state's historical role as a decider and builder of things rather than as a regulator, and the underdevelopment of regulatory practice on the part either of regulator or regulated contributes to the great ambiguity of expectations about the state in this area. These worldviews, inscribed in actors' experiences and the historical traditions with which they identified, have consequences for their practice.

The Logistics

The 1997 law declared that water use could be subject to charges, that river basin committees should decide the rates and approve spending plans, and that new river basin agencies would be established to collect the payments and implement the plans. Although this may seem straightforward, making it operational turned out to be much more problematic than the designers had anticipated. First, the financial mechanisms that were supposed to guarantee that public moneys would return to the river basin where they were collected ran up against existing budgetary structures that channeled all federal public funds into the centrally controlled national treasury. Second, the constitution is explicit that only official administrative units (defined as municipalities, states and the union) may collect and spend public funds; levying charges through new entities created at the territorial level of river basins, whose boundaries corresponded to none of these, turned out to be a tricky business. There were thus some glaring omissions in the 1997 law's approach to water pricing.

Getting around these institutional barriers required the invention of a completely new set of financial arrangements—something that was accomplished through a daring piece of political entrepreneurship, spearheaded by Jerson Kelman and carried out through the (often contentious) efforts of personnel from ANA and a variety of actors from within the Paraíba do Sul basin. The decision to make the latter a test case for putting in place a system of user fees was made soon after the National Water Agency was created in 2000. That basin seemed like a good choice for a variety of reasons: it is one of the most densely urbanized and industrialized river basins in Brazil; many previous projects had produced a great deal of information about water use there; and perhaps most especially, Kelman had been a central participant in those earlier projects, when he was a professor at COPPE, the engineering school of the Federal University of Rio de Janeiro.

The Paraíba do Sul basin covers parts of three states in the industrial center of southeastern Brazil: Minas Gerais, São Paulo, and Rio de Janeiro. Located between the country's two largest metropolises (the cities of Rio de Janeiro and São Paulo), the region is also home to a highly productive agricultural sector (Gruben, Lopes, and Formiga Johnsson 2002). Although metropolitan Rio de Janeiro lies outside the basin, since the 1950s, nearly two-thirds of the river's flow has been diverted into the neighboring Guandú River Basin, initially for hydroelectric power and eventually becoming the most important source of potable water for almost 9 million of its residents (Formiga Johnsson, Kumler, and Lemos 2007). The basin thus reflected the complexity of water problems and the conflicts over multiple uses that the new management model sought to confront. Because of the region's wealth, there was also a very real possibility that water charges could generate enough money to have a noticeable impact on those problems.

The interstate river basin committee, CEIVAP, predates the national water law.[15] An earlier version was established in the 1970s as an attempt at interagency coordination but had become inactive by the 1990s. By that time, there had been various internationally sponsored hydrological and water management projects, most of them run out of the hydrology laboratory at COPPE that Kelman headed. The research team in one of those projects experimented with setting up a different kind of committee, in which 50 percent of seats were destined for civil society and water users (Interview 13, Brasília, 2002). As a result of that initiative, the Comitê de Integração da Bacia Hidrográfica do Paraíba do Sul (CEIVAP) was formally inaugurated in 1996. Lacking an agenda for action, the committee quickly got bogged down in administrative busywork. Once he became president of the newly minted National Water Agency, Kelman set out to reactivate it.

In 2000, ANA contracted COPPE's hydrology laboratory to provide technical support for CEIVAP, as a first step toward creating a basin agency. A year later, the agency offered a carrot to try to get river basins to implement water pricing: ANA would pay half the cost of building new sewage treatment plants (a municipal responsibility) if water charges paid for 25 percent and other sources could be found for the rest. The first municipalities

---

15. Comitê de Integração da Bacia Hidrográfica do Paraíba do Sul (Committee for the Integration of the Paraiba do Sul River Basin).

to sign up for the program were in the Paraíba do Sul basin, but the funding could go through only if water charges had begun to be levied (Formiga Johnsson et al. 2003; Formiga Johnsson et al. 2007, 102).

Water user communities mostly stayed out of the early debates about water pricing that went on in CEIVAP. But when the committee passed a resolution in March 2001 to begin charging the largest industries and water utilities for the water they used, they paid attention. Both industrial and sanitation utilities particularly objected to proposed exceptions for farmers, energy producers, and the Guandú diversion. For more than a year, vehement debates took place over these issues at 10 committee-organized seminars and about 50 presentations on the proposal (Formiga Johnsson et al. 2003). According to Ioris (2008, 70), "During this phase of debates, CEIVAP meetings became a battlefield, where representatives of economic sectors, particularly industry, expressed their disapproval."

By the end of 2001, CEIVAP had decided to postpone charging user fees until after the committee had approved a river basin plan and set up a basin agency. Furthermore, it demanded federal assurances that revenues would revert to the basin, warning that if they did not users would immediately cease to pay (Formiga Johnsson et al. 2003). This put the onus on the National Water Agency to resolve these outstanding issues as fast as possible.

Over the course of 2002, many observers noted the beginning of a shift in user discourse on water pricing—especially among industrial firms (Gruben, Lopes, and Formiga Johnsson 2002; Formiga Johnsson et al. 2003; Sousa Júnior 2004, 108; Formiga Johnsson et al. 2007; Ioris 2008, 69). Instead of opposing water charges altogether, they recognized that the policy could benefit the basin but were willing to go along with it only if certain conditions were met. Midway through that year, CEIVAP approved the creation of Brazil's first river basin agency, a nonprofit organization called the Associação Pró-Gestão das Águas da Bacia do Rio Paraíba do Sul (Association for the Management of the Waters of the Paraiba do Sul Basin—AGEVAP) and lowered its proposed base rate for water charges; the National Water Resources Council ratified these decisions soon after. In anticipation of a meeting set for December 2002 to decide how the new agency would be run, industrial groups made a critical move to guarantee their control over it. They convinced other users and some civil society organizations that AGEVAP should be governed by a general assembly that would include all CEIVAP members and by an administrative council that assembly would elect. Ratification of this proposal was followed by elections for the administrative council and presidency of the agency. The industrial users managed to rally enough support to win both a majority of seats in the council and the presidency (Sousa Júnior 2004, 108). If on the one hand the users had finally agreed to support water pricing, on the other they had definitively taken over the decision-making process. Water pricing would happen on their terms.

The terms were these: that all users (including those using waterways under state domain) would pay something, that the rate would be acceptable to them (read: "low"), and that the money would return to the river basin. The first condition was meant to ensure that any increase in production costs from water charges would affect all users in the basin. One precondition was that states would have to begin charging as well. The problem was that CEIVAP could charge only for the use of federal waters, but the Paraíba do Sul River Basin included many waters under state domain, such as any tributary that did not cross state borders. Until state governments instituted user fees, competing firms using waters from those tributaries would have an economic advantage over those using federal waters. A second requirement for starting to charge at all was that there had to be a basin-wide registry of water users. Since there was no such registry, the quick solution was to provide incentives for users to sign up voluntarily. Early signers were offered discounts on their rates and more water security. These incentives worked, persuading 3,645 water users to sign up by the deadline, 85 percent of which were from the agricultural sector, a fact that Pereira and Formiga Johnsson (2003, 55) attribute to the low rate that had been established for that group. A significant number would be classified as using negligible quantities of water and thus would pay nothing. Getting states to start charging for water was more complicated, as we shall see below.

In practice, with the commitment to obtaining prior user support for the pricing scheme, any idea that either technical or market criteria would determine the so-called right price was totally abandoned; the goal became simply to find one that was politically acceptable (Formiga Johnsson et al. 2007, 90). Besides lowering the basic rate, the new formula negotiated in CEIVAP incorporated a user demand that firms that treated their effluents pay less. With negotiated rates, the onset of water charges proved relatively uneventful. The first bills went out in January 2003. Of the 240 high-volume users charged during the first year, around 43 percent were industries, 27 percent were water and sanitation providers (mostly municipalities), and 24 percent were large farmers. There were also seven hydroelectric dams and a small number of other types of users (Agência Nacional de Águas 2003). By 2007, the number had increased only to 359 paying users (Agência Nacional de Águas 2010a), paying annual amounts that ranged from 20 reais (about 12 dollars) a year to millions.

Nonetheless, the conditions imposed by users meant that two major problems had to be settled if the system were to avoid coming to a screeching halt. First, there was still no formal guarantee that the funds would return to the river basin. For the first two years of water charges, the National Water Agency provided a temporary fix, effectively a (preemptive) wager made by its leadership that the problem would be solved. The federal government collected the user fees, and as expected the money was absorbed into the federal treasury. In 2003, in a highly unusual (and somewhat risky) move, ANA transferred an equivalent sum out of its own budget to the basin to implement CEIVAP's investment plan. Dissatisfied with the fragility of this mechanism for returning the funds to the river basin, in late 2003, the biggest water consumer in the basin, the pig iron factory Companhia Siderúrgica Nacional (CSN), went to court, claiming that ANA's promise was not enough of a guarantee for the committee to feel secure about making investments. The company won an injunction allowing it to pay the 3 million reais[16] a year it owed (a quarter of the yearly revenues for the whole basin) into an escrow account until the case was resolved. The pressure was certainly on to find a more satisfactory solution, but the authority to resolve it resided in the national Congress.

Second, in the name of fairness, CEIVAP required all users in the basin to pay, including those who used waters under state, rather than federal, jurisdiction. The most significant problem here was figuring out how to get the users of the water diverted into the Guandú basin to pay. The Guandú diversion rerouted two-thirds of the river's waters into a state domain river basin, ultimately to provide drinking water for the Rio de Janeiro metropolitan region. Despite the huge proportion of the river's total volume involved in the transfer, CEIVAP could only levy charges on users of water from the part of the river that remained under federal auspices. CEIVAP issued a declaration that if the Guandú users did not start paying by 2004, the whole system of payments would stop. As one interviewee put it, "Jerson Kelman had a knife to his throat" (Interview 32, Rio de Janeiro, 2010). But the solution to *this* problem would mean changing *state* water laws.

Resolving both of these problems would require further institutional entrepreneurship, strategic maneuvering, and political action at new territorial levels. In the process, new actors would have a chance to influence the design of the water pricing model. Experiments with putting the system into operation in a single river basin had had reorganized relationships and resources in ways that supported a new set of proposals for lawmaking.

---

16. Equivalent to about 1 million U.S. dollars in 2003.

THE SECOND WAVE OF NATIONAL LAWMAKING

The lead actors in the passage of the National Water Law and the creation of the National Water Agency in the 1990s were technical specialists in state agencies and universities. The second round was led by users, mostly from the industrial and energy sectors in the Paraíba do Sul basin, and by key actors at the National Water Agency. Industrial users from the Paraíba do Sul basin were the first to sound the alarm about the insecurity of the provision that revenues return to the basin. The evidence was from legislation passed in 2000 that transferred part of an existing levy on hydroelectric revenues to be allocated according to the water pricing provision in the 1997 National Water Law.[17] Industry representatives pointed out that despite this requirement no one had consulted river basin committees on how those funds would be spent.[18] The obvious conclusion was that the 1997 law did not guarantee that river basin committees could actually control the revenues from water charges (Interview 23, Belo Horizonte, 2003).

Although no one had said so when the 1997 law had passed, by 2003, legal experts had concluded that the National Constitution required that public money be controlled by a "federative unit"—that is, by a municipality, a state government, or the Union—not a river basin entity. If river basin agencies could not levy the water charges themselves, there needed to be a mechanism through which the federal government would be obliged to transfer funds collected in the basin to a basin agency controlled by the committee. In 2004, a group of CEIVAP members, led by representatives of industry, worked with Kelman and Minister of the Environment Marina Silva to figure out a solution.

And then, in a classic example of how multiple streams of institutional reform can interact (Pierson 2004), a separate reform process provided the legal instruments to solve the problem. As part of the broad administrative overhaul in the mid-1990s discussed in chapter 2, the government introduced legislation designed to facilitate public-private collaboration, specifically by allowing the state to transfer public funds to certified nongovernmental organizations. One key law passed in 1998, a year after the National Water Law, turned out to provide the mechanism that would legalize the financial relationship among government, river basin committees, and river basin agencies. While prior rules greatly restricted the government transfers to nonprofits, this legislation created a new kind of

---

17. The 2000 law in question was the same one that created the National Water Agency (ANA).

18. Indeed, they discovered, much of the money had been sequestered by the Treasury Department to meet budgetary requirement for a high primary surplus.

management contract (*contrato de gestão*) that would make it possible for government agencies to subcontract complex services to NGOs. This legal mechanism provided an avenue for transferring funds from user fees, still collected by government organs, to nonprofit river basin agencies, which would in effect be employed by river basin committees to do their administrative work and implement programs. The contracts could thus oblige the government to transfer revenues back to the basin (through the basin agency) and allow the committees to ensure that the agencies' expenditures follow the approved investment plans.

Throughout 2003–2004, industrial users from the Paraíba do Sul basin worked with ANA representatives in the National Water Resources Council's technical subgroups to draft a law making these connections explicit. They convinced the government to issue the legislation by executive decree (Medida Provisória) in early 2004 and oversaw its transformation by Congress into ordinary law a few months later. The legislation stated that the National Water Council could delegate the powers of a river basin agency to NGOs. ANA could sign management contracts with such organizations on the condition that the contracts stipulated that control over the agencies be shared between ANA and the river basin committees. The key provision was the requirement that ANA transfer revenues collected in a basin back to the delegated organization for that basin. Within months, AGEVAP—CEIVAP's basin agency—had taken this route, thus satisfying the first set of user complaints.

MULTILEVEL PRACTICES: GETTING THE STATES ON BOARD

Demands that all users in the basin pay—including those using state waters, especially in the Guandú basin—meant that even with the advances in national legislation the whole project was at risk unless states passed laws of their own.

Designers of São Paulo's 1991 Water Law, whose negotiation we discussed in chapter 3, intended the question of water charges to be resolved in a subsequent, separate law, whose passage was expected to follow soon after the basic law. However, this phase of the process encountered vociferous opposition not only from the private sector but also from SABESP, the state-owned water and sanitation utility (Interview 31, Brasília, 2010). Leaders of reform efforts organized numerous projects and task forces that drew up pricing scenarios and discussed ways to overcome operational problems (e.g., lack of a complete registry of water users and the fact that no resources had been allocated to create one). Eventually, a draft bill authorizing implementation of water charges was written, and Governor Mario Covas submitted it to the state assembly in 1997 (Barth n.d.). It took eight years to get the law passed.

The 1997 bill received hundreds of amendments and was sent back to the governor's office for revision, since assembly rules do not allow a bill with more than 80 amendments to come up for a vote. Then the government submitted a revised version in 2000. This revised bill took five years to come to the floor for a vote, as a variety of interest groups (small and medium-sized businesses, small farmers, and the entire electric sector) sought exemptions from water charges (ISA 2005) or demanded, as textile firms did, that there be a cap on charges for pollution emissions (Folha de São Paulo 2003). Then, in 2003, when the bill actually reached the assembly floor with a good chance of passage, the governor had it taken off the agenda at the last minute to add a proviso that charges could not be passed on to consumers.

Alongside resistance from water users, many in the state government were not at all convinced that river basin organizations and not government agencies should control water revenues from user fees. Some officials were less concerned with rate setting than with the fact that the money would go directly to each committee's account in the state water fund; they drafted a counterproposal that half the proceeds should remain in state coffers. Representatives of powerful industrial and agricultural user groups, who wanted to be able to influence how any money collected was used, roundly rejected this proposal (Viveiros 2003).

That phase of the legislative process finally ended in 2006, with a decision that all users would have to pay but farmers only after 2010. The revenues generated by each river basin would go into the respective committee's subaccount in the state water resources fund. Firms were legally forbidden to pass the charges on to final consumers (Martinez and Lahoz 2007). Water pricing finally began in 2007 in the basins where those using federally owned waters were already paying (the Paraíba do Sul and the Piracicaba, Capivari, and Jundiaí basins) and was slowly expanded to the rest of the state.

The lawmaking process in the state of Rio de Janeiro was quite different. In spite of all the activity around the interstate Paraíba do Sul basin, the state government showed little interest in reforming water management and passed basic water management legislation only in 1999, emulating the 1997 federal law. The only river basin under state domain where a basin committee had been set up by 2003 was the Guandú. Although a State Water Resources Council was established in 2001, it foundered and had to be reestablished in 2003 (Interview 33, Rio de Janeiro, 2010).

The explicit threat that CEIVAP would halt water pricing unless the users of the water diverted into the Guandú were also charged gave Kelman and his collaborators a strong motivation to find a solution. As a first step, they got the State Water Resources Council to pass a resolution in May 2003 authorizing charges in the parts of the Paraíba do Sul basin under state domain, beginning in January 2004, and calculated according to the pricing methodology already approved for CEIVAP. Fearing that a council resolution did not carry sufficient legal weight to ensure that water pricing actually begin on time, a group of high-level officials in Rio de Janeiro hoping to improve the state's water management capacity pushed hard to get legislation passed on the subject. Providentially, Ícaro Moreno Júnior, the head of the state agency responsible for water management at the time, was a Kelman ally who was also close to the governor. At the annual conference of the Brazilian Water Resources Association (ABRH) in November 2003, the two brainstormed with other Rio de Janeiro-based water experts (mainly from COPPE) and worked out a strategy. They persuaded the governor to propose legislation that would initiate pricing throughout the state by January 2004. Demonstrating both the power of the executive branch over the legislature when there is interest in a law and the general lack of mobilization around water issues in Rio de Janeiro compared with São Paulo, it took only three days for the bill proposed in December 2003 to be brought to the floor for a vote and passed (Interview 32, Rio de Janeiro, 2010).

The Rio de Janeiro law offered a singular solution to a political roadblock that was common in many parts of the country. The state government would start charging all state users in 2004, whether or not a river basin committee existed or had approved the rates. The money would be placed in earmarked accounts for each river basin and would not be touched until committees were created. The rates charged for water use would initially be set at the same level as those set by CEIVAP for federal waters in the Paraíba do Sul basin, but once committees were formed they could establish their own methodology. This solution thus violated the principle that water pricing should always be decided by river basin committees but confirmed that they should control revenues and should ultimately set the rates. The law also solved the Guandú problem, by designating 15 percent of the user fees collected in that basin for transfer to AGEVAP as payment for the diversion.

CHANGING CONCEPTIONS OF WATER PRICING

Finally, the system was in place, the CEIVAP users were satisfied, and paying for water became routine in the Paraíba do Sul basin. Nonetheless, whether the pricing system was worth all the effort that went into it was far from evident. Ramos (2007, 57) calculated that the water charges amounted to less than one U.S. dollar per inhabitant of the basin per year. Generally speaking, rates for water use are a fraction of those paid in European countries where similar schemes have been put into place. In the first six years of charging for water, the water users in the parts of the Paraíba do Sul basin under federal auspices paid only about 53 million reais (U.S. $31 million) (Agência Nacional de Águas 2010b). By contrast, the estimated cost of the master plan CEIVAP proposed in 2007 for dealing with the basin's most urgent problems was around 4.7 billion reais (U.S. $2.8 billion) (AGEVAP 2007, VII: 7).[19]

Furthermore, it has turned out to be very hard to spend what money has been raised. The 1997 federal water law limits the portion of revenues that can be used to cover administrative costs to 7.5 percent, but even in a wealthy river basin like the Paraíba do Sul, this is not enough to run a viable agency. Lacking the in-house technical capacity to design the components of the CEIVAP investment plan, mostly small sewage treatment plants budgeted less than 1 million reais each (U.S. $2.8 million), AGEVAP subcontracted project design and oversight to the federally owned bank Caixa Econômica Federal. But even though new legal mechanisms were supposed to facilitate more flexible relationships between state and nonstate organizations, the bank has stuck to a conservative interpretation of the rules governing public spending, as a result of which the vast majority of funds collected after 2003 and deposited in the AGEVAP account remained unspent in 2010 (Interview 29, Brasília, 2010).

The decade-long story of instituting water charges in the Paraíba do Sul basin illustrates both how ideas about policy change through the process of making them work in practice and that this process is not reducible to a rationalistic conception of "social learning" (Friedmann 1987, 181–223). Those who believed in the power of market mechanisms to change the conduct of the business sector have been confronted with a fundamentally liberal dilemma: it is exceedingly difficult to get economic actors to act collectively to protect public goods, particularly if it means paying for something they previously got for free. For market mechanisms to change behavior, the liberal prerequisites of such a model require that firms voluntarily submit to the discipline of markets. But in Paraíba do Sul, local users used what influence they could muster mainly to lower the price of water, thus reducing the revenue that

---

19. Dollar equivalents in this section are for October 1, 2010.

charging for water could generate. The generation of self-regulating governance of natural resources, long studied by Elinor Ostrom (1990), does not appear to transfer to very complex settings like the one in the Paraíba do Sul basin, where decision making by economic stakeholders led instead to what some have called the legitimation of shirking (see, e.g., Ioris 2008; Ioris 2009).

Even those who viewed user fees mainly as a form of cost recovery—a way to prod the economic groups using water to invest in water infrastructure—turned out to have been overly optimistic. It is safe to say that in the years following passage of the national law, most Brazilian water specialists agreed with the statement made by the water management staffers in the Brazilian World Bank office: "The implementation of the national water resources management system [depends] almost exclusively on water fee revenues" (Azevedo and Asad 2000, 335). Ten years later, when revenues from user fees turned out to be minuscule even in such a wealthy river basin as the Paraíba do Sul, they were not so sure. In relation to the kinds of problems highly urbanized, industrialized regions face, the sums raised were a drop in the bucket.

For pessimistic observers, the CEIVAP story is yet another example of the continuing influence powerful economic sectors have over public policy, this time with a veneer of democratic procedures (Ioris 2009). More optimistic reformers, however, have been rethinking the purpose of water pricing and its place in a more integrated management system. One alternative expounded by an interviewee who remains deeply committed to change is to think of water user fees not as investment funds for resolving big problems but as seed money for jump-starting a process of seeking solutions.

> We used to think that pricing was everything....As a whole, the educational effect [in which users recognize the true value of water] has not had much effect in Brazil. The other major objective, which is to raise revenues, is hogwash, at least if you think that it will come close to the full amount of investments. But it's not hogwash if you think that the money can be used intelligently to give autonomy to the committee, to create incentives for collective action and for mobilization to get other resources. It provides them with minimal conditions for leveraging other resources. (Interview 32, Rio de Janeiro, 2010)

This kind of reformulation represents a reinterpretation and reconfiguring of the relationships and resources that make up the new organizational domain or field of water management. For example, one of our key interlocutors, who spent years working for the consolidation of CEIVAP and now works for a state government agency, lamented the difficulty of getting things done amidst the proliferating decision-making forums of the new water management system. Many decisions, she noted, have to be ratified by state committees, federal committees, technical subcommittees of those committees, the State Water Council, and both the General Assembly and the administrative council of the water agency. Sometimes the same individuals have seats in several different stakeholder bodies. Multiplication of participatory arrangements seems to have increased the number of people inside and outside the state who have veto power over policy making—often not for the sake of democratization and social justice but rather as a way for specific individuals to gain influence. In 2010, for example, someone from a Rio de Janeiro university occupied a civil society seat on at least seven different collegiate bodies related to water management at once and purportedly used them to block government proposals every step of the way (Interview 32, Rio de Janeiro, 2010). Institutional change, it might be said, sometimes adds new layers of complexity to the institutional setting, not always in ways that make things work better.

INSTITUTION BUILDING, EXPERIMENTATION, AND ORGANIZATION BUILDING

In 1999, when we began to conduct research on these reforms, the enthusiasm among experts in the sector was contagious. The passage of the water law was expected to provide both political legitimacy and the practical means to implement a more integrated, participatory, and decentralized approach to water management. Power over water policy had been wrested from the hands of the energy sector and placed within the Ministry of the Environment. Although some worried about the implications the creation of the National Water Agency might have for recentralizing the system, most of these enthusiasts thought that the speed with which it occurred reflected a high level of government commitment to water policy. Over the course of the 1990s, more than half of Brazil's states had approved water laws, some in emulation of the São Paulo legislation, while later laws copied the federal one. By the early 2000s, the remaining states followed suit. In their opening sections, all of these laws claimed as their principles ideas that cohered with those of the international integrated water management movement: integration, participation, decentralization, river basin planning, and the introduction of economic instruments.

At the time, water specialists we met rarely mentioned the enormous lacunae in the legislation; most of those who began to collaborate with us in the Watermark Project seemed more focused on other aspects of the new system. Particularly striking was the fact that several years of fairly intensive research exchange passed before we met anyone who mentioned that guaranteeing the return of revenues from user fees to the river basin where they were raised was, at the time, technically impossible. Many of the politically more progressive actors involved in water policy were particularly excited about the democratizing potential of the river basin committees. Few of them seemed concerned with how little civic groups had participated in the process thus far. Although seats were allocated on river basin committees for civic organizations, there were no mechanisms in the law to guarantee that these groups had the resources or information to enable them to participate effectively. Nor did our collaborators and interviewees seem to worry that—in the absence of clear legal mechanisms forcing governments to create river basin committees, provide them with technical and financial support, and follow the plans that they approve, let alone create new executive agencies at the river basin level with the power to raise funds and implement projects—the whole endeavor seemed to rest on the willingness of a large number of organizations to collaborate voluntarily.

In retrospect, it seems clear that the cards were stacked against such collaboration, because many powerful actors had little incentive to invest in the new system. How can we explain the apparent contradiction between the enthusiasm among reform-minded specialists and the weakness of the legal infrastructure being erected? One explanation may be that water specialists were caught up in the liberalizing narrative of the 1990s, which accompanied a worldwide trend promoting collaborative governance, the results of which—like the revenues raised by water pricing—would be felt only later on. Key leaders of the reform process clearly expressed at the end of the 1990s the belief that a participatory approach to pricing would work better than top-down approaches. Kelman (2000, 103) wrote, for example: "In countries with limited institutional capacities, such as Brazil, strategies that demand government enforcement should always be replaced by strategies based on the self-regulation of stakeholders." Many believed that economic actors in Brazil were eager for market discipline.

Another explanation is simply that despite the lost battles and the weakened language, the specialists were encouraged by political recognition of a new policy field in which they were the protagonists. Although their proposals were still contested and could not simply be legislated into effect, the fact that they had been instantiated in law gave them a political legitimacy that they had not had as advocates of positions in technical debates. Part of this may have to do with the sense of ownership that technical experts had with respect to the new legislation and with some of the incipient organizations that were created through it. Over the course of the 1980s and 1990s, engineers and other water specialists had insisted on what seemed like obscure concepts. As chapter 3 showed, this process forced those experts to go beyond intellectual debate in order to get these concepts into the laws. They had to use practices less associated with technical knowledge and more with politics: generating publicity, building networks, and leveraging personal ties with powerful authorities (see Gutiérrez 2006a; Gutiérrez 2009). By the 2000s, they had become experts in this kind of technopolitics, too, to the point that a number of them eventually took on political jobs in the organizations they had helped create. Through such institution-building practices, they essentially created a new policy field—however imperfect—and then occupied that field themselves through its organizations.

Institutional entanglement and the multiplicity of actors involved in institutional reform made it impossible to resolve all issues at once. The pragmatic solution was to construct the new institution in law and in practice, bit by bit. Logically, it might have been much more sensible to settle first the prerequisites in the federal legislation (e.g., operationalizing basin agencies) and at the state level (guaranteeing a simultaneous initiation of water pricing throughout the basin) so that the system could have begun in the Paraíba do Sul more smoothly and with fewer potential obstacles to overcome along the way. Yet this did not happen, in large part because no coalition of political actors was yet mobilized to pressure for those changes to occur. It was the halting efforts of the experiment itself that restructured the political scenario, mobilizing political actors—especially water users, who had not been involved previously. The institutional changes at the federal and state levels that occurred from 2004 on were simply much more possible once the pilot experiment of pricing in the Paraíba do Sul River Basin had set the ball rolling and, in so doing, committed a variety of actors to getting those changes made.

Like other models, integrated water resources management contains a set of ideas about how the world works, about the interests of different categories of actors and the way to build in mechanisms by which new institutions can constrain and motivate behavior consistent with the set of goals the model is intended to reach. But ideas do not leap from the drawing board into a set of well-established routines. They are mediated through the experiences of the actors whose actions will constitute the institutions in practice. All of the elements of the institutional design package—the goals, the interests, and the expectations about how different mechanisms will work—were continuously transformed through these actions. The institutional reform process described in these chapters is still under way, a continual process of institutional creation nourished through practical experiences that, while testing ideas, also transforms them.

CHAPTER 5

Becoming Committees

Diversity, Problems, and Processes

The idea that river basin committees should play an important role in an integrated water management system was a recognition of diversity. In each place, different combinations of actors, activities, soils, rainfall patterns, and terrains (along with many other factors) make for different sets of problems and possible solutions. Although the basic planning unit in the new approach was generically taken to be the river basin, in fact, Brazilian states drew up their own water districts, some that were drainage basins, others that were parts thereof, and some that were organized on other principles. In planning this study, we expected that the establishment of committees would follow systematically from the legislative mandates described in chapter 3 and that we would be able to explain variation in results on the basis of different combinations of problem situation and socioeconomic or political factors, much as Putnam and his collaborators (1993) do for Italian regional governments. As we saw in chapter 4, lawmaking and the implementation of the system on the ground were and continue to be recursive; committee formation also turns out to be at least as much a constitutive element as it is an outcome of these more general processes. Thus, distinguishing cause from effect, condition from outcome, however simple it appeared in theory, turned out to be almost impossible when applied to any particular committee setting. As with climate change, general systemic tendencies do not tell us much about what happens in any specific location.

Basin committees were intended to serve as planning and deliberative organizations for the new water management system, for which they were to bring together representatives of significant public and private interests who would share information, resolve conflicts, and build consensus about what should be done to better allocate and protect freshwater resources.

The distribution of committee seats among categories of possible members (state agencies, users, public interest organizations, etc.) is normally established in the legislation. This new focus of attention, water management, had to be carved out in the midst of a complex institutional ecology in which many of the actors already had different, well-established habits of interaction, and many other foci competed for their attention and energy. In effect, it proposed a reconfiguration of existing functions and networks, along with the addition of new ones. It counted on the willingness of people from a variety of government agencies at different levels, alongside representatives of firms and civic organizations, to reorient their existing relationships to collaborate on a new project, shaping a policy arena that did not previously exist, often with very little in the way of additional resources.

A great many of the system's building blocks were missing at the outset. When provisions in the water laws charged committees with prioritizing investments that could be funded partially with the proceeds of water pricing, they implicitly assumed the prior existence of information gathering and regulatory capacity that had yet to be created (Akhmouch 2012, 12). They assumed that relevant public authorities were willing and equipped to carry out their plans, despite the conspicuous shortage or lack of specialized personnel in many—perhaps most—regions of the country. They assumed that shifts in the primacy of particular agencies at different levels of government would be assimilated without much difficulty

Yet over the 12-year period we studied them, river basin committees sometimes also became spaces in which actors committed to the project's integrative goals attempted to reshape the scale or scope of its ambitions to fit local circumstances, at the same time as they worked hard to increase the capacity of local authorities. They could do this because, while responsible for planning and deliberating about the integration of a complex system, river basin committees were also microcosms of that system, a paradox that underpinned both their weaknesses and their strengths. On the one hand, members representing state agencies and private-sector actors could rarely make major decisions binding upon the organization they represented. On the other hand, precisely because they brought together actors from throughout the system, when committees did gain influence there were ripple effects. Notwithstanding the enormous gap between the responsibilities assigned to committees and the capabilities with which they started out, they remained in many respects the linchpin of the system—the guardian of its integrative aspirations. It is hard to imagine any other explanation for their continued proliferation in spite of a conspicuous absence of major achievements.

In fact, river basin committees have been set up by the dozens over the two decades since the first laws were adopted in Brazil, well ahead of the system's other formal components. In 1997, when the federal water law passed, there were 26 state river basin committees in operation, mostly in São Paulo. As other states adopted legislation, the numbers soared. In 2003, there were 85 (Abers and Dino 2005, 9), and by 2010, there were more than 160, in addition to eight interstate committees created under federal legislation.

Some of these were false starts, committee initiatives that for one reason or another never got off the ground. Not every region had a group of people prepared to take on this new project, nor were the advantages of seeing problems in river basin terms always immediately apparent. However, a surprising number contained at least one highly motivated person, sometimes inspired by the image of waterways connecting people and places rather than delineating borders between them. Others began from a pragmatic standpoint, the belief that working with a river basin perspective offered an approach to problem solving that could bypass persistent blockages in the existing policy process. Still others understood committees as part of a broader participatory project intended to deepen democracy in Brazil. Some of these people worked for public agencies, others for the private sector, universities, or nongovernmental organizations (NGOs). Most of them invested long hours and years of their lives seeing to the nitty-gritty details of building a new organization. They were caretakers and incubators as much as visionaries.

When we started this research only a few years after the National Water Law passed, we expected to find variation in how successfully river basin committees were able to exercise the roles attributed to them and hoped to identify sources of variation and the mechanisms by which they operated. We did not anticipate that *none* of the committees we studied would stick to the designated script. When they did not, we had to reexamine our own assumptions and expectations and pay more attention to the evolution of committees over the period of study. Among other things, we had to problematize the lists of expected facilitating conditions and recognize that they did not necessarily exist in advance of the committee actions that were supposed to be facilitated by them. In order to fulfill their designated planning and supervision roles, committees had to call together the necessary expertise, to produce (or commission) planning instruments, and to establish action priorities. In addition, the other public and private institutions whose actions these plans and priorities were intended to govern had to be, or become, functioning organizations, capable of evaluating and implementing innovative projects and affecting behavior. We did not fully understand at the outset that none of those conditions really pertained in any of the places the water committees were organized. Their first challenge, then, was to help establish the conditions under which they could themselves operate and to inspire others to work with them.

As we saw in previous chapters, the committees operated under a tenuous legislative mandate. They could not compel public or private actors to do anything. Their legal attributions carried weight only insofar as public authorities took them into account and provided the means to exercise them. Initially, the idea that water pricing would provide an autonomous funding base for the new system's components, including river basin committees, deflected questions about where the money would come from to get the process off the ground. Especially during a period of recession combined with a squeeze on state spending from new federal requirements for fiscal probity, no agency was prepared to sacrifice either budget or functional turf to a new process that, by definition, would reduce its own autonomy. Intended as a space within which to combine forces, committees were neither designed nor equipped to enter into a competition for public funding. Thus, resources for administration were often cobbled together out of meager state funding and contributions in kind from the committee's members.

Other tensions sometimes emerged among public and private actors being summoned to work together. Municipalities viewed river basin management as encroaching upon local control of land use zoning; state agency personnel saw municipal actors as irrevocably parochial; much of the private sector remained convinced that the water reform was a thinly veiled effort to raise taxes; farmers were certain that water charges would ruin them; civic organizations were in the main uncertain about what they were being asked to do and whether it was worth their time. Outside of the relatively small world of professionals and those directly affected, the water reform process had almost no public visibility. In other words, before they could carry out their legal functions, river basin committees had to become credible organizations, using the capabilities they could assemble to make plans and undertake projects with consequences that made sense to people and gained them recognition from broader publics. This did not happen automatically. The remainder of this book explores how some committees and not others achieved this kind of practical authority.

THE CASES

As we related in the prologue (and explain further in appendix 1), we began this research in 2000 with a collaborative study, the Watermark Project (Projeto Marca d'Água), whose goal was to follow the development of river basin committees in a variety of basins[1] over an extended period (initially

---

1. As we noted above, some of the water management areas are not "river basins," in fact, but are either segments of a basin or districts comprising more than one smaller, similarly situated watersheds.

5 years, increased to 10). Aware of the sampling issues posed by the large number of potential variables coupled with the relatively small size of the universe of cases, our main goal in selecting cases was to ensure diversity in the sample, paying attention to regional, socioeconomic, demographic, political-institutional, and environmental characteristics. After assembling relevant socioeconomic and demographic information, researchers carried out qualitative baseline studies of committee organization in 23 basins. A number of different research activities followed over the next decade involving many of these basins and one other where a committee formed later.[2] We treated committee formation as a founding event, tracing back and forward from that moment. By the end of the period, we were able to put together fairly sustained narratives of institutional evolution for 16 river basins (see the map in the prologue).

Organizing this material has proven a daunting task, and for most of the committees studied, we limit ourselves to summary accounts that illustrate the complex institution-building processes we survey in this chapter. Other chapters explore aspects of five of them in more detail, beginning with the account in chapter 4 of implementation of water charges in the Paraíba do Sul basin. In chapter 6, we situate the process of committee organization in a context of broader power relations in Brazil through the lens of conflicts over interbasin transfers in the Piracicaba and São Francisco regions. In chapter 7, we zoom in on the slow accumulation of practical authority in cases where civil society organizations were the main protagonists: the Velhas basin in the state of Minas Gerais and the Itajaí basin in Santa Catarina.

Table 5.1 presents some basic data about the committees we studied. Three of our cases were interstate river basin committees: the Paraíba do Sul committee discussed in chapter 4; the Piracicaba, Capivari, and Jundiaí committee (where a state committee was formed in 1993 and an interstate one in 2002); and the giant São Francisco basin committee. The rest are committees under the jurisdiction of states. They are charged with water management planning for areas ranging in size from 400 to 639,000 square kilometers and with populations ranging from 10,000 to more than 19 million. Of the committees we studied, the smallest area was associated with

---

2. The São Francisco committee had not been formed at the time we started our research and was not initially included in the study. For this reason, our treatment of that basin in chapter 6 relies almost entirely on secondary sources for that important case, one of which was a dissertation written by a participant in the Watermark Project (Empinotti 2007). The Paranoá committee was created long after the study began, but we followed that delay from the beginning, having included the activities of a commission proposing the committees creation in our baseline studies. This turned out to be a precious opportunity for studying a non-institution-building process.

Table 5.1. RIVER BASIN COMMITTEES STUDIED

River Basin	Year Created	Population[a]	Size (km²)	Water Problems at Time of Creation	Organizational Form and Strategy
Interstate River Basins					
Piracicaba, Jundiaí and Capivari (PCJ)	1993/2002[b]	4.7 million	11,320/ 15,320	Water scarcity, reservoir management, degradation of water sources by deforestation and urban growth, transfer of water to São Paulo	Synergistic organizational layering. Consortium predates and later supports committees and has municipal and business backing and problem solving experience, resulting in strong negotiating position vis-à-vis state government.
Paraíba do Sul	1996	5.5 million	62,074	Widespread, untreated industrial and domestic pollution, transfer of water to Rio de Janeiro	External investment helps build organization but also mobilizes for broader institutional changes. Pilot project for water pricing with support from engineering institutions and National Water Agency mobilizes actors to build organization and fight for federal and state laws to make pricing work.
São Francisco	2001	16 million	639,219	Conflicts among irrigators and pollution of water supply by small towns. Proposed transfer to other states.	Conflict between river basin actors and federal government/other regions occurs prior to organization building effort. Non-water-related political dynamics intervene in the process.
State River Basins					
Gravataí	1989	1.3 million	2,020	Major pollution from lack of urban sanitation infrastructure and from draining of marshlands for agricultural use	Reworking missions–transgressing boundaries of water policy to gain problem-solving capacity. Activist group with environmentalist bent predates legislation. Spends years discussing plans but efforts frustrated. Refocused mission on creating protected areas when river problems well beyond capabilities, lack of state response.

Alto Tietê	1994	19 million	5,900	Severe pollution from metropolitan waste, destruction of water sources, floods, water supply dependent on interbasin transfer	Shifting scales to gain problem-solving capacity and allies. Stalemate among powerful agencies and interests. Moving action to subcommittees and specialized working groups, where collaborative problem solving on small measures proves possible.
Santa Maria	1994	220,000	16,400	Over-withdrawal for irrigation, scarcity in urban water supply	Negotiations around feasible problem solving efforts build organizational cohesion. Strong community of interest among rice growers transforms committee into sort of interest organization making demands on state government.
Litoral Norte	1997	231,000	2,000	Urban growth in environmental protection areas (which cover 80% of jurisdiction), water source degradation; seasonal pollution and water scarcity.	In small region, initially focuses on connecting water policy with other issues, integrating efforts. Activists predominantly from state sector promote integrated regional planning among municipal, other administrative units; strong environmental commitment.
Itajaí	1998	1.2 million	15,500	Devastating floods; increasing pollution	Synergistic organizational layering (committee, university, water agency, and nongovernmental project). Committee building bolsters support for alternative approach to flood control. Fund project implementation, mobilization campaign with external grants; conflict with state government; partnerships with municipalities.
Pirapama	1998	160,000	700	Industrial pollution of water supply; high urban demand; droughts, human displacement by a dam	Truncated organization building—created with international funding for environmental planning project, committee folds while waiting for others to implement its plans. Demobilization in absence of concrete returns.

Continued

Velhas	1998	4.6 million	28,300	Extreme industrial and domestic pollution of rivers, affecting health, fishing, other activities	Synergistic organizational layering: Network built out of local and larger-scale problem-solving projects develops capabilities and recognition and then appropriates committee, increasing political clout of both; partnership with state government and municipalities.
Baixo Jaguaribe	1999	229,000	6,900	Extreme scarcity, conflicts for water supply between metropolitan area and local farms; intermittent waterways, state investment in linking.	Organizational layering without synergies: Committee competes with other participatory model; state control reduces organizational capacity; river basin scale less compelling than other scales of action.
Lagos São João	1999/2005c	520,000	3,800	Pollution of Lagoon affected fishing and tourism economies; water supply and sanitation problems	Synergistic organizational layering: state employee initiates intermunicipal + business consortium with civil society involvement with problem-solving capacity; committee built on organizational basis of consortium. Both influence and sometimes act in lieu of various government agencies.
Itapicurú	2000/2005c	1.3 million	39,000	Extreme scarcity, reservoir management, degradation of water sources in rural area	Truncated organization building. State government shifts models midstream; external funders provide fickle foundation, leaving local actors frustrated and demobilized.
Araçuaí	2000	302,000	16,300	Extreme scarcity, poverty, conflicts among large producers, small farmers, towns	Reworking mission. Thinly organized, active members rework mission by reducing aspirations, developing role as broker for small grant making, especially from state water fund.

Continued 5.1

Lagoa da Conceição	2000	397,000	400	Pollution by urban–domestic sewage in urban lake	Truncated organization building. Committee formed out of NGO lawsuit against state government and relies on goodwill and member funding for organizing: overwhelmed by tasks for which not equipped; internal conflicts lead to premature collapse.
Lago Paranoá	2010	2.5 million	3,700	Destruction of water sources by urban expansion	Organizational layering without synergies. Committee project on back burner for a decade while activists focus on municipal planning debate and wait for government to support for water management reform; committee provides second front in mainly environmental struggle.

Note: Cases marked in bold are discussed in-depth in other chapters.
(a) Population and size from National Water Agency website (http://www.cbh.gov.br/#not-interestaduais, accessed September 17, 2012).
(b) The first date refers to the state committee, the second to the interstate committee.
(c) The first date refers to the creation of intermunicipal consortiums, the second to the creation of committees.

the Lagoa da Conceição committee, a portion of a single city, and the largest was associated with the São Francisco committee, covering six states and the Federal District. Several river basins in our sample include large parts of major metropolitan areas, such as Belo Horizonte (the Velhas River Basin), Porto Alegre (Gravataí), and São Paulo (Alto Tietê). Some contain smaller portions of large metropolitan areas, such as Brasília (Lago Paranoá), Florianópolis (Lagoa da Conceição), and Recife (Pirapama). Two basins are in coastal zones, with tourist economies and fluctuating populations (Litoral Norte and Lagos São João). Some had significant rural populations (Araçuai, Itajaí, Santa Maria, Itapicurú, Baixo Jaguaribe). We studied river basins in highly impoverished semiarid regions (Araçuai, Itapicurú, Baixo Jaguaribe, São Francisco) and others in much-better-off regions of rural and urban Brazil.

Even when basins share other characteristics, the types of problems the committees were created to solve vary. Among predominantly rural basins, the Itajaí has experienced disastrous floods, while the Itapicurú, Araçuai, and Baixo Jaguaribe basins are plagued by recurring drought. Committees also operate in very different economic, institutional, and political contexts. Both levels and patterns of economic development differ among regions; local- and state-level political institutions reflect both different histories and distinctive relationships with the federal government; and elected officials at all levels have diverse partisan and coalitional allegiances. We had to consider the obstacles and resources associated with these diverse elements—geography, water-related challenges, economic development, institutional capacity, and political support—because they influenced what local actors could do (or thought that they could do) as they sought to create or make use of new policy organizations.

But none of these variables fully determined what those actors would end up doing. In order to build practical authority, committee organizers had to use the resources and relationships available to them to find a way of approaching problems that made sense to people around them, in light of which they could assemble the skills and the credibility (or recognition) necessary to address them. Preexisting personal and professional networks mattered, as did the existence of organizations that had already pioneered the idea of water management, such as intermunicipal consortiums. In several cases, where university personnel played important roles in committee organization, universities served as organizing platforms and provided a basic material infrastructure (offices, Internet). When local committee organizers had good connections with the "water community"—that is, with the groups of professionals and legislators discussed in chapters 3 and 4—they could sometimes gain access to resources outside the basin (Cardoso 2003). Nonetheless, resources and facilitating conditions were mainly of interest insofar as people sought, recognized, and used them. The actions that people took as they worked to organize these committees and the processes they unleashed were at least as important as the conditions under which they had started and the outcomes we had expected to see.

COMMITTEES, PROBLEMS, AND PROCESSES

At the point where we realized that we were no longer comparing conditions and outcomes, many of the advantages of our research design came into question. A longitudinal comparative study is normally an investigation into how different combinations of variables (actors and conditions), over time, correlate with (or, even better, cause) different outcomes. In *Making Democracy Work*, Robert Putnam et al. (1993) and his collaborators came up with measures of institutional performance for Italy's new regional governments and correlated these with other variables—economic development, political equality, and civic community—to conclude that the civic community (or social capital) best explained strong institutions. But we had no such clear measures of institutional performance or, better, the ones we had (whether a committee has approved a basin plan, commissioned a river classification, established an information system, and begun charging for water) told us very little about the organizations and nothing at all about whether they had any impact on the management of water.

Correlation of such outcomes with variation in conditions did not tell us much, either. Processes are diverse, not just because contexts—or configurations of contextual aspects, as Ragin (2000, 71–89), would call them—are always different but also because actors combine ideas, resources, and relationships in different ways. A major problem was that committees that managed to gain some momentum did so in entirely different ways, and not always according to plan. The Araçuai committee in Minas Gerais settled into acting as a clearinghouse for local organizations seeking funding for environmental and development projects. The Litoral Norte committee in São Paulo tried to coax state agencies and the four municipal governments in its jurisdiction to coordinate programs and integrate planning efforts among policy areas such as coastal zone management and tourism development. The Lagos São João consortium in Rio de Janeiro (whose leaders later set up a committee) moved right into confronting and then negotiating directly with industries and water utilities to help clean up a lagoon. Benchmarks for whether committees were meeting the formal criteria defining their institutional mandates did not measure this much more convoluted—and lengthy—process by which diverse groups of actors attempted to make these committees into institutions in the first place. If we were studying a process of institutional change, how would we know when it had ended?

A further problem in characterizing and assigning values to outcomes was that some cases jumped unexpectedly from one category to another. Our initial sample was results-blind; we did not know in advance where these organizations would be 5 or 10 years later. We therefore observed while committees went through periods of stagnation and paralysis in addition to enthusiasm and vitality and came to see these as ongoing processes rather than outcomes. Some were fairly consistent, but others underwent surprising turnarounds. Committees that our first publications expected to fail became energized; others experienced the opposite.[3] As Sabatier (1987) notes, in policy research covering a decade or more, any simple classification of success or failure breaks down. Thus, we had to make two adjustments: First, we had to be more modest in drawing conclusions; and second, we had to recognize that the time line imposed by our study bore no relation to the complex temporal dynamics of the organizational processes we were examining.

Another complication was that our case studies influenced one another. Some cases turned into examples of success, which other committees emulated, often by inviting people from those committees to visit their river basins and help them organize. Over the period in question, a network of river basin committee organizers emerged, meeting annually to share ideas at the National Forum of River Basin Committees and in other venues. A core group of people circulated from committee to committee, often hired as facilitators of committee planning efforts and other projects. As more national meetings and exchanges among committees took place, it became increasingly difficult to treat our cases as independent or to ignore the probability that they would increasingly influence one another over time.

Just as the identification of outcomes became more uncertain, the predictive power of contextual conditions also turned out to be unexpectedly problematic. Although contexts clearly provided both advantages and obstacles to making committees function, organizational efforts in apparently similar contexts had radically different trajectories. It turned out to be more useful to think about those characteristics in terms of perceived problem situations—judgments about resources available and obstacles to be overcome to build something new. To map these trajectories without attempting to squeeze them into preexisting containers, we needed to recognize and describe the tentative and provisional moves that constituted the becoming of the river basin committees as they experimented with

---

3. The Watermark Project's baseline studies are summarized in Formiga Johnsson and Lopes (2003).

new ways of doing things and built relationships that would help them to acquire the kind of influence that we call here practical authority.

Finally, conditions were not static; they changed, sometimes because people worked hard to change them. Committee organizers, faced with conditions that made it more difficult for them to act—for example, foot dragging by other government agencies—worked to transform attitudes and sometimes capabilities, what we might once have thought of as independent variables. Committee organizers worked not only to make their organizations function but also to reshape the institutional environments within which they were located. River basin committees do not develop in isolation; they draw on the powers, resources, and meanings associated with existing institutions and organizations in both public and private sectors and on "logics of appropriateness" (March and Olsen 1989) or "organizational repertoires" (Clemens 1993) grounded in their histories. Institutions appear in the form of artifacts endowed with meaning, and new concepts become institutionalized as they are embedded through experience, as individuals and groups use them to solve problems. As this occurs, they come to occupy positions in wider institutional ecologies, and their meaning may become constrained by their linkage with other concepts implied by these relations. At the same time, as an ecology becomes more complex, an increasing number of possible combinations become imaginable, opening up the possibility of more margin for maneuver for creative actors (Ansell 2011, 31–32). Thus, committees interacted with their environments both through the networks and ideas that their members brought with them and as organizations whose very existence served as an often fragile example of what changing the way water resources were managed might mean.

The extent of political or institutional support for the creation and activation of basin committees mattered a great deal but not always in the same way. Some committee organizers were deputized by relevant state government agencies, with budgets and timetables and administrative backup; other organizing processes involved the establishment of looser sets of contacts between state government personnel and individuals in different localities who expressed interest. Sometimes organizers had strong local ties; in other instances, these were built on the fly. Personal and professional networks were crucial for flows of information and resources, and many committee activists became networkers at regional or national levels, creating forums and listservs in which committees could exchange ideas and experiences and support each other's efforts. In some instances, where state agencies failed to back committee decisions or to provide them with the information or tools they needed to operate effectively, committee activists pragmatically shifted direction to fit the available capacities and opportunities. In others, committee organizations tried to compensate for the failure of other organizations by investigating problems, producing missing data, executing projects of their own, or monitoring private behavior. In still others, we found committee organizers facilitating interagency coordination or providing training to help public employees do their jobs better, for example on environmental management.

Finding room to maneuver in such diverse institutional contexts was a significant challenge for the organizers of basin committees, reflecting the diversity of tasks involved in activating new institutions. Building capabilities and recognition required framing ideas about what the committee is for that made sense both locally and in the broader picture framed by the new legal-institutional water management system. These ideas had to be anchored in an organizational structure that had a material presence in offices, staff, event promotion, documents, websites, and other elements that helped the committee to attract the attention of an audience—creating a broader public. And it had to link this new organization with other organizations, institutions, and agencies whose actions were necessary to make a committee's actions viable and effective. Where those components of the system did not exist, had no interest in collaboration, or did not have the skilled personnel or resources to fulfill their functions, committee organizers needed either to find ways of changing those conditions or to reorient their own activities in order to take advantage of capabilities that did exist locally.

These three tasks—translating formal missions into something meaningful in their locations, building organizations, and finding (or creating) a supportive local environment in which to embed their organizations and activities—were the substance of the effort to build practical authority. These things did not happen in the same order or the same way or even to the same degree, but all were part of the formative experiences of the committees examined here.

REWORKING COMMITTEE GOALS

For most people, water resources management is not a meaningful category of political decision making. We are more likely to think of water policy in relation to things such as flood control, provision of potable water to households and communities, sewage evacuation and treatment, access to irrigation water, fishing, or transportation of goods. As Latour and Le Bourhis (1995, 64) point out in an assessment of the French water management system that inspired many of the Brazilian reformers, there is nothing "natural" about a river basin as a decision-making unit: "The trajectory of the drop of water, even if it defines a river basin, does not by itself define a community of political interest." For that to happen, there need to be relays that connect geography to politics. In effect, for river basin committees to function, they had to find ways to nest local narratives about conflicts over water into a larger one describing how water resources could be managed differently.

For the most part, legislation left ambiguous the amount of discretion that river basin committees had to shape their own agendas. Setting parameters for water permits and rules for water pricing were roles that worked well for committees like the Paraíba do Sul in industrialized areas where user fees could be expected to raise significant amounts of money to cover the cost of new infrastructure. The Piracicaba, Velhas, and Alto Tietê committees were the only others in our sample that fell into that category. There was a long delay before any of them could begin charging for water, and even when they did, revenues were lower than reformers had expected. Without the funding source that had promised to facilitate concerted action, these committees had to figure out how to operate in situations where the scale of problems—pollution, flooding, and providing an adequate supply for the population—was immense. But for most committees, especially in poor regions (such as the Itapicurú, Pirapama, and Araçuai basins), user fees did not offer much hope for revenue, as there were few nonagricultural enterprises whose extractions met the threshold volume for charges. For reasons discussed in chapter 4, when levied at all, water charges for agricultural uses have been quite low. However, even in countries where water tariffs are well established, it is rare for charges to irrigators fully to cover the costs of operating and maintaining existing infrastructure, let alone to defray the investment costs for building new waterworks (Molle and Berkoff 2007; Garrido and Calatrava 2010).

Sometimes people became demobilized by the lack of fit between the water problems they thought needed to be addressed and a committee's formal warrant. An embryonic Paranoá basin committee faced a situation in which Brasília's chaotic expansion had destroyed green areas that protected essential water sources, stretching the capital region's water and sanitation system to its limits (Interviews 120, 122, 124, Brasília, 2001). A group of environmentalists, community activists, and public employees began organizing to set up a committee in 2000 but encountered resistance from the government. The reaction was not to give up on the project but rather to put it on the back burner, paying more attention to other activities until a more supportive administration was in office (Interviews 116, 117, Brasília, 2001; Interview 140, Brasília, 2012). In the meantime, many of the same people thought their time would be more productively spent fighting the government's proposed revision of the city's master plan. This was a high-stakes battle, since the possibility of real estate bonanzas enticed local politicians to support relaxing land use restrictions in protected areas. Compared with organizing a basin committee with little influence over urban sprawl, the master plan battle seemed a more direct way to address the same problems.[4]

In other cases we studied, committees redefined their missions to fit the problems they perceived. This usually involved infringing on environmental or land use jurisdictions, where the law gave them little authority. The Gravataí committee, in Rio Grande do Sul, whose establishment predated the legal reforms discussed earlier, is a good example of such boundary crossing. The Gravataí River flows from a rural area of marshlands and rice production into the metropolitan area of Porto Alegre, the state capital. Concerned about pollution of the river, a coalition of environmentalists and state employees in the sanitation sector originally joined forces to try and save marshlands being degraded by rice production in the rural part of the basin, something that remained a central concern through much of the committee's 20-year history. Its first decade was spent enthusiastically drawing up plans, culminating in a water quality code (*enquadramento*) whose standards were so unrealistically high that the code was impossible to implement (Gutiérrez 2006a; Gutiérrez 2006b). Subsequently, however, the committee lost momentum when several other projects went awry and negative feasibility studies scuttled a proposal for a dam to protect the marshlands (Pereira, Zatz, and Frank 2008).[5] As the Gravataí committee was one of the oldest in Brazil and its members were among the most dedicated, its inability to actually improve the state of the basin's water was discouraging. A 2009 assessment by the National Water Agency designated the Gravataí River one of the most polluted in the country (IHU online, April 13, 2009).[6]

Resolving the problems of a highly polluted basin was well beyond what the committee was equipped to handle, even if all the management tools mandated in the water resources management legislation had been fully operational. The Gravataí committee had started out as a forum in which public employees who were frustrated with the state's failure to tackle the big problems could coordinate efforts to try to keep them from getting

---

4. Process reconstructed from interviews with environmentalists and other actors in the basin in 2008 and 2009 by students of Abers at the University of Brasília. The committee was finally created in 2010.

5. Conclusions of a 2008 Watermark Project workshop with members of the Gravataí committee to discuss results of a 2004 survey and the committee's plans for the future (Pereira, Zatz, and Frank 2008).

6. http://www.ecodebate.com.br/2009/04/13/rio-dos-sinos-e-rio-gravatai-os-piores-do-brasil-entrevistas-especiais-com-mauricio-colombo-e-silvio-klein, accessed July 23, 2012.

worse. As in most metropolitan areas where water pollution is a central issue, it is hard to separate water management from environmental policy areas, nor does doing so make much sense. After its dam proposal proved unviable, the committee began to focus on so-called soft nonengineering measures that could improve the state of the river, mainly by doing a better job of protecting its headwaters. This took it well into the formal jurisdiction of environmental legislation. In the late 2000s, the committee worked closely with NGOs to raise the level of environmental protection around the headwaters, convincing the state environmental agency to establish a large marshland protection area in addition to a smaller wildlife reserve where an endangered species of deer was found to be living. Environmental and water management entities are thoroughly entangled here in terms of mission. As some committee members are also members of the management councils for these protected areas, discussion of their activities has spilled over into committee meetings. The entanglement of two policy areas is perhaps most aptly expressed in the committee's logo, a drawing of the endangered deer (Interview 143, Porto Alegre, 2011).

Not surprisingly, such jurisdictional transgressions occurred in almost all the cases we studied where river basin committees managed to gain some form of practical authority. To address the problem of chronic flooding in the Itajaí valley, for example, the Itajaí committee promoted riverbank restoration projects (a policy area supposedly regulated by Brazil's forest code) and later tried to collaborate with civil defense agencies in an effort to deal with the aftermath of floods. The Litoral Norte committee encouraged municipalities to integrate hitherto unconnected planning efforts. The Alto Tietê's subcommittees successfully crafted subregional water source protection plans, working on land use regulation with the municipalities whose responsibility it was. In all of these cases, the committees went beyond their mandates to engage problems that were immediately apparent and that they were more organizationally equipped to address than the formal planning and regulatory instruments they were designed to produce.

These redefinitions also helped committee activists explain what they were doing to larger audiences. In many instances, these activities drew upon understandings of problems that had built up over decades and networks that had begun to link actors in state agencies, municipalities, and nongovernmental organizations in search of joint remedies. River basin committees offered the possibility of enlarging the scope and scale of earlier efforts but, as the Gravataí example illustrates, were not in a position to take on remedial projects on the scale of eliminating the pollution of a river by mountains of untreated waste. The investments required to address problems produced by generations of neglect were many orders of magnitude larger. What such committees could do was enhance the visibility of a problem and build credibility for an integrated approach to addressing it on the basis of intermediate accomplishments more suited to the limited means they had.

ORGANIZATION BUILDING

For supporters of participatory water management reform who saw committees essentially as deliberative arenas, sometimes even calling them water parliaments, the new organizations were not expected to function as organizations capable of taking action. Instead, the proposals their discussions generated would be implemented elsewhere, normally by state agencies. This view of river basin committees classed them with the numerous other participatory councils, mainly at the municipal level, being set up in Brazil during this period for participatory budgeting, health, education, and consumer protection, among other purposes. Many authors studying these phenomena have viewed them through a Habermasian lens (Avritzer 2002; Lüchmann 2002; Fung and Wright 2003; Cunha 2009). It seemed logical to imagine that river basin committees would serve as spaces in which people would come together to resolve conflicts and set priorities but not to expect that they would actually *do* anything.

Yet even to begin deliberating, a committee had to take on some of the characteristics of an organization. It needed an office, computers, a secretary, a car. Someone had to schedule and call the meetings, reserve a meeting space, mobilize civil society organizations and water users, craft a meeting agenda, and carry out other mundane but essential tasks. Furthermore, when committee members found that agencies or organizations they depended on to provide information to support their work and implement their proposals might not have the capability (or will) to do so, committees had to develop their own operational capacities. They had to design proposals, write projects, find funding, do their own research, communicate with the local population, organize events, and even implement small-scale projects and programs. This meant that from the beginning, committees had not only to represent different interests but also to carry out some of the functions usually associated with executive agencies.

From committee to committee, there was tremendous variation both in the capabilities (skills and access to material resources) that new committee members brought with them and in the degree to which the institutions or constituencies they represented were committed to the process. In one committee, the member representing an environmental agency might be able to draw on the resources of a skilled and experienced corps; in another, she might be backed up by one or two others who tried to fill all the same functions with neither resources nor skills. In one, an environmental organization seat might go to an NGO with a paid staff and a geographic information system mapping capacity; in another, it might be occupied by an organization made up of a handful of volunteers. In one, a seat for private-sector organizations might be occupied by a representative of Brazilian or foreign multinational enterprises and in another by someone who spoke for an association of barely surviving small firms. Moreover, especially with respect to the public sector, the fact that a committee member evinced a strong personal commitment to the organization's goals did not necessarily reflect an institutional commitment on the part of the state or municipal agency the member represented.

As we saw in chapter 4, government support for creating committees and for providing administrative and operational resources also varied substantially state by state. São Paulo systematically created river basin committees over the course of the 1990s, and during the late 1990s and early 2000s, both Rio Grande do Sul and Minas Gerais followed suit. The Piracicaba, Alto Tietê, Litoral Norte, Araçuai, and Santa Maria committees in our study were all created under the aegis of these systematic efforts to expand the committee model. In these cases, government agencies provided money and personnel for organizing an election process, convening organizational meetings, communicating among members, writing up bylaws, carrying out some preliminary diagnostic studies, and so on. Other states were less consistent in supporting committee formation, often depending on use of consultants hired with money from international agencies without developing an institutional commitment internally.

Organization building is a slow process and frequently demands not just sustained investment of resources but also some material accomplishments to sustain people's support (what Ansell and Gash 2008 call "intermediate outcomes"). As Sabatier et al. (2005, 10–17) observed in *Swimming Upstream*, a study of watershed management institutions in the United States, creating participatory, collaborative institutions is ultimately not enough to keep people engaged if they cannot produce discernible improvements in the state of the watershed. People need to see some results.

The thwarted organizational process in the Pirapama basin in Pernambuco is a good illustration. The Pirapama River flows through a sugar-cane growing area into a section of metropolitan Recife, a city of nearly 4 million people plagued by dire poverty, chaotic land use, and weak sanitation infrastructure. In 1997, with funding from the British Department for International Development (DFID), the state government initiated a project to increase the city's water supply by combining construction of a long-contemplated storage reservoir for potable water on the Pirapama River with elaboration of an Agenda 21 sustainable development plan. Taking advantage of the impetus from passage of both state and federal water laws that same year, organizers from the state environmental agency decided to set up a basin committee in the region instead of the "community forum" that had originally been proposed to draw up the plan (Gama 2002). Having a defined mission, along with funding for organization, the committee appeared to get off to a good start.

For three years, DFID supported an executive secretariat's office within the state environmental agency to coordinate logistics for a variety of activities. The committee got large numbers of people involved in discussing the expected impacts of the new dam. Crafting the Agenda 21 sustainable development program involved countless workshops, studies, and training programs; the committee also produced an ecological-economic zoning plan and even submitted a plan for water charges to the State Water Resources Council (Gama 2001, 2002).

When the DFID funding ended in 2001, organizers from the state government expected the committee to be able to continue on its own, especially after the State Water Resources Council approved water charges in 1998. However, as it did elsewhere, charging for water proved a political hot potato, and a new state government backpedaled on the proposal (da Silva et al. 2003, 16). None of the committee's carefully prepared documents became operational; instead, along with others in Brazil's massive archive of plans, they served as artifacts of briefly mobilized hopes, markers of impasse. Although committee members kept meeting for some time afterward, they took no initiatives, waiting for revenues from water charges to revive their organizational budgets (Lalonde 2005). In 2008, when we visited the region for a workshop with the committee, only a small group participated, lamenting the impasse reached but seeing no options for getting past it.

In stark contrast with the Pirapama example are other cases in which individuals and groups made long-term investments in organization building and found ways to produce concrete, visible gains that built a foundation for energetic river basin organizations. In several cases, committee organization piggybacked on other organizational processes. In the Velhas basin, a seemingly moribund committee was revitalized when it joined forces with (or was taken over by) a university-sponsored network of grassroots river restoration committees, building on active community support and practical problem-solving capabilities throughout the basin. In the Piracicaba River Basin, a committee was built on the foundation of a preexisting consortium of municipalities and industries, giving the committee substantial social capital and practical authority from the start. We explore both of these cases in more detail in later chapters.

We find a similar pattern in Rio de Janeiro's Lagos São João region, where a basin committee was established after a consortium of local governments, industries, and civic groups gradually built up capabilities and a reputation for problem solving. Organized and initially coordinated by an activist employee of the state environmental protection agency, the consortium sponsored seminars and workshops to discuss the region's environmental problems and, with funding from the German Cooperation Agency (GTZ), conferred with specialists about practical ways to generate positive results that did not need significant financing. Material improvements from these early experiments in turn built both member confidence and a reputation in the region (Pereira 2007, 52). Eventually, consortium leaders also decided to set up a basin committee, both to give the association stronger legal clout and to benefit from the implantation of water pricing, then just beginning in Rio de Janeiro. Organizational support from the consortium gave momentum to the committee from the beginning.

However, municipal and intermunicipal forms of organization were not by themselves the answer; they had to be backed up with genuine local commitment and resources, and even then, they needed time to acquire skills and experience. Clearly, collaborative experiments that combined the assets of municipalities in well-off regions with plentiful skilled personnel and other resources to call upon were in a position to make more ambitious plans than those without them. Organization of municipal water committees and intermunicipal consortia in the Itapicurú basin in Bahia was much more fragile than in the aforementioned cases and could not easily be converted into the organization of a basin committee. As in the Pirapama committee discussed above, organizing in this basin depended largely on organizers and funding from outside the basin.

The Itapicurú basin—in the extremely poor, arid backlands of the state of Bahia—was first "mobilized" through a World Bank-funded Bahia Water Resources Management Project that combined efforts to reinforce the technical capacities of the state's water administration with investments (much more desirable from the state's standpoint) in irrigated agriculture. Up to that point, the state government had explicitly rejected the committee model, and its 1995 Water Law was highly centralized. Under pressure to promote water user participation, the government hired an NGO and personnel from a local university to go into the field and help small farmers' unions, community groups, and municipal governments to form "municipal user commissions" and subsequently a consortium of such commissions (Leal 2004, 65–68, 77–95). Yet not long thereafter, the state government changed its policy, deciding to adapt to the federal water model. Once again, the government hired outsiders (this time, a consulting company) to get people involved and to run the meetings (Watermark Project 2002; Ribeiro 2006). Not surprisingly, this policy switch irritated consortium members, who felt that the time and work spent building an organization had been wasted, and most of them abandoned the project (Ribeiro 2006). At a Watermark Project workshop in 2008, participants recalled a fairly intense period of organizing for the consortium that had just begun to have some momentum when the state government changed course. Several participants noted that it was difficult to convince local actors to try again, especially since the few proposals they had worked on the earlier period were never implemented.

The Itapicurú and Pirapama cases suggest that although state government and international agency sponsorship of organizers can help local organizations get off the ground, external organizers can be fickle. Yet longer-term government involvement in water resources management did not necessarily translate into activist river basin organizations. In Ceará's Baixo Jaguaribe River Basin, the ascendancy of the state's water management agency, COGERH, seems to have crowded out local initiative. By far the most technically qualified water management administration in the Brazilian Northeast, COGERH has a special office just for organizing user commissions and river basin committees, the Department of User Organization (Departamento de Organização de Usuários, DOU). Although the DOU's institutional fortunes waxed and waned with shifts in the political winds, hitting a low point in the mid-2000s (Lemos and Oliveira 2004), compared with the Pirapama and Itapicurú cases it provided fairly consistent support to committee functions.

The result of this sustained support, however, was that the DOU dominated committee meetings. At a 2008 meeting of the Baixo Jaguaribe committee that we attended, COGERH officials had set the agenda and ran the meeting. The main order of business was to vote on an action plan COGERH had drawn up for the following year. It passed without opposition. Gutiérrez's (2006a) study of the same river basin found that COGERH technical personnel believed that committee members lacked the knowledge and management skills either to make decisions in the face of perennial water shortages or to maintain the infrastructure required to confront them (Gutiérrez 2006a, 202–217). Taddei (2011) similarly observes that, despite the COGERH team's obvious dedication in principle to participatory decision making, in practice, it reinforced the committees' dependency by controlling funding for committee activities. This had a positive side—Taddei argues that COGERH's control over both committees and the user commissions prevented their takeover by clientelistic politicians, as would normally be expected in a region traditionally dominated by local bosses. But it also meant that members could not even meet or communicate with one another without going through the agency.

These examples suggest that poorer regions, where civil society and local governments are fragile and resources are scarce, may have less capacity to build sustainable organizations because they rely on outside resources, the flow of which can be unstable and which may inhibit local mobilizing. Yet even in relatively wealthy regions, in situations in which local actors have their own resources, it does not follow that they can generate a sustainable organization. The Lagoa da Conceição committee, located in an upscale district of the city of Florianópolis where local organizations and business groups had already shown support for environmental protection, illustrates this point. Certainly there were resources around for putting a new organization together. Indeed, the process of forming and maintaining the committee was largely paid for by local NGOs, especially one local businessman who headed an environmental organization and who, not coincidentally, became the committee's first president. But after a year, tensions within the committee drove him to resign. With no one to take on his role, without his leadership and resources the committee quickly ran out of steam (Frank 2002; Watermark Project 2002).

BUILDING NICHES, MOBILIZING INSTITUTIONS, REORGANIZING PROCESSES

While identifying missions that resonated with local understandings of problems and developing the resources and skills to function as organizations were both crucial tasks, the purpose of doing them at all was to enable committees to become operational in relation to other parts of a complex and evolving system. They could not very well serve as arenas for resolving conflicts and generating new ideas if the other actors and institutions that were supposed to make up this new field of water resources management either ignored their existence or actively opposed their initiatives. Thus, for committees to become effective elements of the system, committee organizers had to become active in creating the system in which they were supposed to have a place. This helps to explain why the more active committees seemed to be taking on activities well outside their mandates, operating not only as participatory arenas, representative bodies, planning organs, and mediators but also as instigators, gadflies, and provocateurs. In a complex system, however, efforts to disrupt old practices and catalyze new ones may not have predictable results, and the ensuing adaptations may not be favorable to those whose actions prompted them or, indeed, for the system as a whole.

If river basin committees were intended to help generate a new approach by assembling people with different ideas, interests, and resources, the committees' actions could be expected to both reflect and affect changes in the situations they represent. The roles assigned to committees in the system hinge on the performance of functions assigned to other public institutions (usually state or federal). These include setting up systems to monitor water use by major consumers and other relevant information, evaluating and granting applications for water permits, coordinating among administrative areas and levels on matters in which jurisdiction is shared, and putting into effect programs and solutions proposed in water resource management plans. Very few states possessed the ability to carry out these activities at the time the committees were set up, and even when they did, as in São Paulo, the agencies involved often saw no reason to add a new layer of participatory decision making to their existing workload. Organizers found that for committees to make a difference, they either had to build relationships with organizations and institutions that could provide real support for resolving problems they identified (which sometimes involved reframing their missions), or they had to galvanize (or assist) other components of the system to do their jobs better, a process we refer to elsewhere as "mobilizing the state" (Abers and Keck 2009).

In either case, committee builders had to find an organizational niche, a space within the complex environment where they received the support from other institutions and actors allowing them to thrive. This was a dynamic process, in that many of those who became active in committee organization started out with expectations about the interests, capabilities, and likely behavior of other actors and institutions that were proven wrong or at the very least were misleading—sometimes because they misinterpreted the situation but sometimes also because the configuration of actors and orientation of institutions changed along the way. This problem of establishing an institutional niche when the parameters are changing around you, what some sociologists call coevolution (Oliver and Myers 2002, 8), characteristically involves adaptive learning and diffusion, albeit recognizing that what is learned may not be the right lesson and what is diffused may not be appropriate to the receiving situation.

More or less coterminous with the São Paulo metropolitan area, the Alto Tietê basin appeared to be a favorable context for creating a committee. Organizational resources seemed plentiful, along with abundant state capacity, clearly identifiable problems to solve, a wide range of organizations active in the area, and diverse repositories of knowledge and skills. For all the same reasons, however, São Paulo was an extremely competitive institutional environment. Efforts to carve out an organizational niche for river basin committees took place in a densely occupied terrain, where functional turf was hard-won in partisan and interagency struggles. The same conflicts that had turned some water specialists in that region into proponents of a new water management system continued with equal furor after it had been legally established.

The committee was one of the two whose creation was explicitly mandated in the state water law.[7] Momentum in favor of the committee's formation also came from a major civic mobilization demanding a cleanup of the fetid Tietê River, led by the Eldorado radio station and the NGO SOS Mata-Atlântica and supported by numerous banks and businesses (Keck 2002). The committee's organizers included a number of state employees dedicated to both an integrated vision of water management and its democratization.

Awareness of the scale of the river's problems, together with opportunities provided by the 1997 passage of a long-negotiated revision of the state headwaters protection law (*lei de proteção aos mananciais*), prompted a decision in 1997–1998 to create five subcommittees. The new headwaters law required that each subbasin of the Alto Tietê formulate locally specific land use rules for controlling urban expansion in water source areas, thus designating a concrete, difficult, but feasible task for smaller-scale river basin institutions (Formiga Johnsson and Kemper 2005).

However, although the full committee commissioned and adopted a river basin plan and served for a while as a forum for discussion, its ability to influence policy in the state depended largely on the influence of individuals within it. In 2001, two political events—the death of Governor Mario Covas and his replacement by Vice Governor Geraldo Alckmin and the election of a Workers' Party mayor of São Paulo who also became the committee's president—complicated the committee's relations with the state government. Not long after, the state environmental secretary sidelined key employees in the agency who had been committed to a decentralized approach and successfully resisted demands that controversial pollution-control plans, including one to restore the Billings dam's hydroelectric potential by using flotation to extract pollutants from the Pinheiros River, be passed through the committee.

Unable to contest decisions at this level, the main Alto Tietê committee essentially deactivated; nonetheless, those who had been pushing for a new approach remained active in a number of technical working groups and in the five subcommittees, which became arenas for discussing all kinds of water issues. In the Billings subbasin, for example, where environmental activists had long protested degradation of the Billings reservoir, the subcommittee did not restrict its mission to drafting the zoning plan required by the headwaters legislation, finished in 2007 (Alvim 2008). It also produced an environmental protection plan, had heated discussion of the construction of a new ring road that would cut through the region (the Rodoanel), and debated the Rio Pinheiros flotation proposal that had

7. The other was the Piracicaba, Capivari, and Jundiaí committee.

bypassed the main committee (da Cunha 2004). At the subcommittee level, there was also a much more congenial collaboration with the very active intermunicipal consortium in that region (Consórcio Intermunicipal do Grande ABC), allowing for working across functional boundaries that state government offices in the capital were hardwired to defend. In essence, like the Gravataí committee discussed earlier, the Alto Tietê committee shifted scales in order to find a niche in a difficult institutional ecology.

Although in some cases, basin committees drew strength from alliances with other local organizations (such as municipal consortia), in others, local alternatives played a part in crowding them out. The state water agency COGERH had begun in Ceará not by organizing basin committees but with the creation of councils of water users around storage reservoirs, later joined up in user commissions at the river basin level. The councils included only the direct users of the stored water, mainly farmers, and not public authorities or civil society groups. Their job was not to engage in broader planning efforts but rather to negotiate yearly a schedule for release of the reservoir waters according to their different needs. COGERH specialists drew up scenarios illustrating the probable implications of different choices to inform these annual negotiations. Although not legally binding, decisions made at these meetings about when and how much water should be released from reservoirs and how much each user could extract had considerable practical authority and became a key management tool, albeit for a system in which the orientation toward water was decidedly productivist (Garjulli et al. 2003; Ballestero 2004; Lemos and Oliveira 2004; Formiga Johnsson and Kemper 2008; Taddei 2011).

When the DOU began to set up basin committees in the state in 1997, including in the Baixo Jaguaribe basin, it intended for them to scale up from the reservoir level, broadening the range of issues discussed and people involved.[8] But high-volume users preferred the user commissions model because it allowed them to participate in water allocation decisions that affected them directly, creating something closer to common pool resource management system than to a broader system that took into account interests other than the economic needs of direct users. It was difficult to expand decision making from negotiations over allocation to long-term planning and policy, especially when in Ceará's water management system so many such decisions were centralized.

Yet not all committees had as much difficulty finding a viable niche in the system as the ones in the Alto Tietê and Baixo Jaguaribe basins. In several

---

8. The DOU got a special funding line from the World Bank's PROURB program to mobilize the committees and between 1997 and 2002 set up six basin or subbasin committees.

of the cases we studied, committees built collaborative relations with other government agencies and nongovernmental actors in their regions. Besides the Velhas committee, discussed at length in chapter 7, a good example is the Lagos São João consortium (and later committee), whose origins were described above. The consortium involved a flexible grouping of governmental and nongovernmental actors to fill a vacuum left by state agencies unable to fully implement their own mandates—what network theorists might call bridging a structural hole, a kind of linkage that can easily break but that if maintained can be particularly robust (Burt 1995). Specifically, a local network of municipal authorities, businesses, and NGOs got essential backup from the Ministério Público and from Rio de Janeiro's state environmental agency, in part because the initial idea for the consortium had come from an employee of that agency and in part because Rio's environmental agency during this period made water pollution a priority and was sympathetic to collaborative initiatives of this kind. The organizations involved exhibited considerably more flexibility, without the kinds of closely guarded functional roles and turf that we saw in both of the two previous cases.

The consortium racked up its first major accomplishments from negotiating problem remediation with polluters, with the backing of the state environmental licensing agency (whose regulatory failures had allowed the situation to occur). Its first target was the Companhia Nacional de Álcalis, a huge salt and lime mining company whose dredging machines were operating closer and closer to the lagoon beaches, disrupting tourism. NGOs protested that the company did not have a permit for dredging so close to the shore. The consortium became the arena in which an accord between the state environmental agency and the company was worked out. The deal not only put an end to dredging activities but also persuaded the company to dig a channel that environmentalists hoped would draw more seawater into the silted up lagoon, improving its water quality (Pereira 2007, 53–55). By brokering this deal, the consortium essentially took over a responsibility that the state government had failed to fulfill: the enforcement of environmental licensing (albeit with the participation of the responsible agency).

Another consortium project was to renegotiate municipal contracts with private water supply and sanitation companies. In Brazilian law, water supply and sanitation are municipal responsibilities, but a majority of municipalities transferred the concession for those services to state sanitation companies in the 1970s. Upon the expiration of those concessions in the 1990s and 2000s, some municipalities decided to replace inefficient state companies with private ones. This was the choice made by a group of municipalities in the Lagos São João region, where most urban waste was discharged, untreated, directly into the lagoon. In the contracts they negotiated, the concessionary firms promised to expand water services but put off sewage treatment even though the lagoon's problems were already urgent. Monitors detected deterioration in the lagoon's water quality just a few years after the contract was signed (Pereira 2007, 56).

In the face of what it considered a looming emergency, the consortium brokered a creative (though unorthodox) solution that involved rapidly reducing the emission of sewage into the lagoon by using the region's storm drain system. The concessionaries protested that it was technically ill advised to mix rainwater and sewage water systems. Consortium members put pressure on the companies to change their position, mobilizing the local population and activating the Ministério Público. Finally, the companies agreed to amend their contracts and move up the investment schedule in exchange for a more rapid increase in water and sanitation service rates than originally planned. To ensure that this increase happened, the consortium leaders once again brought in the Ministério Público, which in turn convinced the regulatory agency responsible for water services to allow an exceptional rate increase for water supply and sanitation services. Agency directors, worried that the price increase violated strict pricing rules it was required by law to follow, still resisted, until—in an inversion of the water wars scenario[9]—local NGOs held a demonstration in front of the regulatory agency's offices *demanding* the increase to pay for sanitation infrastructure (Pereira 2007, 58). The new installations eventually reduced the amount of sewage expelled into the lake by 75 percent (Pereira and Barreto 2009). The rather astonishing number of limits bent and boundaries bridged in this story by actors behaving in ways not easily predicted highlights the degree to which in collaborative governance processes, actions seem as often to emerge out of experimental practices as from deliberate design.

Another river basin organization that built practical authority by promoting coordination was the Litoral Norte committee, in the northern coastal area of São Paulo. This is one of São Paulo's smallest river basin committees, responsible for only four municipalities in a region of beach tourism and weekend homes and where 80 percent of the area falls within environmental protection areas. The prime movers included the committee's executive secretary (in this case, an employee of the state environmental agency), other employees of state technical agencies, and municipal

9. The "water wars" case was the massive confrontation in 2000 between the public of Cochabamba, Bolivia, and a newly privatized municipal water company, which inaugurated its short tenure in the city by raising rates on piped water steeply and by laying claim to wells and other water sources habitually used by the population.

government officials. Because the region was relatively small and adminis-trative offices tended to be clustered together, there were plenty of oppor-tunities to share information and imagine joint activities. As elsewhere in São Paulo, the State Water Resources Fund (FEHIDRO) provided ini-tial incentives for local actors to participate in the committee, especially municipal governments. This interest in resolving local problems was transformed by committee leaders into an opportunity to get policy mak-ers from the four municipalities together to discuss common issues. This included joint meetings between the water and coastal planning groups and other groups in the region charged with producing plans in relevant areas—solid waste planning, for example—and the coordination of plan-ning efforts on all these fronts. The committee also established a close working relationship with the local Ministério Público to pressure other state agencies (particularly SABESP, the sanitation utility, and DAEE, the water agency) to complete planned sanitation projects and, especially, to fulfill the monitoring and licensing activities that they were required by law to undertake.

The Litoral Norte committee benefited from being far enough away from the capital of São Paulo to avoid the competitive climate that para-lyzed some of the efforts of the Alto Tietê committee but close and well connected enough to take advantage of access to information and a well-informed strategic understanding of water politics in the state. Rosa Maria Mancini, the executive secretary of the committee during the expansive period just described, had been part of the planning team that worked under Stela Goldenstein when the latter was assistant secretary of the envi-ronment to Fabio Feldman in 1995–1999. Mancini had worked with the FUNDAP team that studied the state water management system and in the early 1990s had been one of the organizers detailed from São Paulo to set up a basin committee in the Piracicaba River Basin, discussed in chapter 6, where a consortium of municipal governments had pioneered river basin organization in the region. These experiences prompted her as executive secretary to focus on enhancing a collaborative intermunicipal context in which to embed the committee during a period where state support was weak. Later on, her experience with institution building at the commit-tee level shaped her approach when she was appointed head of the water resources section of the Environmental Secretariat during the governorship of José Serra from 2007 to 2011. This trajectory illustrates the way people navigate these complex settings, moving among locations and levels of gov-ernment and acting on both small and large territorial scales. Moreover, to further entangle the picture, from early on, Mancini was a participant in the Watermark Project.

NAVIGATING ENTANGLEMENT

The accounts here and in the next chapters of efforts made by different kinds of actors to set up river basin committees are in some ways remarkably diverse and in other ways surprisingly similar. Although organizers had a wide range of personal histories, most of them were well educated, generally with at least a decade of professional experience. Many, but by no means all, were engineers or had some technical training. Although some had political organizing experience, many did not, and most did not imagine at the outset what they were getting themselves into. Most of them saw in river basin committees a vehicle for combining optimism about possibilities for change with professional knowledge. Most had strong connections with both public and private (generally nonprofit) organizations. They usually had a strong sense of place but had also usually spent some considerable time elsewhere.

Generally speaking, committee organizers expected the new water management system to work the way its design principles promised, if not immediately, then very soon. They imagined that, with the creation of this new field of water management, the institutional reconfiguration necessary to make the system work would fall into place. Early experiments were undertaken in anticipation of the project's full effectuation and not with the idea that by experimenting, they were the ones building the system. When they did realize it, some doubled down and worked harder.

They were bricoleurs. In the absence of some of the system's fundamental building blocks, they jerry-rigged replacement parts, mobilizing one state agency to get another to do its job and finding alternative platforms like university departments to provide them with organizational infrastructure or bully pulpits. When the state failed to treat them as public institutions, they acted like civil society organizations, to the consternation of some of the system's original designers, who frequently lamented that basin committees were not supposed to be like NGOs. Sometimes committees simply ignored the limits of their formal responsibilities, trespassing into other areas, especially environmental policy, because it was impossible to resolve water-related problems without doing so. In some committees, organizers waited for the system to reach them; some are still waiting.

Where committees were constructed on top of other organizations or networks, such as intermunicipal consortia, the new did not replace or even necessarily absorb the old. Activists hedged, recognizing the advantages of keeping their possibilities open in multiple forms of organization. In some cases, organizational layering created important synergies, as when the Manuelzão Project in Minas took over the Velhas basin committee or when, alternatively, members of the Itajaí basin committee created a nonprofit organization to campaign for watershed restoration, the Piava project, and got funding from a private foundation.

Some people moved between different levels of government or between private and public sectors. Ricardo Gutiérrez (2006b) notes the surprising continuity of individuals in the Gravataí basin committee, such that at one moment a particular individual might have held a seat as a representative of a state government agency and at another as representative of a university or a professional association. Just as these individuals were hybrids in terms of the roles they played, the committees themselves were simultaneously organizations striving to strengthen the system of which they were meant to be a part and arenas within which participants with different ideas about how to approach water problems could generate new ideas and practices.

In a great many of the cases we studied, river basins—however appropriate for planning and decision making—were not a scale at which committees could actually build networks, mobilize resources, and solve the kinds of problems that concerned them. For some committees, this lack of fit was paralyzing. Others responded by focusing on particular parts of the basin, as with the Gravataí's headwaters project or with the shift in organizational attention to subbasin committees in the Alto Tietê that encouraged inter-municipal networks to provide support that was not coming from the state.

Such actions had wider implications, affecting how other actors interpreted what was possible. As one component of their efforts, committee organizers and those with whom they interacted were continuing to experiment with the institutional design, attempting to mold it in sync with local realities. They did this not only through local actions but also in interactions with one another (through visits to other basins and conferences of basin committees) and in conjunction with national and often international organizations. How did the evolution of these committees affect other aspects of the wide variety of systems in which it was embedded? If what we are examining is process, rigorous demarcations of success and failure seem at best premature and at worst to miss the point. What began as an adjustment of our research methods began to acquire an ontological dimension for which we were unprepared. Studying committees in their process of becoming could not be reduced to the before and after of an entity, much less a collection of them. By adding time to the mix, we had admitted a force that was both revealing and rambunctious. We became aware of the sometimes divergent temporalities governing the careers and experiences of individual activists, terms in office of policy makers, project deadlines and closing dates, and agency creation and dissolution, to say nothing of the rush of waterways.

All of these practices fall outside of the formal benchmarks with which most would measure the success or failure of basin committees—whether

they had approved master plans, water quality classifications, user registries, pricing, and so forth. The problem with the formal benchmarks was
that they measured conformity to an established agenda (the production of
plans and documents) without necessarily revealing anything about how
or whether these were materialized in the world. A basin plan that lived
only in a file cabinet should not have the same value as one that guided
action. It was evident from our case studies that the second did not automatically follow from the first. Insofar as committees themselves took on
the job of making sure that their deliberations acquired tangible form, and
not all of them did, we had to make sense of what they were actually doing.
What goals were they setting themselves, and how were they assembling
the human and material means to accomplish them? Had they found common purposes, whether reactive or proactive? Had their activities built the
capabilities of the committee and its members and won it recognition from
others? Had these advances in turn helped them to develop influence over
the behavior of other public and private actors? Exploring how these processes worked in concrete settings would help us understand the construction of practical authority.

CHAPTER 6

Diversions of Authority

Power, Perseverance, and Struggles over the Control of Water Resources

In this chapter, we explore two conflicts over interbasin water transfers that demonstrate vividly how actors have asserted competing claims to legal authority and have mobilized different kinds of power to influence key decisions. A central characteristic of these cases is the layering of different forms of power, whose legitimation drew upon different kinds of political mandates, expert knowledge, legal attributions, democratic process, and religious belief, to say nothing of the power of tactical advantage, coalitional bargaining, and the weight of precedent. Yet, as we will see, the *power to act* is not entirely reducible to the degree to which superior resources give particular actors *power over* a situation. Prior accumulation of practices and practical authority made it possible for the Piracicaba, Capivari, and Jundaí River Basin Committee to make its case in multiple arenas, giving it much greater leverage than might have been expected over management of a 30-year-old diversion of water to the city of São Paulo. Members of the brand-new and territorially dispersed São Francisco River Basin Committee, charged right away with ratifying or opposing a monumental diversion of the river, had no such history. From a purely formal standpoint, the two committees had essentially the same legal authority over such decisions, but in practice, their power to influence the process differed markedly. Thus, the outcomes of these high-profile political battles did not simply indicate the balance of power among contending territorial and economic interests but rather reflected a gradual accrual of capabilities and recognition over time, expressed in a *politics of perseverance*.

The intensity of these conflicts belies any notion that changes in the freshwater management systems meant creating a system based on subsidiarity, with decisional authority vested in the smallest viable unit. Although there may well be river basins and water districts whose management bears very little on neighboring (or sometimes even distant) ones, this relationship is contingent on both natural forces and political decisions. The management unit may be as small as a few municipalities or larger than several states, and the graduated territorial designations within which they are nested (microbasins, basins, macrobasins, and water districts formed from other criteria and the political units of the federation) overlap, making some degree of shared jurisdiction inevitable. Numerous human interventions, such as dams, canals, and aqueducts, were in place long before the idea of decentralized river basin management was introduced. Moreover, the system's reorganization was meant not only to divide formerly centralized power but also to integrate the capabilities of fragmented functional entities. Finally, because the preexisting regulatory situation was not really that water was managed too centrally but rather that it was not managed at all, the challenge in most places was not to transfer power but to generate it in the first place.

As discussed in chapter 3, reformers differed on the status of the new territorial inventions. Were they intended as planning units for a technically based process, arenas for direct negotiation of conflicts among contending interests, or new venues for making authoritative policy decisions? Local actors were usually the ones who espoused the third, more radical interpretation, seeing water reform as an opportunity to gain more control over policies affecting their regions. At the limit, the idea was not so much to provide a new planning arena but actually to create a new policy *jurisdiction*. Like the political units of the federation, this functional jurisdiction would possess some autonomous capacity to generate revenues (water charging), to decide what to do with the money (through the committee), and then to execute those decisions (through the water agency).

The water laws left unsettled the question of how much authority committees had over the way water rights should be allocated. The fulcrum of any water management regimen is the establishment of an effective system for granting and administering water rights, meaning usufructory rights to withdraw, store, or otherwise use a determined quantity of water from a natural source for a determined period of time along with rights pertaining to the amount and condition of the water to be returned. In most countries, the same administrative process normally regulates diversions, extraction of gravel, and other activities that alter the course, quantity, or quality of a waterway (Hodgson 2004, 13–19). In Brazil, this process is known as *outorga*, translated here as "water use permits." At the time most of new water legislation was passed, *outorga* was notable by its absence.

The state and federal laws all reserved the power to actually issue such permits for public agencies. But by providing that committee-approved river basin plans should set the priorities according to which permits should be allocated, the federal law by implication granted the committees some influence in this area. The legislation was silent, however, regarding the issuing agency's obligation to act in accordance to those priorities or how that would be monitored.[1]

The efforts of the institutional activists in the new river basin organizations to gain influence over water permits provide a good illustration of how practical authority acquired through bottom-up capability building can help to translate apparently zero-sum power struggles into something else. As Allen (2008, 1614) reminds us, not all power is "wielded at somebody else's expense." By building capacities that no other organization previously exercised, new organizations can develop the "power to make a difference in the world" without having to take it away from others, something that tends to arouse greater resistance (Allen 2008, 1614). This does not somehow level the playing field in which committees face off against political actors deploying superior economic or political resources. However, if given the time to build capabilities and recognition under the radar—that is, without having to engage in high-stakes conflicts with more powerful institutions— new organizations are better positioned when such conflicts do arise.

In both of the examples discussed in this chapter, basin committees contested (or contested the terms of) giant water transfer projects that would export water to other river basins. In São Paulo, the Cantareira system, built in the 1970s, supplied 9 million residents of the city of São Paulo with water piped in from tributaries of the Piracicaba River. The water permit for the system came up for renewal in 2004, a decade after the creation of the Piracicaba, Capivari, and Jundaí River Basin Committee. In the São Francisco case, the proposal to divert a part of the river's water to states to its north and northeast had not yet been implemented. This is a giant river basin, covering parts of six Brazilian states and the Federal District, from Minas Gerais in southeastern Brazil through much of the semiarid Northeast. The river basin committee for the São Francisco River—formed in 2002—had very little time to organize before dealing with the highly contentious transfer scheme.

---

1. The only exception is the state of Minas Gerais, where the water law required committees to approve high-volume water permits. This was a decision that, apparently, made it into the law under the radar screen, a suggestion of technical personnel in the government who hoped it would promote a more radical decentralization (Interview 54, Belo Horizonte, 2003; Interview 138, Belo Horizonte, 2003).

The conflicts around these river diversions cut to the heart of the issue of the authority of new river basin institutions. How much power should they have over the allocation of the water in their own basins? Could central government agencies be allowed to divert water away from river basins against the wishes of the river basin committee? With legislation giving permitting power unequivocally to state and federal governments, the simple answer would seem to be yes. But river basin actors would try to counteract that simple answer through political practice.

THE PIRACICABA RIVER BASIN

The coverage area of the Piracicaba, Capivari, and Jundaí River Basin Committee includes the second-most-populated urban region in the state of São Paulo, a region whose rapid population growth in the late 20th century was built on both commercial agriculture (mainly sugar cane) and industry. The constant need to compete with metropolitan São Paulo for access to state funding provided an incentive for local politicians to cooperate across party lines; the region also boasted several excellent universities, including the prominent State University of Campinas. A major source of interregional contention was the Cantareira system, a complex network of canals and pumping stations owned by the state and federal governments that diverted 31 cubic meters of water per second from tributaries of the Piracicaba River to provide water for the residents of São Paulo, less than 100 miles to the southeast. When pollution of the Piracicaba River became a public issue in the 1980s, a group of mayors, industrialists, and water engineers in the river basin joined forces to try to get that water back—or at least some of it.

As we saw in chapter 3, their struggles ended up influencing the design of São Paulo's water law and, indirectly, also the federal one. While negotiations over the law were under way in the state government, organizers in the region established a self-funded intermunicipal consortium for the Piracicaba and Capivari River Basins, pulling together technically skilled individuals and agencies and a regional political alliance to back their efforts. This gave them the momentum to insert an article into the São Paulo water law passed in 1991 stipulating that river basins should have their own executive agencies, making the state system more decentralized than originally intended. Although its powers remained vague, the idea of an executive agency became a central part of the model that was ultimately codified in the federal water law.

As Castellano (2007) recounts, turning the consortium into a strong regional institution took years, with an enormous investment of time on the part of its leadership.[2] The mayors who joined in 1989 agreed to deposit 1 percent of municipal revenues into the consortium fund, of which five-sixths had to be invested in programs and projects and one-sixth could be used to fund administration. By 1992, the consortium was raising $1 million a year (Castellano 2007, 124). This situation changed in 1993 when newly elected mayors decided that the portion of their contribution targeted for infrastructure was no longer necessary, since the 1991 state water law had created a Water Resources Fund (FEHIDRO) to be fed from royalties from hydroelectric dams and water charging. Quickly realizing that FEHIDRO funding would not be enough to replace the municipal contributions, the technical staff had to find another source of funding. The solution they proposed was to allow industries to join the consortium. In 1996, the representatives of municipalities agreed to give half the consortium seats to paying industrial members. A year later, municipal governments resumed their payments under a new system: instead of linking payments to tax revenues, both municipal and business members would pay according to how much water they used, at the rate of 1 Brazilian cent per cubic meter (less than U.S. $0.01). This would later be touted as the first practical experience in charging for water use in São Paulo (Castellano 2007, 124–128).

Meanwhile, the 1991 state water law posed an institutional challenge for the consortium. The legislation called for two river basin committees to be created immediately: one for the Alto Tietê River Basin, roughly corresponding to the São Paulo metropolitan region, and the other for the Piracicaba, Capivari, and (adjacent) Jundaí River Basins.[3] The law's instigators thought these would be ideal sites to test the new approach. Both had visible, acute conflicts over water use, but both also were regions with enough technically trained and experienced people to address them. One ingredient was shared: the Cantareira system, which transferred water from one basin to the other. The leaders of the Piracicaba and Capivari consortium had reservations about the state government's design for basin committees, which granted state government agencies a significant role that they did not have in the consortium (Castellano 2007). They worried that a basin committee would increase centralized control over water management in the basin.

2. Castellano (2007, 122–123) relates that mayors who became consortium presidents spent around half of their time on consortium business, which also required a lot of travel through the basin; many were thus more interested in the vice-presidential slot when elections for consortium leadership came around.

3. To make its boundaries compatible with the committee's, the consortium incorporated the Jundaí basin beginning in 2000 (Castellano 2007, 112).

Over two years, designated organizers from state agencies (CETESB, DAEE, FUNDAP) worked with a task force comprising representatives from municipalities in the basin to set up the committee. The most contentious issue at the more than 40 meetings held with civil society groups and municipalities was the committee's composition (Lopes 2003, 127; Barbi 2007, 77). By law, state and municipal representatives were to have an equal number of seats, and representatives of civil society (a catch-all category for nonstate actors) were to have no more than a third. As a temporary expedient, the task force decided that each group would get a third of the seats, a formula that became the model for all committees in the state (Interview 136, Piracicaba, 2003). The effect was to give actors from within the river basin a two-thirds majority on the committee, reducing the fears that the state government would dominate. Each of the three categories was to set up its own mechanisms for designating representatives. The civil society category was split in two, with half its seats going to university and civic associations and community groups and the other half to user associations (representing industry, farming, and other economic sectors) (Barbi 2007). The task force also divided up selection of the committee officers, with the municipalities choosing the president (perceived as politically most important), civil society choosing the vice president, and the state government holding the position of executive secretary (and supplying administrative support to the committee). Intended to establish a balance of power between municipalities and state government, this became the standard format for officers in the São Paulo committees (Interview 94, Ubatuba, 2002; Interview 137, Piracicaba, 2003).

The state government did take steps, however, to keep the Piracicaba committee from being totally controlled by the consortium. At the first meeting of the committee, in November 1993, the president of the consortium, Frederico Polo Muller (the mayor of the city of Americana), announced his candidacy for president of the committee as well. According to Castellano (2007, 138), organizers from the state government, fearful that this would allow the consortium to take over the committee, convinced Antonio Carlos Mendes Thame, then mayor of the city of Piracicaba and ally of the governor, to run against him and asked the state governor to urge the region's other mayors to vote for Thame, who was duly elected the committee's first president.

Despite these initial tensions, the two organizations gradually established a division of labor, with the committee responsible for formulating plans and rules and the consortium for implementing projects and programs (Castellano and Barbi 2006; Barbi 2007; Castellano 2007; Eça and Fracalanza 2010).[4] Underlying this rapprochement was an unwritten accord

4. Only in 1997 did the committee decide to allow the consortium a seat (expanding at that point the number of members so that each category would have 17 seats).

that the consortium would become the executive agency for the basin once water pricing was implemented. Since the committee was responsible for deciding on the allocation of FEHIDRO funds, mostly to small-scale municipal sanitation and water treatment projects, this function provided another way to build local support for the committee and complementarity between the two organizations.

Continuing on the trajectory the consortium had begun, the committee first set out to strengthen regional autonomy over water management decisions by trying to set up an agency and charge user fees. However, as the legislation necessary to commence charging stalled for years in the state legislature, the committee's agenda shifted to other issues, like deciding how to spend funds from FEHIDRO or analyzing projects which involved high-volume water use from public agencies such as the state-owned electric company (Xavier 2006; Barbi 2007). Sometimes the committee rejected major proposals, as with two thermoelectric plants that required large amounts of water for cooling systems, which came up for deliberation in 2000 and 2001.[5] The energy agency respected these verdicts, which were reached after extensive public consultations and sophisticated technical studies. By the end of the decade, most of the committee's work happened in its technical subcommittees and working groups, which met much more often than the full committee itself and where heated debates went on about specific projects, proposed laws, and plans for the region's future. Thus, despite the delay in implementation of the formal management instruments, the committee congregated capabilities and gained recognition as an authoritative interlocutor in regional planning, capable of influencing significant decisions about what kinds of water use the state would authorize.

In 2003, with the support of committee and consortium members, state officials initiated a process of transforming the PCJ into an interstate committee, in the hope of speeding up the onset of water charging. Because the headwaters of tributaries of the Piracicaba begin in Minas Gerais, the river falls under federal domain, even though only a tiny portion of the basin's territory is actually in the neighboring state. Since the consortium's requirement that members contribute according to the amount of water consumed was already an experimental version of water charging, there was much less resistance to the idea than in many other basins (except from farmers, who opposed it vehemently but who were barely represented on the committee and not at all in the consortium). A further motivation was the hope that

---

5. The committee also regularly took a position in more general debates, making recommendations to the state government on legislation about water charging, water agencies, and water source protection.

under federal auspices, the PCJ committee might gain more leverage over the Cantareira water transfer system (Interview 30, 2011).

Members of the state committee artfully navigated the differences between state and federal laws through lengthy negotiations and maintained control over the new interstate committee. In addition to including federal government representatives, the federal law required a composition that awarded half the seats to civil society and water users, giving the latter a categorical status they did not have in the state law.[6] The PCJ leadership was able to ensure that a majority of people elected to the interstate committee (29 of the 50 members) were already members of the state one. With that majority, the PCJ leaders easily approved the election of a nearly identical executive board.[7] Everyone agreed that the committees should also share their technical subcommittees. Eventually, the two committees began to meet together as an integrated assembly of 72 members that issued all their decisions jointly. This unusual arrangement seems to have worked without major problems essentially because the well-organized, densely networked group of actors involved in the state committee had been able to establish so much continuity with the new one (Barbi 2007; Eça and Fracalanza 2010; Interview 30, 2011).

Thus, by the early 2000s, Piracicaba had three well-organized, overlapping river basin institutions: the consortium, the São Paulo committee and the interstate one, with almost a dozen shared permanent technical subcommittees in which the experts from the region's universities and research centers, from the consortium, and from the regional offices of state water agencies participated actively.[8] The consortium had years of experience in promoting collaboration among regional actors. Its staff had extensive knowledge of the region and had made important contributions to the design of water treatment and other environmental protection projects and plans. It also had substantial experience in implementation of projects ranging from environmental education to reforestation to the installation

---

6. While the state law called for three categories and included users in the civil society segment, the federal law had four, one of which was users. In the São Paulo system, furthermore, private users could not participate directly, only through their associations, while the federal law allowed the participation of individual users. Another hitch was that some members of the National Water Resources Council—which would have to approve creation of the committee—questioned the inclusion of the Capivari and Jundaí River Basins in the federal committee, since those are state-owned rivers. Eventually, the majority of council members approved the idea, however, agreeing that water charging would be easier to implement if the state and federal waters were governed jointly.

7. The only addition is that of two vice presidents, one from Minas Gerais state and another from the federal government.

8. Later on in the decade, Minas Gerais created a state committee for the part of the basin that is located in that state.

of water monitoring equipment throughout the basin. This kind of local technical capacity was unusual in Brazil and can be attributed to presence in the region of some of Brazil's country's most advanced university and research centers as well as corporate headquarters and municipal governments with sizable budgets of their own.

The Piracicaba institutions got a chance to flex their muscles in 2004, when the Cantareira water permit came up for renewal. The state water and sanitation company (SABESP) had been granted a 30-year permit in 1974, at the height of the military dictatorship, to divert water from the Piracicaba River to the metropolitan region of São Paulo. For Piracicaba actors, this major loss of clean water severely worsened the water scarcity and pollution in the region; in fact, the period from 1998 to 2004 had been unusually dry, and some reservoirs were virtually empty. SABESP's 30-year contract was up in 2004, and the utility would have to negotiate a new water permit under completely different conditions from the ones that pertained in the 1970s. The National Water Agency (ANA) and the São Paulo Department of Water and Electrical Energy (DAEE) shared the permitting authority for the Cantareira system.[9]

Although there were very good reasons for the two government agencies to keep the discussion of the new concession to themselves, pressures from the region made it increasingly impolitic to do so. The system supplied water to 9 million people in urban São Paulo, and the water laws clearly assigned priority to the provision of drinking water over other uses. In addition, it also was an important source of water for São Paulo's giant industrial complex. There were no viable alternative sources available to replace the Cantareira system, so it was imperative that the contract be renewed, despite growing protest in the region over its impact. In 2002, for example, civic groups had organized a well-publicized Day of Lament for the Piracicaba River (Barbi 2007). In December 2003, at the instigation of a federation of Piracicaba nonprofits, the Ministério Público, Brazil's agency for defending the public interest, had won a court judgment awarding 11.4 billion reais (U.S. $3.8 billion)[10] in damages from a lawsuit charging SABESP, ANA, and the state government of São Paulo with environmental harm in the Piracicaba basin.[11] Although it was unlikely that such a fine

---

9. Federal authority over the permit resulted from the fact that much of the water was extracted on the São Paulo side of a river that originated in Minas Gerais, the Jaguari. The state government was responsible for parts of the system fed by state-owned tributaries. Eventually, however, ANA delegated the permitting authority to DAEE.

10. Exchange rate was 2.946 reais = 1 US$ on December 1, 2003; on December 31, 2003, it was 2.9010. Calculation in the text is from December 1. From http://www.likeforex.com/misc/historical-exchange-rates/USD/BRL/2003/12, accessed March 30, 2013.

11. Original case number 2003.61.09.008555-5 2 Vr PIRACICABA/SP; the decision was upheld on appeal in 2005 but dropped in 2011. See Tribunal Regional Federal 3ª Região—Publicações Judiciais I de 15 de Julho de 2011, p. 718.

would ever be collected (and it was, in fact, withdrawn in 2011), the court case escalated the pressure on these entities to repair relations with local actors (Interview 30, 2011).

Thus, even though nothing in the law required that committees have a say in the decision (Barbi 2007), the idea of excluding them from the deliberations was simply not on the table. In addition to the obvious organizational strength of the committees and consortium, the issue was politically sensitive, and as one informant involved in the negotiations noted, "SABESP, with shares traded on the New York stock exchange, could not run any financial risks" (Interview 30, 2011). Furthermore, there was precedent: for years, government agencies had been systematically sending other water permitting decisions for the committee's review and in the cases mentioned earlier had respected the committee's decision to reject permits. Those decisions—about important but less contentious issues—helped build public recognition for the committee as an organization that should be included in any issue directly affecting water resources in the region.

In 2003, the federal and state committees created a joint task force to discuss the Cantareira renewal, including committee members, federal and state government staff, mayors, civil society actors, and SABESP.[12] The group held 11 tense and contentious all-day meetings in 2003 and 2004. SABESP insisted from the outset that there were no alternatives to the status quo. The company had made huge investments in the system that had yet to pay off. Reducing flows to São Paulo would be financially impossible. Representatives from the river basin committees objected that SABESP had systematically failed to invest in the Piracicaba basin. SABESP offered to build water treatment facilities in the basin rather than reducing the water transfer.[13] Civil society groups from the basin demanded a system of shared management of the Cantareira system to protect the region's interests rather than the centralized control SABESP was proposing. SABESP resisted. At one point in the negotiations, the committees increased the pressure by asking the Ministério Público to investigate diminished water supply in the region and proposed that SABESP expand sewage treatment capacity (Moretti and Gontijo 2005; Barbi 2007).

---

12. ANA and DAEE were not members of the group but participated regularly and provided technical support. The consortium also was not an official member of the group but presented many of the proposals that the group considered.

13. A group of professors from University of São Paulo's prestigious Engineering Institute (Escola Politécnica) developed an information support system for the process that produced huge amounts of information and helped the participants examine different scenarios for water use.

The committees approved a final agreement in July 2004 but a few weeks later discovered that DAEE and ANA had made changes in the draft water permit. Once again, committee members used their organizing capacity to mobilize support in ways that successfully navigated the complex institutional setting within which they worked. The committees held a joint meeting attended by 150 people and alerted the Ministério Público to the problem. The latter recommended to the National Water Resources Council that water management should be shared between committee and public agencies in the basin and that civil society participation should be guaranteed. This pressure apparently had the desired effect. The committee and consortium members generally consider the final version of the permit to be a victory (Barbi 2007).

That victory did not, however, reduce water transfers out of the basin. Knowing that radical change was unlikely given high sunk costs and the number of São Paulo residents dependent on this water, the committee leadership proposed something different: the construction of a new system of shared water management of the Cantareira system and the creation of incentives for SABESP to improve water conditions in the Piracicaba basin. A major innovation was the creation of a water bank, a system for making decisions about where water should be stored during rainy periods, to be controlled jointly by the PCJ committees and SABESP. The agreement also gives the PCJ committees a role in the daily operation of the system, limits the quantity of water that can be withdrawn from the river in times of scarcity, and commits SABESP to invest in sewage treatment. To increase the pressure on SABESP to implement these changes, the PCJ participants convinced others that the permit should be valid for only 10 years, a major departure from the past (Moretti and Gontijo 2005; Barbi 2007; Interview 30, 2011; Interview 32, Rio de Janeiro, 2011).

The Cantareira negotiations affirmed the river basin committee's practical authority as an institution based on new territorial boundaries, an authority substantiated by but not enforceable under the law. The capacity of the Piracicaba actors to impose such stringent restrictions on what was formally a joint state and federal agency decision came not from the law but rather from problem-solving capabilities accumulated by Piracicaba mayors, industrialists, and engineers who had been building their local (river basin) institutions for decades and who were adept at mobilizing powerful allies to their cause.

Three factors stand out about those institutions that may help explain this solidity and organizing power. In the first place, specific individuals have held the three organizations together over a long period of time. Mayors came and went, but the executive secretariat of the consortium and a group of key technical personnel have been extremely stable (Interview 32, Rio de Janeiro,

2011). The executive secretary of the state committee, Luiz Roberto Moretti, has been in that position since 1999, and Eduardo Lovo Paschoalotti, a representative of the industrial sector, held the vice presidency from 1993 to 2003 and again from 2007 to 2009 (Carmo and Teixeira 2011).

Second, the dominant actors in all three institutions are technical experts, whose largely shared assumptions and vocabulary increase the likelihood of reaching consensus among themselves. Mayors have added a dose of political savvy to those organizations, but even they were usually skilled professionals; the first president of the state committee, Piracicaba mayor Antonio Carlos Mendes Thame, had degrees in agronomy and law. Rio Claro mayor Cláudio Antônio de Mauro, president of the state committee between 1999 and 2004, and Piracicaba mayor Humberto de Campos, president of the consortium starting in 1999, had both been university professors (Castellano 2007, 157). Actors with less professional training had little presence in these institutions. As Carmo and Teixeira (2011) note, business associations and academics occupy most of the civil society slots. Few environmental NGOs and community organizations participate in the committee and even fewer in the technical subcommittees where most of the real deliberation takes place. Farmers, who were absolutely opposed to water pricing, were also marginalized; they were not members of the consortium, and only had a few votes on the committee. The marginality of other actors may help to explain the high level of internal consensus within the Piracicaba institutions.

Third, besides having resources of their own, those institutions also had the ability to influence the actions of higher-level institutions at key moments, for example, when the consortium's mayors mobilized deputies in the state legislature to introduce key amendments to the 1991 state water bill. Another illustration came six months after the 2004 victory in the Cantareira negotiations, when the minister of the environment nominated José Machado, mayor of Piracicaba and founder of the consortium, to be the new president-director of the National Water Agency, succeeding Jerson Kelman, whose term had ended. As we will see, very different conditions pertained in the São Francisco basin, where government decision makers and the river basin committee took starkly opposing positions in negotiations over a similarly large and politically important water transfer.

THE SÃO FRANCISCO RIVER BASIN

The São Francisco River, known affectionately as the Velho Chico and sometimes called the River of National Integration, extends for 2,830 kilometers, including parts of six states and the Federal District, covering fully 8 percent of Brazil's territory and home to a population of 16 million people. It flows from wealthy Minas Gerais in the southeastern part of the country and through the semiarid backlands of four states of the impoverished Northeast. More than half of the basin's territory is in the semiarid region, where patterns of concentrated landholding restrict access to water. When the region's population began to grow at the end of the 19th century, recurring droughts caused famine, misery, and massive outmigration. Since the early 20th century, public policies have addressed this problem largely through investments in water storage reservoirs, in what became known as the *hydraulic solution* to drought. But these reservoirs, usually under the control of members of the rural oligarchy, actually increased concentration of water resources. The renowned Brazilian author Antônio Callado (1960) memorably called this system, in which local bosses perpetuated social inequality with the help of federal monies, the "Drought Industry" (Christofidis 2001; Empinotti 2007).[14]

Opposition to the view that the hydraulic solution could eliminate misery in the region has a long pedigree, following the classic analysis of economist Celso Furtado, who argued that public works were not bringing economic development.[15] Some grassroots movements in the region have gone so far as to repudiate a development model focused exclusively on economic growth. Advocating alternative development approaches aimed at living with semiarid conditions instead of seeking to eliminate drought, these movements, with the strong support of the Catholic church, insist that the drought industry only perpetuates oligarchic power (Empinotti 2007, 175). With the expansion of rural social movements defending family agriculture, under the wing of the international peasant movement Via Campesina, these criticisms have grown stronger in recent years.

The federal government became involved in drought control schemes in the Northeast in 1909, with the creation of the Inspectorship for Public Works against the Drought (IOCS), later transformed into the National Department for Public Works against the Drought (DNOCS). Several special federal institutions for the São Francisco Valley were also created during the 20th century, such as the Company for the Development of the São Francisco Valley (CODEVASF) and the Hydroelectric Company of São Francisco (CHESF). These three agencies provide one example of the kind of layering we described in chapter 2 and that still exists today. DNOCS, CODEVASF,

14. The São Francisco River figured in the early phases of Brazil's hydraulic ambitions. The nation's first large hydroelectric plant, the Paulo Afonso dam, was built in 1949, followed by five others, all of which regulate the river's flow and harness it for energy. Originally meant to be part of a broader regional development project and modeled after the Tennessee Valley Authority in the United States, the dams flooded huge areas, expelling farmers from their land and impeding navigation and fishing—without noticeable impact on regional development (Mascarenhas 2008, 146).

15. For a review of Furtado's thinking about regional development, see Cano (2000).

and other regional development agencies were housed in the Ministry of the Interior during the military regime. Temporarily weakened during the period of liberal reforms in the 1990s, at the end of that decade, the same ministry, now called the Ministry of National Integration, became a strong political platform for northeastern politicians-turned-ministers. It is mainly dedicated to implementing large-scale infrastructure projects in the region, sometimes appearing to be following in the footsteps of the drought industry.

During the 1990s, in the secretariats and ministries concerned with northeastern development programs, an old idea was revived for dealing with the drought in the Northeast: diverting water from the São Francisco River into neighboring states of Ceará and Rio Grande do Norte. This proposal, referred to as "The Transposition of the São Francisco River," had been resuscitated every few decades since the early 19th century, generally at the instigation of politicians from the two receiving states (Viana 2011, 85). In 1994, political and business leaders from Ceará once again advanced the argument that a diversion would help to mitigate the effects of chronic drought to the north. As we saw in chapter 5, linking the state's waterways and perennializing their flow were central components of the Ceará group's development project, which focused on expanding irrigated commercial agriculture and industry. In 1994, at the end of President Itamar Franco's administration, they won approval for a team of engineers to design such a project, but it remained on the back burner for most of Fernando Henrique Cardoso's (1995–2002) presidency. Nonetheless, in 2000, after another drought prompted pressure from the region's politicians, 80 federal (mainly northeastern) deputies joined a congressional working group to discuss the diversion of the São Francisco River. Fernando Bezerra, a politician from Rio Grande do Norte who became head of the new Ministry of National Integration, commissioned an environmental impact assessment, the first bureaucratic hurdle in getting any major infrastructure project started (Viana 2011, 90–93).

By that time, Cardoso's presidency was halfway through its second term, a bit late in the game for initiating public works that would take years to get off the ground. The Ministry of National Integration continued to commission feasibility studies for the project, and the environmental licensing process began to work its way through the Brazilian Institute for the Environment and Natural Resources (IBAMA), Brazil's environmental agency.[16] Pointing to the absence of credible studies and the lack of any

---

16. To make the diversion project more politically palatable, the ministry proposed actually *increasing* its size, including a second channel that would mostly supply water to Campina Grande, a city in the state of Paraíba (just south of Rio Grande do Norte). This allowed supporters to claim that the purpose was not only to support irrigated agriculture but also to provide water security for human consumption (Viana 2011, 95).

kind of water resources management plan, however, NGOs managed to get the courts to issue an injunction halting the first set of public hearings on the environmental impact assessment. Additional public interest lawsuits paralyzed the environmental licensing process altogether. Opposition from other federal agencies grew stronger during the last years of the Cardoso administration; one of the most vocal opponents, Minas Gerais politician José Carlos Carvalho, was even appointed minister of the environment. Carvalho, who as executive secretary of the ministry for several years before that had fervently opposed the project (Viana 2011, 94–96), convinced the president that it was a mistake (Coelho 2005; Viana 2011, 102).

Considering this resistance, and given that the final year of a second presidential term was not a good time for taking on enormous infrastructure projects, the Cardoso government found it more tenable to make a symbolic move than a decisive one. There had already been some discussion of setting up a new river basin committee for the São Francisco. The National Water Agency (ANA) had an interest in doing so, since an old-style executive committee formed in the 1970s was still operating, under the coordination of CODEVASF, the São Francisco Valley regional development agency. The continued existence of both CODEVASF and the old executive committee—despite the fact that the programs that those institutions had been created to implement had been terminated—provides a perfect example of entanglement produced by the persistence of institutional residues of previous reforms. By replacing the old committee with a new one under its purview, ANA would eliminate one of the competing institutional structures left over from earlier reform processes and thus bring one more of the assorted fragments of the water management puzzle under its aegis. The looming diversion project provided a strong incentive to do so quickly. The head of the agency, Jerson Kelman, had close ties to the political leadership of Ceará state, the main beneficiary of the project. Supporters of the diversion hoped that creating a representative arena for discussing it would ease some of the tensions around the proposal and give it more legitimacy. Minister of the Environment Carvalho also liked the idea. Fiercely opposed to the project, and nearing the end of his administrative mandate, he thought a committee would open up a deliberative arena that would last into a future administration in which he no longer would have the bully pulpit of a ministry (Kleemans 2008, 39–40).

Over the course of 2001–2002, the process of organizing the São Francisco committee laid bare the extent to which intense intraregional competition would come to characterize committee politics. The 19-member provisional executive board charged with setting up the committee had to decide how many seats to allocate not only to each social sector but also to each of the states in the basin.[17] In fact, participants from civil society, users, and state governments joined forces to defend their own states. Those from Minas Gerais wanted a larger share of seats, given their state's larger population, its greater wealth, and the fact that most of the river's headwaters originate there. Representatives of Bahia, Sergipe, Alagoas, and Pernambuco argued that they merited a larger portion precisely because they were poorer. In the end, the organizers allocated more seats to Minas Gerais than to any other state but fewer than its proportion of the population would have dictated. Altogether there were to be 62 seats on the committee. State government representatives, civil society, and water users were carefully distributed among the states. There were also seats for groups understood to operate outside the logic of intrastate conflict: the federal government, hydroelectric power companies, indigenous groups, and (after 2007) traditional Afro-Brazilian communities (*quilombolas*) (see table 6.1).

More than 6,000 people participated in the dozens of organizing meetings, culminating in September 2002 when civil society organizations and water users chose their representatives at 26 state-level meetings and one indigenous community meeting. A total of 1,853 civil society organizations and water users competed for slots on the committee (state governors and the president were responsible for nominating the government representatives) (Mascarenhas 2008, 162; Kleemans 2008, 41–42). In December 2002, in one of the final acts of his administration, President Cardoso personally swore in the committee members.

January 2003 ushered in an entirely new political context. The new president, Luis Inácio Lula da Silva from the Workers' Party, had to build a governing coalition. He appointed Ciro Gomes, the former governor of Ceará who had run against Lula in the first round of the election and had supported him in the second round, to be minister of national integration. The São Francisco River diversion was Gomes's pet project. Despite the president's historical ties to the left and to radical movements, who opposed the project, Lula immediately announced support for it and put his vice president, José Alencar, in charge of a government-wide effort to make it happen. This meant pushing IBAMA on the environmental permit in addition to making sure that ANA issued a water use permit. The prevailing interpretation at

17. This provisional board was established in 2001 as part of a broad-based organizing process required by the National Water Resources Council to document an interest on the part of actors in the basin in creating a committee. Nongovernmental agencies coordinated the process with financing from ANA; a giant undertaking, it involved 120 organizers and professional staff, 43 regional and municipal consciousness-raising meetings, and another 29 plenary meetings at which representatives for specific sectors were elected (Kleemans 2008).

Table 6.1. COMPOSITION OF THE SÃO FRANCISCO RIVER BASIN COMMITTEE
(NUMBER OF SEATS, 2007)

Category/State	Government	Water Users	Civil Society	Indigenous Groups	Total
Minas Gerais	4	8	6		18
Goiás	1				1
Bahia	3	6	3		12
Pernambuco	2	4	2		8
Alagoas	2	2	2		6
Sergipe	2	2	2		6
Federal District	1				1
Federal government	5				5
Hydroelectric concessionaires		2			2
Indigenous communities				2	2
Quilombolas			1		1
Total	**20**	**24**	**16**	**2**	**62**

Note: Between 2003 and 2007, the committee did not include a seat for Quilombolas and had only one seat for indigenous communities.
Source: Mascarenhas (2008, 169).

the time was that the latter could happen only once the river basin committee had approved a water resources plan. The National Water Agency pulled together such a plan in a matter of months and presented it to the committee. Everyone expected that the committee would pass the plan expeditiously and the permitting process would move forward smoothly (Kleemans 2008). They could not have been more mistaken.

At the first meeting of the São Francisco River Basin Committee in May 2003, the members chose their executive board. By then, José Carlos Carvalho, who as federal minister of environment had opposed the diversion a year before, had been named secretary of the environment in the new state government in Minas Gerais, whose governor, Aécio Neves, belonged to the PSDB, the party of ex-president Cardoso and now the leading party in opposition to Lula's government. By selecting Carvalho as their president, the committee members thus inaugurated a new and highly visible arena of resistance to the river diversion.[18]

18. To deal with the huge size of the basin, the committee also set up four nonvoting regional subcommittees made up of the members of the state river basin committees that already existed. Coordinators of these subcommittees would join the executive board members (committee president, vice president, and secretary) on a collegial board that would be responsible for many major decisions (Kleemans 2008; Mascarenhas 2008). Including the subcommittees expanded the reach of the committee and involved the various state-level river basin committees in the debate about the São Francisco.

The vice president and the ministers of the environment and of national integration (Marina Silva and Ciro Gomes) attended the committee's second meeting in October 2003, at which ANA presented its proposed river basin plan. Apparently undaunted by this show of force, the committee passed a resolution that explicitly called into question the whole diversion project and demanded more time and resources to analyze the issue before approving the river basin plan. That resolution provided a taste of the broader debate about development priorities that would dominate committee discourse (CBHSF 2003):

> The CBHSF [São Francisco River Basin Committee] considers that it is more than historically proven that the simple fact of moving water from one place to another in the semiarid region does not resolve the problem of development. An outrageous example of this is the drama that occurs at the edge of the San Francisco River itself, where not far from the water we witness scenes of thirst and misery that multitudes of Brazilian men and women suffer.

Instead of quickly approving the plan, as the government had hoped, committee members went out and mobilized around 5,000 people all over the basin to participate in a series of public meetings in the first half of 2004 (Medeiros 2007; Kleemans 2008, 46). The intention was not just to debate the issue; the meetings were meant to demonstrate how widespread opposition to the proposal was within the basin.

If the public hearings were a way to show its mobilizing power, at the committee's third meeting, in July 2004, it attempted to demonstrate that it had technical capacity as well by contesting the project's figures as to how much of the river's flow was really available to be allocated for new activities. The committee's technical subcommittees estimated the volume of water available at only 1,849 cubic meters per second (m^3/s). This was a much lower figure than the 2850 m^3/s used in ANA's proposed river basin plan, which the committee's experts claimed did not take into account the reduction in flow from the huge dams on the river. The committee's experts also concluded that at least 1,500 m^3/s should flow out to the ocean to maintain ecological conditions in the river delta. This calculation left only 360 m^3/s available for water use permits. For many committee members, the implication was that since users—mostly irrigators—had already received water permits totaling 335 m^3/s of the river's waters, only 25 m^3/s remained for future water permits of any kind. ANA challenged this logic, objecting that most of the existing permits were outdated and underused and should not be incorporated into the calculation. The numbers game was fundamental for justifying or challenging the river diversion, which would use more than 25 m^3/s, at the lowest estimates. By ANA's calculations, this amount was

only 1 percent of the natural flow of the river. According to the committee figures, it was more than what was legally available for water permits
(Fontes 2007; Medeiros 2007; Kleemans 2008, 49).[19]

An actual decision on the diversion was deferred to the next meeting,
in October 2004, by which time the committee finally staked out a position, establishing general rules for transfers from the basin. Committee
Deliberation 18 resolved that the priority for water use permits would be for
uses within the basin and that transfers to other basins would only be per-
mitted for human and animal consumption in situations of scarcity. Water
permits for productive uses (e.g., irrigated agriculture) could be issued only
for activities within the basin. This was the first time the committee took a
formal stand against a diversion of the São Francisco's waters to promote
agriculture outside the basin. Had the government respected that decision,
it would have derailed the project.

Meanwhile, heated debates about the plan's technical merits were also
going on outside the committee. Minister Gomes traveled the country
and appeared regularly on television, presenting a cogent defense of the
diversion and arguing that it would provide drinking water to 12 million
people at only a tiny cost to the donating basin. The Brazilian Society for
the Progress of Science (the country's largest scientific organization) issued
a statement critical of the project at its annual conference in July 2003.
The National Conference of Brazilian Bishops, whose 2004 Fraternity
Campaign had water as its theme, also denounced the project. The members of the Brazilian Water Resources Association debated it on their listserv. A federal accountability agency, the Tribunal de Contas da União (or
National Accounting Court), carried out a major study of the proposal and
held public hearings to debate it. The Ministério Público got involved, as
did numerous other public and private institutions.

After the river basin committee had effectively ruled out the possibility of a major water transfer from the basin to the northern states of the
region, the government decided to go over its head to the National Water
Resources Council, justifying the move on two counts: first, since the decision involved more than one river basin, the national council and not the
donating basin should have the last word; and second, ANA challenged
the right of a river basin committee to veto water permits for any particular
project. The committee had the right to set priorities but not to stop the
diversion altogether. The committee objected, arguing that its resolution

---

19. The committee also approved 10 detailed injunctions on water allocation guidelines, permits, information systems, water charging, and various other issues and rejected a sophisticated
water allocation plan proposed by ANA on the grounds that it was a ruse to try to create a sense
of water security in the basin that did not really exist.

had, in fact, set priorities for overall use, and the diversion project was not one of them. But the government was intent on overriding the decision. Although federal government representatives occupy under half of the seats on interstate committees, they have a majority in the national council. In informal conversations, several government employees who represented specific agencies on the council told us that in the days before the vote, they were called into the Casa Civil—the Brazilian equivalent of the presidential chief of staff's office—and told in no uncertain terms to vote in favor of the project and, more specifically, to approve a water permit large enough to allow the transposition to occur. Navigating entangled institutional terrain is sometimes complicated even for those in power. After finding the committee unwilling to provide legitimacy to the project as its proponents had hoped, the government in effect shifted scales—moving the action to another level of decision making that it could control.

NGOs mobilized. More than 40 signed a manifesto, handed out on the day of the fateful national council meeting in November 2004. Supporters of the committee position shifted scales, too: they appealed to the federal Ministério Público and got a court injunction to prevent the vote on the grounds that the process needed further consideration by the council's technical subcommittees. At the last minute, the meeting was canceled—with the halls already full of councilors.

This temporary victory only delayed matters. In January 2005, the Ministry of the Environment managed to get the injunction overturned, and the meeting took place. As predicted, the council approved the diversion. The water permit that ANA issued soon after did take the committee's views into account at some level, in that although it still approved the diversion of 26.4 m³/s (more than the volume of the water available for permitting in the basin, according to the committee), it restricted its purpose to providing drinking water for people and animals. However, it also provided for exceptions that effectively nullified that concession to the committee. During wet periods, when reservoirs were full, it allowed the diversion of up to 127 m³/s. Thus, by 2025, the diversion was expected to siphon off an estimated 64 m³/s on average, much more than the committee was willing to accept. The permit also allows water to be used for other purposes, such as irrigation, when "real demand is lower than projected demand," also violating the committee's resolution.

Outraged, the committee issued a statement soon after the national council meeting denouncing the decision, protesting that the meeting had marked the "destruction of a national water resources system based on participatory water management" (cited in Mascarenhas 2008, 173). Or as committee secretary Luis Carlos Fontes (Fontes 2007, 66; cited by Kleemans 2008, 64) wrote a few years later, "The federal government's unilateral decision-making had...endangered the whole model of participatory and decentralized water management contained in Law 9.433."

In the following years, the government went ahead with the diversion. IBAMA held a new round of public hearings on a revised version of the environmental impact assessment; several of those meetings were canceled following protests. The agency granted a preliminary license (*licença prévia*) in April 2005. From then on, civic groups focused on trying to stop the project through the courts. Their cause got a burst of publicity when Luis Flávio Cappio, a Catholic bishop in the state of Bahia and longtime activist for the São Francisco River, went on a hunger strike against the diversion. The 10-day strike ended when President Lula promised to hold a new round of negotiations about the project. But these negotiations never happened; instead, the government simply proceeded as before. In late 2006, a federal court invalidated all injunctions against the project, and in 2007 construction began. Frustrated with the outcome, Cappio went on a second hunger strike in late 2007, which lasted nearly a month.[20]

The debate over the São Francisco diversion was the first nationally visible political issue to involve a river basin committee. Consequently, the nullification of the committee's decision helped disseminate skepticism about the new decentralized and participatory model. The first groups to react were the popular movements of the São Francisco basin itself, which decided to abandon the committee in 2005, the next time elections were held for committee positions. Their reasons are interesting, since the majority of the committee had shared their general opposition to the diversion project. In her research on decisions *not* to participate in the committee, Empinotti (2007) found that in the main, they pulled out not because of the national council's action but rather because grassroots rural activists had realized their reasons for opposing the project were entirely different from the ones motivating state governments and high-volume water users who also opposed it—but their arguments were simply not on the radar. Most of the committee members were fighting over where water should be allocated for energy production, irrigation of cash crops, or fish farming. The movements were saying something completely different—that a development model predicated on moving around large volumes of stored water was bankrupt for the semiarid region and that instead, the population needed to adapt its practices to the land and climate that were there. They were speaking a language that other committee members did not even hear (Empinotti 2007, 167).

---

20. The bishop gave up on the strike once he was hospitalized and on the brink of death.

After the council decision, relations between the committee and ANA remained tense, with committee members constantly suspecting that the agency was trying to deceive them in some way or another (Kleemans 2008, 57). They also complained of foot dragging on other issues, such as a request for technical studies on the ideal river discharge from an environmental perspective (whose results might justify even lower levels of water use) and the revision of existing water permits. During a drought in 2007, ANA agreed to allow the agency operating the river's dams to let the river's water level fall below the environmental minimum set by the committee (which had by then been revised to 1.300 m³/s) (Kleemans 2008, 62–63).

Even outside the São Francisco basin, the 2005 decision to override the committee's position made civil society actors more skeptical of the possibilities of creating a more decentralized, participatory system of river management. In 2009, we attended a series of seminars where civil society groups and social movements were asked to discuss why they did or did not participate in river basin committees; activists repeatedly referred to the São Francisco case in explaining why they doubted that the new system offered effective arenas for participation.

THE POLITICS OF PERSEVERANCE

The legislation passed in Brazil in the 1990s through the complex processes described in chapters 3 and 4 left ambiguous the decision-making authority of river basin institutions. Such authority as they possessed had therefore to be produced in practice. In the Piracicaba case, actors from the river basin succeeded in building a counterweight to the central powers of the state government, obtaining significant victories in their efforts to increase their influence over how the river's water would be used. The committee's formal powers in the São Francisco case were quite similar, but there the federal government demonstrated clearly that it had the power of last resort. Why did new institutions gain political authority in one place and not in another?

One reason might be simply the very powerful interests arrayed against the committee's position. For people who were inspired to participate by what they considered the democratizing potential of decentralized governance, the government's refusal to heed the committee's decision was a betrayal. It was not that they were surprised by the political and economic power of the diversion's supporters. But they hoped that the formal authority vested in the committee's collective decision making would stand up to the pressure. The reversal of the São Francisco committee's rejection of the diversion made the limits of the statutory power of river basin committees throughout the country glaringly apparent. For many people, it revealed the decentralizing, participatory design of the new institutions as a fraud. But in fact, although what happened in the São Francisco may have violated their expectations it did not violate the letter of the law, which was imprecise as to the powers of river basin committees but was quite clear in granting a majority of seats on the national council to the federal government. Perhaps the levels of frustration and disappointment reflect a naive reading of the water reform laws. After all, why would government agencies give up power voluntarily in the name of the abstract principles expressed in the law without enforcement mechanisms and even when elected officials had a lot to lose?

Another explanation might focus on the fact that the Piracicaba committee negotiated from a more moderate stance, proposing compensation and co-governance but not an end to the water transfer (which, in any case, had been going on for a long time). In this respect, in the Piracicaba case, the possibility that the government could have forced a decision on the committee was never an issue, because negotiations were successful and demands were contained. The São Francisco case was much more politicized, and the situation polarized into two extreme options. In this sense, one might say that the Piracicaba actors did not really test committee authority over water allocations in the basin because they did not directly oppose more powerful interests, as occurred in the São Francisco case.

That the São Francisco River diversion was linked to the maintenance of a governing coalition did give it unusually high visibility. Most people think about rivers in connection to things that touch their everyday lives—dirty water, droughts, and floods affect everyone, after all. By contrast, deliberation over interventions in river management usually takes place in the context of long-term plans for the future, expressed through abstract debates about water flows, pollutants, land use patterns, and so on, hardly material for prime-time television. But when the ex-governor of Ceará Ciro Gomes designated the diversion as the payment he would require for his part in a delicately balanced political alliance among parties, he pushed the politics of river basin management into a different sphere. Unlike any other case discussed in this book, the São Francisco River Basin Committee operated in the eye of the hurricane of party politics. The project's most powerful northeastern political opponents, led by Bahia ex-governor Antonio Carlos Magalhães until his death in 2007, were part of the political coalition that supported the Cardoso government; in Lula's government, power shifted to supporters of the diversion. Under these conditions, there was no space for adhering to principles that few outside the sphere of water politics had ever really thought about before.

The São Francisco case thus seems to suggest that when powerful groups mobilize they can override organizations with a weak hold on formal power.

But we should be wary for two reasons of the interpretation that powerful mobilized interest groups can always trump creative efforts to build practical authority. In the first place, conventional forms of power and acting creatively are not antithetical. In both institutional processes described here, a plethora of powerful actors—energy companies, government agencies, industries, and so on—have maneuvered constantly to hold on to the influence they have or to gain more of it. Even well-positioned actors often need to use their greater facilities inventively to maintain their positions as novel policy arenas such as water resources management are being configured.

Second, it would be a mistake to attribute the different outcomes in the two cases only to the relative strength of political interests in favor of diverting basin waters. In some respects, the stakes were even more dramatic in the Piracicaba case. While Gomes declared that in the future the diversion would provide water for 12 million people, in São Paulo the Cantareira system already *did* supply water for 9 million São Paulo residents. Yet the Piracicaba committee was treated as a partner in negotiations rather than an adversary. Behind that differential treatment was not simply the fact that the committee took up a more moderate stance; more important, there was a long history of institution building.

In the Piracicaba region, actors had been building new river basin institutions for decades before the Cantareira decision provided an opportunity to demonstrate how much power they had acquired. By the early 2000s, those institutions had aggregated substantial technical capacity and experience. Through a long process of interaction, the committees had established a relationship with the state government in which the latter regularly presented projects for their approval (without being obligated to do so) and the committees occasionally (but by no means always) rejected them. This slow process of building the authority of the Piracicaba institutions occurred both *within* those bodies and *between* them and the state government institutions. That is, it involved building both capabilities and recognition. To build capabilities, the group pooled local resources, designed and executed projects, and accumulated technical and political experience over several decades. Such capability was one of the key means for building recognition (Carpenter 2000; Carpenter 2010). The state government and the river basin organizations incrementally established a relationship of power sharing, in which each side saw the other as legitimate interlocutors. When the time came for a showdown, there was, essentially, no showdown, only an extension of that relationship to a new level of power sharing.

The construction of the São Francisco committee occurred under entirely different conditions. First, it was a proposal that came from outside. The committee had no organizational history of its own; there was no autonomous structure like the consortium that already represented basin interests. Second, despite the fact that the members of the committee brought with them substantial technical and political resources—many were high-level state government officials or worked for large water users—as a group, these actors had little chance to demonstrate those capacities prior to the conflict. Even leaving aside the organizational complexity involved in dealing with a territory as large and as politically fragmented as the São Francisco basin, the committee had to mobilize resources and work through its relationship with the government (the *recognition* aspect) at the moment of the showdown rather than building up capabilities and relationships under less contentious conditions. There just was not enough time to build practical authority.

The effectiveness of the gradual accumulation of practical authority in the Piracicaba basin was less visible to many observers than the public demonstration that the São Francisco committee did not have such authority. Arguing about the meaning of the latter case was itself a practical experience that influenced the water management reform more generally. For some observers, the cup was actually half full. They argued that by taking the issue to the committee at all, the government recognized it as a site of decision making and by appealing the decision to the national council, it was actually validating the law as it was written (Interview 30, 2011). Others credited the committee's efforts, along with the intense mobilization around the issue, with ensuring that the revitalization of the São Francisco River project (the investment the committee supported) remained on the political agenda (Viana 2011). Nonetheless, those who hoped that the water reform would automatically produce new decentralized institutions with authority became much more skeptical after the São Francisco affair. Many of the civil society groups we interviewed in recent years cite it as reason enough for not participating in river basin committees at all. Those who continue to opt in to the system often do so with a much more pragmatic understanding of how hard it is to build practical authority.

CHAPTER 7

Building Practical Authority from Outside the State

The construction of the practical authority necessary to make new institutions operational depends on the ability of organizers to draw creatively on resources and relationships available within the political-institutional context around them. In most of our account so far, this has involved struggles for influence among actors in federal, state, and local governments involved in shaping this new approach to water management. Existing governmental units have responded differently to efforts to set up new kinds of organizations (committees, agencies) at the novel territorial level of river basins. Generally speaking, both supporters and opponents have been widely dispersed among functional units and governmental levels. As an issue that cut across many different areas, integrated river basin management usually has not had either natural allies or adversaries among government agencies. Instead, its supporters or potential supporters were spread out among a wide range of public agencies. They did not necessarily know of one another's existence, and even when they did, it was not always clear at the outset which of them, if any, was in a position to help get things off the ground.

Although the formal recognition of a river basin committee or agency required what we have referred to as state-exclusive forms of authority, this was not necessarily the case for most of the activities involved in setting up and activating these new organizations. Where reforming water management did not elicit strong commitment from well-placed individuals or agencies with the resources to bring others into line, organizing meant assembling support from dispersed supporters and winning new ones, creating networks, and building a core of competent and committed people willing to do the work. Many elements of practical authority could be built from distributed resources and relationships that were not exclusively governmental. Organizers could try to develop new practices by calling on the support of prominent individuals, scientific knowledge, institutional prestige of universities, or the experience and organizing know-how of social movements. In several of the cases we studied, the core organizational practices for activating the new water management system came from and remain to this day located primarily outside the state yet were nonetheless directed at generating practical authority for a public institution. We focus on two such cases in this chapter.

By recognizing the contribution that nonstate actors make to constructing public institutions, we are blurring a number of categorical distinctions. The relationship between civil society and the state is not reducible to making demands and providing services, nor is the relationship between social movements and the state always adversarial. The analytical tools that social scientists use to study advocacy campaigns, social movements, and contestation can be equally useful for studying struggles for influence within state bureaucratic organizations, in which actors mobilize resources, pay attention to political opportunities, and even employ such classic campaign strategies as seeking to leverage the support of an outside agency to win a battle within their own (see, e.g., Tarrow 2011; McAdam, McCarthy, and Zald 1996; Keck and Sikkink 1998). Fligstein and McAdam (2012) make a similar point in their call for a shift in focus to "strategic action fields." These widely used strategies and the practices they generate are not contained within separate arenas of state and society; networks of individuals and organizations that cross those lines meet in the functional equivalents of neighborhood bars or church basements to work out their next steps, not just in Brazil but also all over the world.

In this chapter, we focus on two cases where the struggle to build the practical authority of river basin committees was led by nonstate actors. In the Itajaí basin in the southern state of Santa Catarina, the committee grew out of an initiative involving local university professors and business leaders in the valley. Although formally created by government decree, for much of its history, the state government paid little attention to it or, for that matter, to water management at all. As the committee slowly developed its ability to solve small-scale problems, gained access to funding, and built a broader audience, its stature in the basin grew. Yet even so, it could not convince the state government to invest in the kinds of policies it proposed. Even after a devastating flood pushed the state to finally begin investing in the river basin, the state still managed to sideline the committee, despite its years of building widely recognized capabilities on water policy.

The Velhas committee in Minas Gerais was established by the state government agency responsible for water management. However, early in its existence, it was essentially a formality; the committee came to life only when it was taken over by the Manuelzão Project, an organizing initiative led by university professors that had been promoting grassroots environmental action in communities throughout the basin. The Manuelzão Project eventually accumulated enough expertise and credibility to persuade high-level state government officials to adopt its policy proposals as government priorities. When Manuelzão activists took control of the Velhas committee, they managed to infuse the latter with some of the project's accumulated practical authority, invigorating what had been a relatively weak official body. This rather circuitous path to building practical authority led the Velhas committee to become one of the few river basin committees in Brazil with real power to decide about how government agencies invest in the basin.

As examples of how nonstate actors played central roles in helping committees gain the authority to influence what other government organizations do, these two cases suggest that at least to some extent, practical authority can be built outside the state, without relying on formal mechanisms of state power. Their strategies of *engagement* involved both bringing together people and organizations within the river basin and making connections with other organizations, especially the state agencies that had crucial decision-making power in water management. These actors also sought ways to communicate ideas and demonstrate capabilities to broader publics, broadcasting their goals and achievements. They experimented by identifying problems on a scale where they could address them and by developing their problem-solving capabilities. These processes are linked, often in the same activities.

Engagement has a double meaning in English: it can be an act of mutual commitment or a moment of conflict—engaging the enemy. In the committees explored in this chapter, organizers engaged with other actors and organizations with overlapping claims to authority in both ways: sometimes they managed to find common interests that would entice other organizations to work with them; sometimes they advocated changes in direction that met with intense opposition. The comparison between the Itajaí and Velhas cases suggests that the former strategy may be more successful in conditions where the balance of power remains strongly tilted in favor of traditional decision-making organizations. The leaders of these organizations were not competing for power or prestige with those in state agencies that might at times have come into conflict with them. They portrayed their efforts to influence decisions in non-zero-sum terms, differentiating them from the high-stakes conflicts portrayed in chapter 6, especially the one involving the São Francisco diversion. Both committees did eventually try to influence decisions over major public works, something that could not be done by keeping their heads down. This required becoming involved in public debates not only over technical aspects of water governance but also about state politics and policy. In the Velhas case, activists were more successful than in the Itajaí committee, in part because credit for the solutions they espoused was more likely to accrue to powerful politicians.

THE ITAJAÍ RIVER BASIN (STATE OF SANTA CATARINA)

Civil society actors were behind the construction of the Itajaí committee from start to finish. In fact, their efforts to create a committee were a response to state government omission in flood control and other water problems in the basin. Frustrated with the ineffectiveness of existing policy institutions, they set out to create their own. Beginning with small-scale actions funded by the resources available to members themselves (through the local university, private sector, and municipal governments), the committee managed to put together a strong network of organizations capable of implementing projects and mobilizing large numbers of people. The capabilities they built through those practices helped them win a major grant through which the organization extended and amplified those projects. In this way, the committee is a good example of how to build practical authority from the bottom up. However, the state government's resistance to the committee's proposals set a firm limit to how far that authority could go.

The Itajaí River flows from the interior of Santa Catarina state in southern Brazil to the sea, about 100 kilometers north of the state capital, Florianópolis. With a mixed economy of middle-sized farming, crafts industry, and software development, the region has lower levels of social inequality and poverty than most of Brazil. The largest city is Blumenau, with a population of 302,000 in 2006. The total population of the basin is about 1 million (Mais 2001). It is a mountainous region, where towns and farms often grow up on hillsides and where dramatic floods regularly wreak devastation in the lower valley.

Although the National Department of Sanitation Works (DNOS) began to build flood control dams along the Itajaí River in the 1970s, these failed to prevent horrific flooding in the 1980s. In 1990, DNOS was dismantled as part of a federal structural adjustment program. A year later, another flood inundated towns along the river, especially the largest, Blumenau. Groups in the basin, worried that the state government was not picking up the slack from federal cutbacks, began to organize on their own. They were encouraged by the passage of a new state water law, introduced with little fanfare in 1994.[1] Although the law called for the creation of river basin committees, the state government did nothing to make that happen.

---

1. The law was designed by a commission created to provide an institutional response to the flooding problem, headed by engineers who had connections to the water engineering community in other states and in Brasília (Interview 141, Florianópolis, 2012).

In 1996, Blumenau's Chamber of Commerce and Industry (ACIB) called a meeting of civic and university groups from the region to discuss the continued threat of flooding. Participants realized that the water law offered an opportunity for doing the kind of basin-wide organizing they had long considered necessary. Water specialists at the Regional University of Blumenau (FURB) immediately took the lead. They contacted water users, civic organizations, municipal governments, state agencies, and business associations and assembled a committee of 65 members,[2] which had been meeting for a year when it received official recognition from the State Water Resources Council.[3] Santa Catarina's first committee was thus an initiative of local civil society rather than the state.

The prime movers in organizing the committee were members of a group of specialists critical of the dominant approach to water management espoused by the state government and by the then defunct DNOS. Beate Frank (2003, 47), one of the FURB professors involved, argued that conventional approaches to flood management in the basin misread the cause of flooding and thus misdirected attempts to prevent it. Conventional approaches concentrated on the river channel itself, with a focus on protecting the city of Blumenau. They prescribed hard engineering solutions exclusively, for example, widening the river channel or building reservoirs, and paid no attention to such soft engineering measures as afforestation and land use regulation. Yet the cause of chronic flooding lay in the fact that the broader drainage system was not absorbing enough water before it got to the river channel. Critics of the traditional approach contended that reducing the flooding problem thus demanded construction of smaller-scale infrastructure throughout the basin and soft engineering measures to transform land use patterns and increase lag time before the water reaches the river. Frank became one of the leaders of the effort to promote this alternative vision of water management.

The committee's first initiative was a 1997 workshop to develop an emergency flood prevention plan. Participants produced a series of documents that analyzed current policies and proposed both a new flood alert system and new mechanisms for administering flood control reservoirs. Frank informed the federal Ministry of the Interior, responsible for dam maintenance, that the meeting was to occur. Two weeks later, a ministry envoy arrived in the basin. Soon thereafter, the ministry signed an agreement with

2. It is noteworthy that for several years, the committee held no formal elections for seats—according to committee leaders, the original organizers simply called everyone up in the basin who they thought needed to be there. The first election took place only in 2004.

3. The speed of recognition differentiates the Itajaí experience from some other cases, such as the Paranoá committee, whose organizers waited for years for the government to decree the committee into official existence.

the state government to resume the flood control infrastructure program that had languished since DNOS's extinction seven years before.[4] In effect, by convening a wide array of groups from local organizations, universities, business firms, and municipalities in the basin, the workshop functioned as a show of force that pressured an inactive government to get moving (Frank and Bohn 2003). This immediate response gave the committee a boost of credibility.

This example illustrates the transformative effect of two kinds of engagement. First, holding meetings helped build local networks and also provided venues in which to discuss problems. Besides creating new relationships, this process influenced ideas. People who had previously mobilized on a local scale began to discuss the river basin as a whole. The FURB group took advantage of the new network to disseminate an alternative approach to water management. Many activities combined network building with idea dissemination. In one of the most innovative, a group of mayors, businesspeople, researchers, and other notables traveled to Europe and visited river basin organizations specializing in soft engineering approaches to water management (Mais 2001). Second, the workshop marked the beginning of another kind of engagement. Frank was certain that government support was essential to bring the flooding problem under control, but state officials continued to drag their feet. Her strategy was to shift scales of action: letting more receptive (and better-staffed) federal agencies know that local actors were mobilizing helped put pressure on otherwise unresponsive state agencies. The fact that those initial moves produced concrete results encouraged participants to stay on board. This is the sort of "intermediate outcome" that Ansell and Gash (2008) believe produces organizing capacity and banks the trust needed to sustain future action.

The payoff in terms of recognition of the committee's practical authority appeared to arrive a year later, when the state government requested input on a flood prevention project to be funded by the Japanese International Cooperation Agency (JICA). The original proposal involved investment in just the kind of big infrastructure projects that committee members believed ineffective. The committee held another workshop and came out with the suggestion that JICA incorporate a series of soft measures (e.g., reforestation) and invest not only in infrastructure in the river channel but also elsewhere in the basin. There is no way of knowing whether the committee's proposals would have changed the project, however, because the Japanese funding fell through.

---

4. Interview 79, telephone interview, 2011.

Despite this setback, for participants the process of designing an alternative proposal reinforced agreement on their alternative vision (Mais 2001). Rather than wait for government investments, the committee set off to implement that vision with whatever resources it could garner. A key part involved beginning its own riverside reforestation program, which operated mainly on the basis of voluntary contributions by committee members, including local businesses and municipal governments. This experiment strengthened ties among organizations in the basin and helped develop practical skills. Participants learned the various arts of growing seedlings, persuading farmers to move cattle and crops off riverbank areas, and working with extremely understaffed, underbudgeted rural municipalities. The knowledge and experience that the group gained through this process became the basis for a grant proposal submitted in 2004 to a funding competition for environmental protection projects sponsored by Petrobras, Brazil's state-owned petroleum company. The committee won 3 million Brazilian reais (about U.S. $1,000,000) for the Piava Project (Interview 70, Blumenau, 2007). Thus, small-scale experimentation helped the organization develop capabilities that won it access to more substantial resources.

The money was deposited into the accounts of the Itajaí Water Agency. This was a private foundation that the committee leadership had created in 2001 to operate as its executive secretariat, in the expectation that the organization would need some kind of official existence in order to implement projects and programs. Technically, it was the first officially recognized water agency in Brazil.[5] However, in the absence of water pricing, the agency had been essentially a formality, operating out of FURB's Environmental Research Institute. Now the Piava Project afforded it the means to have its own headquarters and staff. About 25 professionals and 20 student interns began to travel around the basin to work both with municipal government officials, helping them design environmental policy, and with farmers, cajoling them to voluntarily increase the forest cover of riverbanks and hillsides (Interview, 77, Blumenau, 2007).[6]

Besides working directly with farmers and local governments, the committee sought to build a broader audience for its efforts. From 1999 on, it sponsored a yearly educational campaign called Water Week, originally organized to commemorate World Water Day (March 22). The campaign

5. While the federal law requires that agencies can be officially created only after the initiation of water charging, this kind of organization was not even mentioned in the Santa Catarina law. The Itajaí agency was made official by a resolution of the State Water Council. On the origins of the agency, see http://www.comiteitajai.org.br/portal/index.php/agenciaorigem.html, accessed July 12, 2012.

6. http://www.comiteitajai.org.br, accessed September 4, 2004.

involved more than 200,000 people a year by 2003, including members of several hundred local organizing committees and thousands of schoolchildren. Water Week was a way to both broadcast ideas (and enhance public awareness of the committee) and build concrete relationships, since organizing committees in each municipality involved local residents (especially teachers) in preparations for the event. Many of those same people later got involved directly in the committee or in the activities of the Piava Project (Interview 66, Florianópolis, 2007; Interviews 68, 69, Blumenau, 2007).

These various efforts helped build the committee's reputation as an important public actor in the region. The recognition did not come from the state government, which was basically uninterested in water management. The state environmental agency had a sparsely staffed water resources department, whose few employees were badly paid and mostly on loan from other agencies. Many of them sympathized with the committee's efforts and even endorsed its alternative conception of water management. But they could do little to help (Interviews 66 and 141, Florianópolis, 2007, 2012). More robust recognition came from other organizations, especially municipal governments in the interior. Local governments increasingly turned to the committee and the Piava Project as sources of ideas, programs, and even small amounts of funding for local projects (Interview 77, Blumenau, 2007). Although Water Week broadened the audience for the committee's message (Mais 2001), with the Petrobras funding it could scale up its activities. In 2007, this was reinforced by a renewal of the Petrobras grant both for continuing activities within the Itajaí basin and for working in other river basins.

At the same time as the committee and its basin agency built their reputations, its leaders intensified their efforts to get the water management instruments cited in the legislation off the ground, especially the basin plan and water charging. Earlier in the decade, raising the issue of water pricing had proven politically delicate: an attempt in 2001 to discuss a proposal with local communities had led farmers to protest against the committee (Liberato 2004). Although the committee was not going to make that mistake a second time, its members did hope that eventually, user fees could produce an autonomous funding stream for the kinds of alternative programs they defended. After all, the Petrobras money would not last forever, and it seemed unlikely that the state government could be counted on for support. But getting charging off the ground without government help was a tricky proposition.

A first step was to initiate discussion of a river basin plan, something the committee decided to do in the course of Water Week activities. This approach got local groups involved in a participatory diagnosis of water problems in their part of the basin, with a focus on a different theme each year (Interview 65, Foz de

Iguaçu, 2007). The river basin plan, approved in 2010, was built on those local discussions. However, both the planning itself and the eventual prospect of instituting water use permits and fees had to be based on information about how much water was actually being consumed in the basin, by whom, and from what water sources. Registries of water use are hard to put together, as we saw earlier in the discussion of water charging in the Paraíba do Sul basin. It is particularly difficult in a region like the Itajaí basin, where water use is dispersed among many thousands of small users rather than concentrated in a few big ones.

The Itajaí committee spent two years trying to come up with a methodology for registering users, who should do it, with what software, and so forth. With the help of users' associations from different sectors, the committee managed to negotiate an agreement with the state Secretariat for Sustainable Development, in which the user organizations would promote registration and the state government and the Itajaí River Basin Agency would provide training. In a six-month period in 2007, they registered about 8,000 users (Interview 66, Florianópolis, 2007).[7]

A year later, just as the second phase of the Piava Project was getting under way, devastating floods once again hit the region. More than 100 people lost their lives, and 80,000 had to leave their homes, largely because of mudslides. The 2008 disaster was a harsh reminder that dealing with water problems in the basin would require a much deeper commitment by the state government, especially to land use planning. In the view of the committee leadership, most of the impacts of the disaster resulted from the untrammeled expansion of farms and cities on hillsides that did not have the capacity to soak up sudden localized rainfall (Frank and Sevegnani 2009).

However, instead of bolstering support for the committee's alternative vision of water management, the opposite occurred: the catastrophic impact of the floods opened up new sources of funding for building infrastructure in the river channel.[8] One funding agency was JICA, which returned to the state in 2009 and proposed to help the government design a flood control plan. The state agency responsible for public works pulled the plan off the shelf that the committee had objected to years before and

---

7. Frank estimates the total number of users in the basin at around 30,000 but claims that all of the users of significant volumes of water were registered (e-mail communication with the authors, February 29, 2012). See also information available on the website of the Itajaí committee: http://www.comiteitajai.org.br.

8. Even more ironically, the disaster coincided with the emergence in Santa Catarina of a conservative farmers' movement that sought to weaken environmental restrictions on rural land use. Their efforts to change state legislation sparked a movement among actors allied with the agricultural sector throughout the country to change the national Forest Code, leading in 2012 to the passage of legislation that many observers believe will promote further deforestation.

proposed to work with JICA specialists to bring it up to date. Itajaí committee members found out about the initiative when a delegation from Japan came to visit the basin. Since the Japanese engineers were unaware of the prior round of negotiations, Frank took them around the basin, where they met with local leaders and committee members (Interview 144, Blumenau, 2009). A member of the Japanese delegation told us later that they had been impressed by the level of community mobilization and by the technical sophistication of their alternative proposals. But, he noted, there were major disagreements among stakeholders. He meant that representatives of state government agencies were very much opposed to those alternatives (Interview 78, Tokyo, 2010).

Ever since the 2008 flood, the effort to influence decisions about investments in disaster prevention has been at the top of the Itajaí committee's agenda. The JICA plan, the proposal the government had drawn up with the help of the Japanese agency, became the central issue in contention. Revealing fractures within the state government, the Itajaí group managed to get some agencies to support guidelines that would have precluded various components in the JICA plan, while others continued to insist on a hard engineering approach.

Itajaí leaders—especially Frank—began to seek new allies for the committee's approach to water management. Immediately after the disaster, the head of the state science and technology agency—an academic with close personal ties to the conservative governor—invited her and two other committee members to join a technical-scientific task force called Grupo Técnico Científico (GTC) to come up with proposals for disaster prevention. The group produced a disaster prevention and mitigation plan that largely subscribed to the alternative approach the committee espoused. The plan focused on land use management and did not propose any new hydraulic projects, only the improvement of existing ones (Grupo Técnico Científico 2009).

Frank also made use of her position as a member of the State Water Resources Council. The Itajaí committee formally endorsed the GTC plan and then forwarded it to the council in the hope that a higher-level formal ratification would give it more political credibility. Frank had long held a seat as a university representative on the council. When she retired from her university position, she managed to obtain a new seat on a technical subcommittee of the council as a representative of the Brazilian Water Resources Association. In that capacity, she convinced the council to approve the GTC plan as guidelines for state government flood prevention policy and also to ratify Itajaí committee resolutions that directed the JICA plan to follow the GTC guidelines.

A year later (2011), the state government disbanded the GTC and established a new Civil Defense Secretariat, headed by a vociferous supporter of big projects. Although she was by then working as a consultant for the Secretariat of Sustainable Development organizing training courses for other river basin committees in the state and was no longer formally a member of the Itajaí committee, Frank still devoted her spare time to writing technical reports and committee and council resolutions that affirmed the legal status of the GTC proposal (Interview 142, Florianopolis, 2012). The battle, it would seem, had become a head-on collision between the committee and the state agencies involved over who would decide how the government was going to invest in the Itajaí basin. To fight that battle, the committee builders took advantage of the complexity of the organizational ecology by seeking to infiltrate multiple decision-making arenas whose support could bolster their cause. At the time of this writing, the outcomes of this conflict were uncertain.

THE VELHAS RIVER BASIN (STATE OF MINAS GERAIS)

The Velhas committee is one of the few in our sample in which major committee decisions were transformed into government policy. Understanding how this occurred requires zooming out to view the story of the Velhas committee in the context of a broader set of organizational processes, two of which distinguish this case from the others we studied. First, around the same time as the Velhas committee was first established, a separate organizing initiative targeting water-related problems in the basin developed out of the school of public health at the Federal University of Minas Gerais and evolved into a broad-based network of university professors, civil society groups, local governments, state bureaucrats, and businesses. The Manuelzão Project's approach was to organize grassroots community groups in municipalities throughout the basin, focused on local problem solving, with the help of specialists in its network; it was also very good at publicizing its efforts and at mobilizing locally meaningful symbols and images to amplify its message. While the Velhas basin committee was attempting to mobilize a quorum of members to pass bylaws, the Manuelzão committee was fostering widely distributed local capabilities and recognition, building relationships that eventually rebounded to the credit of the committee.

A second characteristic that distinguished this case from the Itajaí committee was the institutional context within which the Velhas organizers (in the committee and the Manuelzão Project) operated: a modernizing state government undertaking an administrative reform (in a state with a history of such efforts) that was looking for tangible goals that would signal the effectiveness of this political strategy. Velhas organizers were able to link into this reform effort, getting the state government to accept and implement their ideas for water resources plan for the basin. This resulted in notable improvements in the condition of water resources in the basin, something that very few of the other organizing efforts we have studied have been able to produce.

More than 700 kilometers long, the Velhas River (Rio das Velhas, "river of the old women") flows through a huge region of dramatic contrasts. The river's upper portion passes through the state capital, Belo Horizonte, the nation's third-largest metropolitan area, where until recently it took on such a heavy load of untreated pollutants that aquatic life could not survive there. Downstream from the city, the river crosses a large, impoverished region of extensive cattle ranching and subsistence farms before flowing into the São Francisco River, whose story was discussed in chapter 6. Along the way, the river receives clean water from tributaries, especially from the Serra do Cipó, a national park known for its waterfalls and mountain trails. Bringing such diversity of interests and problems under the purview of one organization would not be a simple task.

As in Santa Catarina, water management in Minas Gerais has historically been precarious. Until the mid-2000s, the state water agency, Minas Gerais Water Management Institute (IGAM), was understaffed and underfunded. There were no sewage treatment plants serving the metropolitan area of Belo Horizonte until 2002. In 1993, the state government negotiated a loan from the World Bank's Water Supply and Sanitation Program to finance construction of two sewage treatment plants there (World Bank 1993). One of the loan's conditions was that the government produce a water resources plan for the Velhas basin and establish a water agency to implement it. However, soon after that agreement, the state assembly passed a water law stipulating that river basin agencies had to be set up by river basin committees. In 1997, under pressure from the bank to complete the project, the state government resolved to set up a committee to get the agency approved and held a series of rushed meetings over a two-week period to choose members. The state's first river basin committee was thus enacted by government decree, with a predefined agenda. It proceeded to do nothing at all for several years, unable even to mobilize a quorum to pass its own statutes and elect its own executive board (Interviews 43, 47, Belo Horizonte, 2001; Interviews 53, 54, Belo Horizonte, 2003).

The same year that the committee was formed, a group of professors from the Federal University of Minas Gerais's School of Medicine created the Manuelzão Project (named after a popular historical backwoodsman of the region) and decided to focus their work on the Velhas River Basin. The idea grew out of an internship program that sent medical students to work at health clinics throughout the state. Perceiving that many illnesses were related to the lack of clean drinking water, the professors in charge began to encourage interns to work with community organizations to connect water and health problems by organizing river cleanups and public education programs (Interviews 38, 44, Belo Horizonte, 2001; Interview 62, Belo Horizonte, 2008).

The project's leader, Apolo Heringer Lisboa, was a charismatic doctor-activist, with a long history of radicalism (he had been a member of an underground urban guerrilla group in the 1960s and was imprisoned and exiled during the 1970s). Unlike the technical experts who, at that time, were the dominant force on the Velhas committee, Lisboa spoke a fervent, almost millennarian language about the need to revert the devastating environmental impacts of economic development. The approach focused less on technically complicated water management instruments and more on practical problem solving and a transformation of consciousness.

The project started off by setting up Manuelzão committees, loosely organized community groups that brought together schoolteachers, business leaders, volunteers, and politicians. Manuelzão activists—often medical interns—organize these committees around specific problems; the project provides organizing support, locates researchers willing to study specific issues, and brings local committees together to tackle larger-scale projects. By 2005, 80 of these committees had been created. The organizing process was different in each case. For example, the leader of the Cipó committee, concerned with the previously mentioned national park, was the head of a local chamber of commerce who brought in business leaders, scientists involved in research projects in the park, and mayors. Their main focus was controlling the environmental impacts of tourism (Interview 39, Belo Horizonte; Cury 2002). Other committees grew directly out of the medical internship program. An activist in the Alto Vera Cruz neighborhood, who worked in a community center, told us that she watched the local stream become an open sewer over a 30-year period:

> One day, Manuelzão interns began to work at the center. They noticed that the children who came back most often with worms lived near the stream. We did a study that proved that. Then we created a forum of three neighborhoods. The community did not want to turn the stream into a closed sewer. We wanted that stream back...because our neighborhood does not have a park. (Interview 37, Belo Horizonte, 2001)

In effect, by organizing local actors around concrete problems and finding solutions for them, the Manuelzão Project was building many local

networks and helping them develop their own capabilities to solve problems. At the same time, as a sort of umbrella organization, the Manuelzão
Project helped link these different local networks with one another—creating a much broader and more powerful network and accomplishing a
bridging function that simultaneously enhanced Manuelzão's positional
power and prestige (Burt 1995).[9] The effect was both to scale up capabilities and to build recognition. For example, the state sanitation company
was among the first government organizations to recognize the importance
of the Manuelzão Project, a recognition that came in the form of substantial funding for its activities. By 2001, the project had an annual budget of
about 400,000 reais (approximately U.S. $175,000) for 14 subprojects,
ranging from research to ecotourism to environmental education in schools
throughout the basin (Interviews 38 and 44, Belo Horizonte, 2001). For
the most part, the Manuelzão committees implemented these projects.

Gaining recognition involved more than gaining a reputation for problem solving; it also involved a certain amount of marketing, or what we
have called broadcasting. The Manuelzão Project paid a lot of attention to
its communication subproject, carried out as an extension program of the
university's journalism department. Professors and students wrote stories
to publicize the project's many partnerships and to make technical information understandable to ordinary people both for the project's quarterly
newsletter (with a circulation of 100,000) and in other material.

In 2003, the project increased its visibility and dramatized the dire condition of the waterway by organizing a kayak expedition down the Velhas
River, from its headwaters to where it met the São Francisco.[10] To get through
the most polluted area, the kayakers wore gas masks. The Manuelzão leadership and a team of journalism students, researchers, and activists stopped
daily at riverside towns. Manuelzão committees in each locale organized
festive rallies to celebrate the arrival of the expedition, with local music,
dancing, and political speeches. The town of Honorário Bicalho even
decreed a municipal holiday to receive the expedition so residents could
meet the boats. Immediately after the expedition ended, the group organized a march through the city of Belo Horizonte and a closing ceremony
in which it put forward a major policy proposal to the government and the
general public: Meta 2010 (Goal 2010) proposed a broad-based effort to

9. In his seminal work in social network analysis, Ronald Burt (1995) associated entrepreneurship with bridging previously unconnected networks (across "structural holes"), a form of
brokerage that simultaneously holds great promise and is initially quite fragile.

10. Three kayakers rowed the entire length of the river, starting by descending a treacherous
waterfall with rock-climbing equipment. Others joined in as the river got big enough for other
kinds of boats. A beautiful documentary, in Portuguese, can be found on YouTube: http://
www.youtube.com/watch?v=3CYca2Iwf3U.

clean up the Velhas River with the aim of making it possible to navigate, fish, and swim in by the end of the decade. The extent of media coverage of the monthlong voyage surprised participants. In addition to press releases and coverage in the Manuelzão newsletter, the expedition got a total of 72 minutes of television coverage (Mafra 2011, 5).[11]

The visibility of the Manuelzão Project, the expedition, and Meta 2010 gave Lisboa, the Manuelzão leader, the credentials to set up a meeting with the state governor, newly elected Aécio Neves, and José Carlos Carvalho, his secretary of the environment (who figured in chapter 6 as a protagonist in the struggle over the São Francisco diversion). At the January 2004 meeting, Lisboa convinced them to make the Velhas cleanup project a government priority.[12] Immediately after the meeting, staff at the state environmental agency reported receiving the order to put the cleanup on the institutional agenda (Mairinque 2010, 100). In March of the same year, the governor signed a Manuelzão-proposed commitment letter (*termo de compromisso*), promising to invest in sanitation infrastructure, solid waste management, and land use planning to clean up the river (Mairinque 2010, 99).

In sum, the Manuelzão Project had gradually gained recognition based on its capabilities, having assembled for local problem solving and larger project execution a broad alliance of actors throughout the river basin and having won even broader public support. Capabilities grew out of small-scale problem-solving efforts and also from the creation of a network that connected actors throughout the basin allowing Manuelzão to implement broader projects and programs. That network also helped the organization broadcast its mission, for example by organizing the local events around the kayak expedition that gained media attention. That public recognition (from the media) in addition to the organization's reputation as a key problem solver helped produce political recognition in the form of a meeting with high-level political actors, who saw an opportunity to concentrate government resources on a popular proposal.

Although the Rio das Velhas committee was initially overshadowed by the organizing success of Manuelzão, it ultimately benefited from the institution-building practices of the Manuelzão organizers and of state-government politicians, underlining the importance of locating the construction of basin committees in the context of broader organizational

---

11. That experience convinced the professors running the communication program to scale up their efforts, transforming the newsletter into a vehicle for communicating with Manuelzão activists and launching weekly radio programs and systematic public relations efforts to place information about Manuelzão in the mainstream media (Antunes, Fonseca and Mafra 2007).

12. The meeting figured in the accounts of several Velhas committee members and Manuelzão activists interviewed in 2008 and also by Mairinque (2010).

ecologies. The way this occurred tells us a lot about how building practical authority is connected to the people, organizations, and projects that sustain new organizations. In this case, the Velhas committee blossomed when it was drawn under the wing of the Manuelzão Project, to some extent becoming a part of that organization.

Initially, the Manuelzão leadership looked on the official but inactive Velhas River Basin Committee with scorn. "The real committees are the Manuelzão committees," many people told us in interviews in 2001 and 2002. But when elections for committee seats were held in 2003, Manuelzão Project leaders maneuvered to get community leaders and municipal governments associated with the project elected to fill them. More than half of committee members voted in that year were also members of the Manuelzão Project. The reasoning behind this effort was that the committee might be able to provide stronger legal backing for the kinds of programs the Manuelzão Project wanted to see implemented, especially by passing a river basin plan endorsing the kinds of cleanup efforts it proposed.

With the Manuelzão Project the dominant force on the basin committee, its director, Lisboa, was elected president in 2003, and joint members tried to infuse the committee with the project's energy, mission, and political networks. Over the next few years, the Velhas committee became increasingly superimposed on the Manuelzão Project, to the point that by 2008 the committee's offices were actually located in the Manuelzão's headquarters at the medical school. Lisboa was reelected as committee president in 2005 and his chosen successor, Manuelzão member Rogério Sepulveda, won the 2007, 2009, and 2011 elections. This was possible because a majority of committee members continued in some way or another to be participants in the Manuelzão Project.

Lisboa instituted a new style of decision making in the committee—creating various technical commissions and encouraging active member participation by delegating tasks and responsibilities (Costa 2008). Interviews we conducted in 2008 often mentioned the fact that decisions were regularly made only after very long debates and consensus building. This new style reflected how much the Manuelzão Project's way of doing things infiltrated the committee. An important decision was to create subcommittees throughout the basin; by 2005, the committee had created nine of them (Sepulveda 2006). Some of these subcommittees became quite active, designing their own projects and proposals and getting funding for them (Interviews 57 and 62, Belo Horizonte, 2008). In this sense, we could say that the Manuelzão approach, along with the experience and networks that came with it, made it possible for the committee to build a decentralized organizational structure that was better adapted to dealing with the size and diversity of the river basin. It is also a good example of bricolage, in transposing a rich set of organizational repertoires (Clemens 1993) from the world of nongovernmental activists into a public arena that had been starved of both resources and agendas for action.

But the most dramatic effect of the Manuelzão Project's success on the practical authority of the committee involved injecting the river basin plan with a capacity to influence government decision making. On December 10, 2004, the Velhas basin committee approved a river basin plan that was fully directed at meeting the Meta 2010 goals (Jornal Manuelzão 2004). The governor's espousal of the 2010 target date meant that the basin committee's planning process would have resonance in actual policy. This was a major financial commitment, involving the construction of waste treatment plants and sewage interceptors in the major subbasins of the Belo Horizonte metropolitan area as well as watershed restoration, environmental education, and extension services and the establishment of a network of monitoring stations to keep track of water quality. Most of the costs for basin cleanup would have to be borne by the state government. As we have learned from so many other case studies, governments are under little legal obligation to implement river basin plans. Their doing so depended on their recognition that a plan was an appropriate and valid guide to action. The committee gained this practical authority through the political negotiations between the Manuelzão leaders and the state government.

Those negotiations continued well after the plan's passage in 2004. Mairinque's (2010) study of the Meta 2010 argues that the state paid little attention to the project until Neves was reelected for a second term. But in 2007, Neves started his second term with a major planning and administrative reform. He was beginning to position himself as a presidential candidate (he ended up not running in 2010 but is a likely candidate in 2014) and understood that the governorship provided a chance to establish credentials as an administrator, in a tradition of planning and good governance that had important precedent in the state's history (Dulci 1999). The reform involved significant investment in developing strategic planning capacity and in projects that would have a visible impact (Corrêa 2007). One of the 57 high-priority projects was the Velhas River cleanup. The commission that had been created to oversee the project (with both Manuelzão and committee representatives) was reorganized and began to meet much more regularly (Mairinque 2010, 78). Around that time, Manuelzão leadership began to remind the governor that he had promised to swim in the river in 2010 (Interview 62, Belo Horizonte, 2008).[13]

---

13. Lisboa told a reporter for the *Estado de Minas* newspaper that the governor had made the promise (Weil 2007). One of our interviewees suggested that the promise had been made as early as 2004 (Interviewee 62, Belo Horizonte, 2008), but we could find no independent documentation of that.

When 2010 arrived, 60 percent of the goals set out in the 2004 river basin plan had been reached. Water quality improvements were substantial enough to restore aquatic life to parts of the river that had been dead for decades (Lisboa 2010). Although the biggest investments were in sewage treatment plants in the basin (Mairinque 2010, 102), the river remained too polluted in the metropolitan region for swimming. The Manuelzão leadership decided that Neves, then on leave from the governorship while campaigning for a Senate seat, could take his promised swim farther downstream. In exchange for this concession, however, during the publicity stunt, the acting governor—who had been vice governor under Neves and was soon to be elected governor for the 2011–2014 term—signed Manuelzão's new proposal, the Meta 2014, to guarantee continued investment in the project in coming years (Mairinque 2010, 102).

Over the years, the state government also invested in putting other components of the water reform into effect and moved toward a system of water pricing by setting up river basin agencies. A team of dedicated water specialists inside IGAM, the state water agency, was largely responsible for pushing these changes forward. The group had been doing its best to institute the water reform since the 1990s, but its efforts got a big boost from the administrative changes of the second Neves government and from the enthusiastic support of Secretary of the Environment Carvalho (Interviews 53, 54, 55, 141, Belo Horizonte, 2002, 2003, 2012). In 2006, the committee announced the creation of the AGB Peixe Vivo (the Living Fish Executive Association to Support River Basin Management).

For its first three years, while the agency got water pricing up and running, its operation was sustained by voluntary donations from water users. This was not easy to achieve, noted one high-level bureaucrat in the administration: Carvalho, secretary of the environment, had to call many business leaders himself and persuade them to contribute (Interview 141, Belo Horizonte, 2012). In the meantime, the committee discussed and approved a pricing scheme. The bills started to go out to users in 2010. By that year, the same agency had also been hired by five other river basin committees in Minas Gerais and by the huge São Francisco committee to administer user fees in their basins. This was a technical agency, with no political or organizational ties to the Manuelzão Project. To decide how to use the revenues produced by the first water charges, the committee depended once again on the decentralized structure and problem-solving tradition it had inherited from the Manuelzão project. The first four projects were designed by subcommittees, each one addressing a different kind of problem: one to map out urban water sources; another to promote sustainable agriculture; a third to reforest degraded lands; and a fourth to help protect water in conservation areas (Theodoro 2011). They were the natural extension of the localized problem solving that the Manuelzão Project had been doing for a decade.

PRACTICES OF INSTITUTION BUILDING

The two stories told in this chapter have in common a bottom-up effort to build problem-solving capabilities, construct networks of actors in defense of particular ideas about water policy, and produce broader audiences for further support. Yet they also differ strikingly in terms of the extent to which those bottom-up efforts won recognition from the top. In both cases activists established dynamic, cohesive organizations able to coordinate local actors, implement projects, get funding, and push for action on major policy questions. But the Itajaí committee came to be regarded as a thorn in the side of state government planning efforts, while the Velhas committee found ways to transform its proposals into policy. It is undeniable that these different outcomes are related to vastly different political contexts. After all, the state government's commitment to administrative reform and modernization made the task in the Velhas basin a lot easier: the Minas Gerais state government was looking for proposals for change. It was also more open to unorthodox contributions, likely reinforced by the multitude of participatory governance experiments underway in the state, particularly in metropolitan Belo Horizonte. The Itajaí committee was calling for a radical shift of government policy away from a traditional public works focus toward a more ecologically oriented but ultimately less state-centric approach. While it appeared self-evident that cleaning up the Velhas River required big sanitation projects, two opposing views of flood control clashed in the Itajaí case. Given the influence of construction interests in Brazilian politics, it is not surprising that proposals including big infrastructure components had an easier time winning government support than proposals that governments eschew hard engineering solutions.

Thus, focusing on microlevel organization does not imply ignoring the power and organization of political or economic interests. Some problems lend themselves to solutions that make everyone happy better than others do. But such solutions do not simply appear out of the ether and present themselves to the appropriate parties for ratification. Our goal here is to demonstrate that the way actors use resources, define problems and goals, and build networks can sometimes be as important as the context itself for explaining their impact. We should not equate practical authority with particular instances of success in influencing government policy. To be sure, in the Velhas River Basin, committee organizers did engage high-level government officials in negotiations over a mutually beneficial undertaking, in which all sides agreed on a plan of action. The implementation of the river basin plan approved by the committee depended on that negotiation. But if practical authority were only a matter of a governor's decision to implement a plan, then it would be standing on pretty thin ice; with the stroke of a pen or a slight shift in congressional coalition, would the Velhas committee lose all that it has gained?

We argue here that the government's endorsement rests not only on the plan's attractiveness to powerful interests at a particular moment in time but also on a robust process of institution building. Committee leaders invested in creating organizations with the capacity to implement projects, to mobilize complex, diverse networks of actors, and to communicate with a broader public. These accomplishments increased the chances that powerful organizations would support the committee, though of course, they could not guarantee it because the organizers we have focused on here are not the only actors in the ecology of institutions within which they operate. The more the committees developed capabilities and the more often others recognized them as important actors in the region, the harder they were to ignore.

The Itajaí committee's perseverance in the face of powerful opposition from the Santa Catarina state government shows that by drawing on multiple sources of authority and validation an organization can sometimes continue to build practical authority despite such resistance. The Itajaí activists have mobilized public opinion in the river basin, have gained access to the media, have occupied spaces in various public decision-making bodies (such as the technical-scientific group for disaster prevention planning and the state water council), and most recently have begun to strategically set the stage for an eventual legal battle. Although the particular struggle in which they are engaged is far from over, the organization has clearly become an influential actor in water politics, and in this sense, it, too, has practical authority.

We maintain that without such organizational efforts, institutional reforms involving the creation of new sites of public decision making are unlikely to be successful or long-lasting. Without the hard labor of organization building, new institutions remain too dependent on the political will of whoever is in power. By creating organizations rather than just decision-making venues, the more successful committees carved out spaces for themselves in their institutional ecologies. The more consolidated those spaces, the better positioned they were to vie with many others in their company for influence over public decision making. In the following sections, we briefly call attention to some aspects of this organizational process that the two cases described in this chapter help draw out.

Translating and Transcending: Generating New Ideas for Action

As chapter 5 showed, one of the key problems committees faced was how to adapt an ambiguous and incomplete law to the problems local actors identified. The task involved translating abstract water management functions (planning, charging) into specific, situated problem-solving activities. It also involved transcending the limitations built into the water law that focused narrowly on water use, leaving land use and environmental management to other spheres.

In both cases discussed in this chapter, actors broke with the hydraulic perspective on water use, espousing alternative ways of thinking about water management. The Itajaí activists' critique fits with well-established international thinking on integrated water management that emphasizes a holistic view of the river basin. Organizers in the Velhas basin brought in a discourse from outside the conventional world of water management, by focusing initially on preventive health care; they also drew upon organizational repertoires more common to social movements than to expert communities. These alternative sets of ideas about water management provided actors in both basins with ideas about what to do: plant seedlings, build small-scale drainage infrastructure, revitalize streams, build treatment plants. Only after many years of working toward those goals did the committees begin to implement the water management instruments stipulated in the water laws, now reformulated in terms of those ideas. In the Itajaí basin, the abstract notion of a river basin plan was translated into a series of programs that embodied an alternative proposal for disaster prevention. In the Velhas basin, the Meta 2010 served as the basis of a formal river basin plan, thus according legal status to a set of plans and programs that the Manuelzão Project members supported.

While many Brazilian water reformers we spoke to thought the first task of committees was to implement the legally mandated water management instruments,[14] in both committees explored in this chapter, the organizers put off this task until after more basic capacities were developed. Creativity involved more than just alternative ways of thinking about water management. Actors also had to rethink expectations about what river basin committees should do. In both Itajaí and Velhas, the leaders realized that before tackling the formal mandates of the new water reform laws they should engage in smaller-scale actions that would help them hone their ideas more precisely, develop local capabilities for understanding specific situations and devising specific solutions, and build alliances of actors around those alternative ideas. The elaboration of a river basin plan took on an entirely new meaning when built on the basis of these experiences.

---

14. We could not possibly count either the number of times we have heard the complaint that a committee is acting like an NGO, that it has not begun to implement the water management instruments, or how many training courses were premised on the idea that members of such committees are doing it wrong, somehow, because they do not properly understand the meaning of the law and the precise nature of their formal attributions.

More than Just Good Ideas: Experimentation and Engagement

Devising alternative ideas could not be separated from action. To make their ideas speak, committee organizers had to experiment with actions that produced effects or resonated with local communities; they also had to actively engage with other organizations in their environment. We found that actors developed authority only as they practiced engagement and experimentation, part of a perpetual process of reshaping how their institutional ecology was understood and who or what was included in it.

Engagement involved not only making and energizing connections among people and organizations within the river basin but also establishing ties with other organizations, especially the state agencies that retained crucial decision-making power in water management. It also involved broadcasting, communicating new ideas and experiences to the broader public. Experimentation meant developing problem-solving capabilities through what were often initially small-scale problem-solving endeavors.

Engagement and experimentation were not separate activities. The Itajaí committee's riverside reforestation program was an experiment in problem solving through which members developed ideas, resources, and relationships around a specific task: getting farmers to plant seedlings on their lands. This was experimentation, because the committee members were learning how to do something new through practice. But it was also an opportunity for engagement—for activating and extending networks—as the leaders of the program made contact with municipal governments, identified local coordinators, brought them into the network. In the Velhas case, the kayak expedition down the river is a good example of how broadcasting ideas relies on prior experimentation and engagement. The television images of crowds arriving at the riverside to welcome the kayakers were possible only because after years of experimenting with problem solving at the community level, the Manuelzão Project could mobilize the support of a network of local Manuelzão committees.

Building Support for Authority Claims

The chances that an organization will gain practical authority depend largely on whether it can win support for its claim to legitimately make decisions that influence the actions of others. Such support can be built in several ways. When new organizations develop problem-solving capabilities, other key actors are more likely to view them as credible decision makers. Committees build a variety of skills in the course of negotiating and implementing plans and projects. These include institution-building skills: getting information about one's environment; learning about users; identifying presence or absence of positive or negative activities (observation); writing reports, formal letters, resolutions, and so forth. These, in turn, involve communication and sometimes legal skills, such as calling and running meetings, facilitation, visualization, presentation, imagining futures, evaluating progress, sometimes creating artifacts (T-shirts, logos, folders, posters, and banners), and fund-raising. These skills are learned socially and internalized and are likely to get better over time, especially as people who have them teach them to others.

Those immediately affected by a problem are likely to show allegiance to an organization that has helped solve it. But problem-solving activities, even when less immediately or obviously successful, can also create alliances by building a network of actors committed to those activities. Even though the Itajaí committee's riverside reforestation program never achieved dimensions sufficient to effectively reduce flooding problems, putting it into practice helped the committee connect with people throughout the basin, some of whom had substantial power, such as local mayors and business owners.

The greater success of the Velhas case suggests that being able to scale up media attention—demonstrating the existence of a broader-based popular support—can be critical for gaining recognition from key decision makers. The governor's decision to invest in cleaning up the Velhas River was the direct result of the publicity the Manuelzão Project was able to generate. But we should be careful about drawing a simple causal connection between media attention and political support for two reasons. In the first place, the publicity afforded the Meta 2010 proposal did not come out of nowhere; it grew out of the years during which the Manuelzão Project implemented projects and systematically communicated with the public about them. Television and newspaper coverage would have been very unlikely without this backstory of organizing. In the second place, the Itajaí case reminds us that media coverage can intensify opposition instead of generating support. According to Frank, for example, a headline in the Itajaí committee newspaper declaring that the committee questioned the JICA plan led to an escalation of tensions between the committee and actors in the state government.

The ability of the Velhas committee to write a river basin plan that would actually be implemented depended in the end on a complex web of support for the Meta 2010 project, based in part on the reformist project of the state government. Fundamentally, the Manuelzão Project had established dozens of problem-solving organizations, each with skills and a local network of actors committed to cleaning up the river. Larger-scale programs of environmental education, agricultural extension, research, and so on, helped build connections not only with community members but also with people in state government agencies, such as the water and sanitation company (which funded many of its initiatives). These were all connections that generated support within the state government for the Manuelzão Project. Through its communications programs, the project also worked at building broader-based, more amorphous support, something akin to the name recognition that businesses and politicians prize. Although we did not conduct any systematic research proving that those efforts worked, informal conversations with friends, taxi drivers, waiters, and others in Belo Horizonte made it clear that ordinary people who were not involved in water politics had heard of the Manuelzão Project. All of these factors converged in 2003, when the project was able to mobilize the media and request a meeting with the governor. The governor signed on in part because he knew that the Velhas cleanup would be a politically popular project that cohered with his reformist ideas. But that popularity was not something that came out of the blue—it was built over time through practice.

Garnering support for decisions also required navigating entanglement. River basin committees were intended to be a new site of decision making in an arena already riddled with overlapping jurisdictions. This meant that if, on the one hand most policies could not be implemented without the collaboration of various public entities responsible for different pieces of a policy problem (liberating funds, building infrastructure, monitoring natural resources, providing environmental permits, etc.), on the other hand, it meant that institution builders could look for support in various places.

Both committees sought support at multiple territorial scales and *shifted scales of action* when necessary. The Manuelzão Project grew up simultaneously at the local and the river basin level into a sort of double-decker network. In the absence of support from the state government, the Itajaí activists often strategically shifted scales to gain support from more amenable allies. On several occasions, for example, the Itajaí leadership built connections with federal authorities in the efforts to pressure the state government, such as when they informed the federal Ministry of the Interior that they were holding an emergency meeting to discuss measures for flood control. As in other places where state governments resisted giving committees decision-making power (e.g., in the Alto Tietê committee in São Paulo), the Itajaí organizers worked with municipal governments and other actors to get things done.

Activists also used *hedging*—getting involved in more than one organization—as a strategy for building support for their ideas. The Manuelzão activists took over the committee as a means to supplement their project's effectiveness, seeing it as a sort of legal arm for nongovernmental initiative. The Itajaí leadership worked to build support for its proposals by participating in as many other relevant decision-making arenas as possible. Frank was almost omnipresent, sitting not only on the

Itajaí committee but also on the State Water Resources Council and the government-created technical-scientific group for disaster prevention, besides participating prominently in national organizations such as the Brazilian Water Resources Association. From each of these spaces, she advocated positions and supported decisions that enhanced the credibility of the Itajaí committee's proposals. She recognized that the committee's claim to have a strong influence on disaster prevention policy was relatively weak, and she hedged by getting other decision-making bodies to ratify those positions.

The Importance of Leadership

The importance of visionary leaders is not specific to these two cases of committee building. In all of the committees we studied that were able to build committees into working organizations, it was easy to identify one, sometimes two people who were behind it all. Yet it is hard to generalize on the precise role that leaders play in institution building. Lisboa was primarily a communicator. He found other professionals to make sure that meetings were called, proposals written, projects implemented. Frank, on the other hand, was involved in the details of running the organization, writing resolutions and reports and projects and even revising the meeting minutes. The former strategy is probably more effective for building a sustainable network of organizers who will outlive the original leader. This seems to have occurred in the Velhas committee, still dominated by the Manuelzão Project but led by a completely different person.

Students of collaborative governance have long noted that the existence of a facilitator or a convener is fundamental for ensuring that an agenda is set and decisions are transformed into actions (Wood and Gray 1991; Johnson et al. 2002; Leach and Pelkey 2001; Huitema and Meijerink 2009). The cases we have examined have also emphasized the importance of people willing to dedicate their daily lives to getting the new organization moving. Despite the importance of people like Frank and Lisboa as visionaries, it is important to understand their work less in the heroic vein as Schumpeterian political entrepreneurs providing a vision of the future and more in the domestic role of caretaker. In Philip Selznick's (1957, 82–86) classic work on leadership, he stresses that organizational roles are adaptive, responding to an individual's decision about how he or she ought to work—as idea person, as questioner, or something else—within the social system of the organization itself. Organizations need people who make sure that meetings take place, documents get written, and who undertake the many personal calls and visits necessary to build networks of collaboration and support. Such work generally involves more than one person. Indeed, even in the Itajaí basin, where Frank seems to have operated both as vision-ary and administrator, she put together a team of competent collaborators who did much of the everyday work of organizing.

If leaders should thus be understood as fundamental to getting organi-zations moving, they are also products of the organization-building pro-cess. In many of the cases we studied, their work at the river basin level gave them credentials that they used not only for helping the committee gain support for its decisions but also for taking on jobs at higher levels. Lisboa became a major leader in the São Francisco committee, first as a member of the commission that helped organize it and later participating on the committee itself as a vocal opponent of the diversion project. Frank moved to the state capital to work for a state government program aimed at training members of other river basin committees. Some of the com-mittee builders whose careers we have followed have risen to higher posi-tions. Luis Firmino Pereira, the leader of the Lagos São João consortium, became the head of Rio de Janeiro's environmental agency. Rosa Mancini, the leader of the Litoral Norte committee, headed up the water resources department in São Paulo's environmental agency during José Serra's gov-ernorship. In taking on these jobs, they connected their local experiences with broader processes of institutional reform. Pereira spearheaded an effort, for example, to integrate water management with environmental management. Mancini invested in participatory planning efforts in river basins (Interview 114, 2011). Over time, this kind of new leader began to bridge the experience of organization building at the river basin level with that of building a new water management system at the state and national level. Bilingual, able to speak both the language of institutional models and the language of practice, such people become crucial translators in pro-cesses of institutional change.

CONCLUSIONS

Public policy reforms often have a strong aspirational component. Rather like the baseball field in the movie *Field of Dreams*, there is the hope that "if you build it, they will come." It is not uncommon for legislation to include standards that are not enforceable at the time of writing.[1] Frequently, new institutional designs that do not correspond to existing organizational structures have been imposed anyway, in the hope that the latter will adapt. This kind of reform can unleash a cascade of moves intended to establish the preconditions for implementation. Efforts to make reality conform to the law do not always occur and, when they do, are not always successful. Sometimes nothing changes at all.

Brazil's water management reform created an assortment of new institutions and mandates but did not eliminate the ones that were already there—it presumed that in a process of mutual adjustment, new and old would gradually reconfigure themselves into a coherent field. Today, the policy area is composed of myriad institutions, organizations, and rules, with no clear hierarchy among them; some fragments resist integration, while others are aligned in name only. Creating a new decision-making organization within such a complex, entangled environment raises particular challenges, because authority not only can be vetoed by but also must be recognized by actors with very different understandings of what is being created. It is hard to fit this kind of reform process into conventional discussions of democratization. Debates about democracy entered the Brazilian public sphere in the mid-1970s (a decade before military rulers left power), exploded in the run-up to the 1987 constitutional assembly, and have continued since. Brazil's democratic landscape has seen changes to political parties and their configuration, to federalist arrangements, and

---

1. Charles O. Jones (1975) notably characterized the passage of "technology forcing" environmental legislation in the United States in 1969–1970 as an example of policy escalation responding to an aroused public producing a bandwagon effect but without a fully formed policy community around it; he referred to this as legislating beyond capabilities.

to the degree of centralization of policy governance. A political culture in which politicians in the 1980s ridiculed the notion that workers could represent themselves in politics was transformed over the next two decades into one in which a former trade unionist could be elected president and finish out two terms with an 80-percent approval rating. Since the 1990s, many scholars have followed the growing role of innovative participatory mechanisms in Brazil's democratization process. The participatory budget, policy councils, and other deliberative institutions afford civil society organizations systematic access to decision-making processes throughout the country (see chapter 2). However imperfect these new decision-making institutions may be, they mark something distinctive about the Brazilian democratization process in relation to other countries in Latin America. When we started to study river basin committees, we understood them principally as part of this participatory experiment.

From the start, we expected democratization to be a central element of the study—and we, along with many of our collaborators, spent quite a lot of time asking questions about participation and representation. The answers were elusive, because neither the policy arena nor its constituency is clearly mapped and it is hard to depict the emerging set of relations in principal–agent terms. More people certainly participate in deliberation over water issues than in the past, but we need to be careful about equating more participation with more democracy. Greater numbers of participants do not necessarily make a policy more democratic, either in the sense of who decides or who benefits. Moreover, democracy's purposes may require not only making government more inclusive but also making it function better. River basin committees have often been better at performing this role than they have at serving as arenas for representing different views and claims. Indeed, most citizens are unaware of their existence and have no clear opinions on the policies they make.

Most studies of new participatory institutions locate them in a kind of public space in construction, in which there is an expectation that by promoting inclusion or collaboration, they will make a political system more democratic and accountable. The (democratic) political system, in this view, is heterogeneous, with room for majoritarian decisional and executive structures, occasions for direct democracy, and deliberative spaces in which participants attempt to achieve consensus or negotiate agreements among a wider range of interests and views than would likely be found in legislatures or state agencies, albeit regarding a limited range of issues.[2]

2. Parkinson and Mansbridge (2012) refer to these as deliberative systems. See Almeida (2011) for an analysis of Brazilian participatory politics in these terms.

However, many studies have shown that the expansion of deliberative arenas does not necessarily transform government decision-making processes.[3] Where deliberation fails to affect outcomes, it tends to lose legitimacy (Abers 2000; Lubell et al. 2005, 280–285), and many erstwhile proponents of participatory councils today worry that they mainly function to legitimate the status quo. These concerns seem most likely to discourage societal actors: if potential participants do not think that the structured public deliberations of participatory governance bodies will produce concrete results, they will most likely take their energies elsewhere—to an NGO, for example—unless participating has other benefits, such as affording them an unusually good platform for voice or for networking (Hirschman 1970).

The organizational process we have been studying is only partly comparable with better-known experiments with municipal participatory institutions in Brazil. Both the territorial and the functional boundaries of water management as an interorganizational field (Fligstein and McAdam 2012) are contested. As a result, basin committees have been both more than and less than participatory representative forums. They have been more, in that as one of the most consistent organizational forms in a new policy field they have sometimes been attractors, or focal points, serving to pull other actors into novel relationships, not only with the committees but also with one another. In this respect, they have acted as catalysts for field reorganization. Notwithstanding this important function, in some respects, the committees have been less than their proponents hoped. Representation and deliberative participation are highly relational activities; they depend on recognition by both sides and clarity about who is representing what and to whom the representative claim (Saward 2006) is being made. More complicated than the representation of interest organizations on these committees was the representation of the state, which held the ambiguous three-sided position as defender of functional bureaucratic interests, facilitator of implementation, and—simultaneously—the only committee members potentially accountable to the public at large. This ambiguity is rarely noted but has to be taken into account when we think of these organizations in terms of their representative capacity (Abers and Keck, 2008).

Those river basin committees that gained some practical authority had to invest energy in establishing the preconditions for their own operation— that is, strengthening the capabilities of the governmental and nongovernmental organizations whose collaboration they were supposed to promote.

---

3. Some of these works are Abers (2000), Avritzer (2002, 2003, 2009), Borba and Lüchmann (2007), Dagnino (2002),), Santos Júnior, Queiroz, and Azevedo (2004), Tatagiba (2002) and Wampler (2007).

This activist role seems far removed from the concerns raised in most scholarly debates about participatory governance and even more so from conventional accounts of decentralization. Yet without a view of deliberation that links it to action, the idea of participatory or collaborative governance is a sterile conception. It seems pointless to evaluate whether river basin committees' role in decision making democratizes public policy without addressing the question of what might make the policy acquire a public presence in the first place. Yet by focusing on their practices and not just on their (in)ability to perform the formal roles attributed to them in water management legislation, we discover unexpected agency in the stories of these new participatory institutions.

FROM PRACTICES TO PRACTICAL AUTHORITY

We have reiterated on numerous occasions in the preceding pages that the reform process this book explores did not take place in the way we expected when we started our research. This is a view that many of the people who helped make the reform happen share with us and is a common part of institutional change processes. Scholarship on institutional change tends to focus on the exogenous factors that cause it to occur, such as alterations in the economic environment, social structure, political regimes, and other macro-elements; more recently, scholars have turned their attention to teasing out more gradual endogenous change processes. In complex institutional configurations, the line between what is exogenous and what is endogenous is difficult to draw. In any case, we find that these mesolevel institutional approaches, for all they have contributed to our understanding of the fact that a change occurred, stop well short of explaining the particular direction a reform effort takes, the way that reform projects are instantiated in actual laws, organizations, programs, policies, or action. Exploring such *how* questions requires focusing on processes and not just on conditions. It also means looking at micro-processes, the actual practices in which people engage. A focus on the micro scale is not a negation of the importance of what Tilly (1984) called "big structures" and "large processes" but a recognition that even these most macro phenomena comprise multitudes of specific acts of debating, reworking and testing ideas, building organizations, engaging in conflicts and negotiations, connecting people, and building capacities.

In political science, we rarely ask how people organize, gain influence over others that they did not previously have, and make institutions work. What do they actually do? What enables them to do it? It is not enough to affirm that action matters. In this book, we have tried to develop a theoretical vocabulary for thinking about how agency works in processes of institutional change. In chapter 1, we presented a schematic outline of our argument about the relationship between agency and institutional change. Each step in the argument is a possibility, not a necessity. Institution-building practices, we argued, involve two overlapping types of activities: engagement and experimentation. When these activities are mutually reinforcing, they can have a transformative effect on ideas, resources, and relationships which can potentially produce new capabilities and build recognition. When this occurs, those organizations have achieved some degree of practical authority.

In Brazilian water politics, proposals for institutional reform originated in a set of technical ideas that developed mainly in the course of intellectual debate among experts. Yet chapters 3 and 4 demonstrated just how messy the process of transforming those ideas into a legal framework was. Even at early phases, participants often did not recognize the existence of multiple and sometimes contradictory understandings of reform ideas. Interests also intervened: local actors tended to defend more decentralization, those in central offices more centralization, and actors in particular agencies sought to defend their decision-making turf. The disputed nature of the process resulted in an ambiguous, incomplete, and internally contradictory legislation.

Blyth (2001) argues that ideas can function as blueprints for action. But what happens when an institutional design is too ambiguous to really tell people what they should do in particular circumstances? Trying to use the water management system design as a blueprint hampered the imaginations of those doing it. As Blyth argues, blueprints can produce "cognitive lock," making it hard to adapt ideas creatively. Institutional activists on the ground must translate abstract ideas and ambiguous legal frameworks into a way of seeing local problems differently. River basin committees we studied usually had to redefine in profound ways those generic ideas about the roles and responsibilities of the new institutions. Often this meant transgressing boundaries set up by reformers that separated water resources management from other areas of policy making.

Although thinking creatively was a fundamental part of building new river basin institutions, we have argued that making them work required much more than just good ideas. Testing out ideas on the ground—such as water pricing in the Paraíba do Sul basin—helped reformers not only rethink ideas but also build coalitions of actors in favor of certain interpretations. While the effort to implement pricing in the Paraíba do Sul basin had dramatic impacts on national institutions in a relatively short time, experimental practices often involved starting small, in practical, collaborative action that helped organizations build capabilities over a long period of time: the design of an emergency flood prevention plan in the Itajaí basin; dozens of community-based river cleanup projects throughout the Velhas basin; a successful negotiation with a dredging company in the Lagos São João basin. Those problem-solving efforts were essential for building trust among actors, demonstrating capacity for action, and creating a public reputation and legitimacy. Working together on small projects also afforded committee members the opportunity to build and strengthen networks with each other and with those they wanted to attract to their activities. Broadening these networks in turn amplified the committee's resource base.

Although the stories told in the later chapters of this book suggest that starting small and slowly building capacity from the bottom up can help new organizations accumulate practical authority in contexts where other institutions may resist that process, creating practical authority in complex environments also usually means going beyond localized efforts. Committee organizers had to develop good relationships with other organizations on which they relied for information and resources and whose collaboration was necessary for plans to be implemented. Sometimes they did more than build connections; they worked to transform other organizations, helping them carry out the tasks they needed. This occurred, for example, when the Itajaí committee took over the process of registering water users, an administrative task that was normally the responsibility of the state government, not a deliberative body.

Since, by definition, practical authority involves the ability to influence the behavior of other actors or organizations, assembling it requires the consent of those particular others. Developing capabilities helps build such recognition. When an organization can solve problems, it becomes useful to other organizations. The Piracicaba consortium, for example, slowly won recognition as it became the main repository in the region of specialized knowledge and experience with small-scale water-related projects, such as revitalizing water sources, identifying causes of pollution, and working with local actors to deal with those problems (chapter 6). Yet organizational capabilities alone do not translate into influence. Getting other organizations to collaborate also depends on the political positions of other institutions. Political processes unrelated to water policy often intervene: in the São Francisco case, the formation of a national party coalition mobilized the government against a committee decision; in the Velhas case, a governor's reform project created an opportunity for a committee plan to be taken seriously.

In these larger political settings, the project of building practical authority encounters the problem of entanglement. Organization building cannot be separated from the complex environment in which it occurs or from the consequences of entanglement. The construction of new water management institutions in Brazil depended on the ability of organizers to make surprising connections among various arenas. After years of stagnation, water charging moved forward in the São Paulo legislature largely because industries, historically against it, began to pressure state governments to implement the policy. The reason industry leaders changed their minds had to do with their role in a concurrent and overlapping process, the evolution of federal legislation, and the Paraíba do Sul experiment in water pricing (chapter 4). Water specialists in the Piracicaba basin followed a similarly circuitous route: they developed particular notions of water management through cooperation programs with French water specialists and then managed to get those notions signed into law by mobilizing mayors, who used party ties to influence state legislators. Reformer Flávio Barth persuaded the governor to sign the São Paulo law by mobilizing his professional ties with staff at an international agency, who threatened to cut off funding for river cleanup if the bill was not signed (chapter 3). This is the way things are done in entangled environments.

Where political processes work through interlocking networks, power is associated with being able to bridge previously disconnected networks (Burt 1995). Where multiple jurisdictions overlap, the same is true: those who have connections in various action arenas have a greater capacity to influence outcomes. A clear example of such a person is Jerson Kelman, the first president of the National Water Agency and a main character of chapter 4. By the time he participated in the creation of that agency, Kelman was a respected figure in the engineering community, participated in water politics in Rio de Janeiro, and consulted extensively in the state of Ceará, where he developed strong ties with a leader of the PSDB, Tasso Jereissati, through whom Kelman was in contact with Brazil's president, Fernando Henrique Cardoso.[4] As an institution builder, Kelman was powerful, because he could connect easily with resources and disseminate ideas in multiple places at the same time.

Yet entanglement also means that less powerful actors, trying to implement alternative ideas, can also seek support in more than one place. Entanglement thus may be conducive to a *politics of perseverance*, through which actors avoid direct conflict by finding allies in arenas of action that are under the political radar screen. When committee organizers in the Itajaí and Alto Tietê basins faced resistance from state governments, they shifted their scale of action and built ties with municipal governments. The

---

4. After leaving the National Water Agency, Kelman became the head of the even more powerful National Electrical Energy Agency (ANEEL) and from there became the chief executive officer of the Light Electric Company. He thus continued to navigate different policy arenas with expertise.

stories we have told in this book are replete with such strategic redefinitions of the scale of institution building, in which actors sought out the paths of least resistance in order to guarantee that their organizations could keep on operating.

When institutions have overlapping jurisdictions and it is not obvious which ones are going to prevail, organizers *hedge* by working in multiple action arenas at the same time. In the Piracicaba basin, a group of water specialists allied with businesses and mayors managed to dominate three overlapping arenas at the same time: the consortium they had created, a river basin committee created under state law, and another created under federal law. For a time, the consortium even acted as river basin agency in the basin, through which it administered the incipient water pricing program (chapter 6). In the Velhas basin, leaders of the Manuelzão Project were central actors both in the state-level Velhas committee and in the interstate São Francisco committee and helped create the Velhas River Basin Agency, which later also became the water agency for the São Francisco basin (chapter 7). By helping to construct all of these organizations, they helped build different types of practical authority: some organizations (e.g., consortiums, universities, and agencies) were better for project implementation and fund-raising; others (e.g., the committees) brought the legitimacy of representative elections and legal sanction. While in those cases hedging built synchrony among overlapping organizations, in other cases it was not so productive, serving as a way to stay in the game without investing very much.

In a sense, the entire integrated water resources management project is a call for organizational bricolage The construction of the new water management field in the Brazilian federal government centered on a coalition of specialists from policy sectors that had in common mainly the desire to limit the domination of the energy sector. Institutional designers intended that river basin planning and basin committees would impel experts from different policy arenas to work together. Yet building support for integration also meant being selective. Ironically, the new institutional design integrated some policy fields while it sidelined others. As shown in chapters 3 and 4, water reformers chose not to attempt to integrate water use management with either land use policy or environmental licensing, despite the fact that internationally these fields are generally considered fundamental parts of river basin management.

When they started to apply the new institutional design at the river basin level, committees were confronted with the fact that the design provided policy tools for influencing water use but not land use or the use of other environmental resources. Yet the problems they faced often could not be solved from a water use perspective. In some of the cases that we studied, the disconnect between the institutional design and the nature of water problems led to a stalemate. Committees in big cities, such as the Pirapama (Recife) and Paranoá (Brasília) committees, had difficulty translating the abstract ideas presented in the water laws into missions for their committees (chapter 5). In most of the more successful cases, however, committee organizers tried to stitch environmental and land use management back into water management, through practice. For example, the Itajaí committee tried to promote the reforestation of riverside farmland and more recently— in the attempt to have a stronger impact on flood management—has started to dabble in civil defense policy. This web of connections being established in practice is likely to become even more important as the energy sector recovers from its period of relative eclipse from the mid-1980s to the mid-2000s and the lobby for expanding irrigated agriculture grows ever stronger.

Such efforts to reconnect the pieces lead us to suspect that the process of institutional becoming that we have considered here may never reach an end. In the 1990s, institution builders wove a coalition around an institutional design that separated water use policy from environmental management. In the 2000s, as they attempted to implement that design, the organizations created under its auspices came up with new ideas for solving water problems that called for integrating water and environmental policies and tried to build new political coalitions for institutional change. In Rio de Janeiro state, for example, a group of activists who started by working in river basin committees eventually took on key positions in the state environmental bureaucracy and used them to promote the integration of environmental licensing and water use permits. In this way, after 30 years, actors in Brazil continue to create new water management institutions. Given the multiplicity of its objectives and the entangled nature of the setting within which it occurs, there is no reason to believe that those institutions will ever reach a state of equilibrium or that path dependence will set in. Indeed, resilience may demand a continuous process of change.

BECOMING INSTITUTIONS

This study is part of a broader trend in the social sciences that seeks to explore how actors construct institutions. This is problem-driven research, an attempt to decipher the complex relationship between institutional design and the active political work of institution building on the ground. Although our study has focused on only one country and one policy area, many other studies exploring institutional change in a wide variety of contexts and from various social science disciplines have identified similar processes. Most cite Mary Douglas's (1986) classic work, summarized in her book of lectures *How Institutions Think*, in which she develops ideas about reasoning by analogy and of bricolage. Her work serves as a fundamental building block for understanding how, absent the ideal, people make do with what they have. Many scholars besides us have also developed an appreciation for the organizational insights of Philip Selznick (1957), the pragmatism of John Dewey, and the possibilism of Albert Hirschman, particularly in their explorations of the open-endedness of organizational life and of process.

Understanding institutional becoming may require studying processes that would not be visible to someone approaching them with a traditional institutionalist lens. We are not afraid of studying the underrated: scholars of political parties and of fiscal policy saw Keck's (1992) doctoral research on the formation of the Workers' Party and Abers's (2000) work on the development of participatory budgeting in Porto Alegre as somewhat naive choices of subject matter, certain to be marginal. The creation of those institutions, too, was decidedly messy. Although at this remove we can come up with many good reasons for why both of them survived and thrived, these reasons are not explanations. Our research during the period of their organization makes us quite certain that they could easily have been— and almost were—derailed at numerous moments before they were fully integrated into national political life. They could easily have *not* become institutions.[5]

As in the case of Brazilian water management, institutional layering provides the context for many other studies of creative institutional construction. Stark's (1999) study of firm behavior in postsocialist Eastern Europe discovered, for example, highly complex patterns of interfirm ownership. In a landscape of great uncertainty and multiple simultaneously operating logics, no one knew who the important actors would be in the future, so firms diversified, hedged, and in remarkably creative ways transformed their relationships into resources with which they acquired shares of one another's firms. In some respects, the system constructed by Hungarian firms resembled the pawning system of the farmers in rural Senegal studied by Galvan (2004, 104–130). In both, the appearance of capitalist property relations was grafted onto a quite different set of relationships and historical practices. The ingenuity of creative actors in uncertain landscapes was to become bricoleurs, recombining the familiar with the strange to make

---

5. Even well-established institutions once had to be constructed. For example, Snowiss's (2003) study of the history of the U.S. Supreme Court shows that the power of judicial review—today taken for granted as a crucial part of the American political system—was slowly constructed through incremental, multilevel, legal-political interactions over the course of the 19th and 20th centuries.

something that served its purpose. Meijerink and Huitema (2010) similarly made political entrepreneurship central to their analysis of 16 cases of water policy transition around the globe.

The problem raised by complexity for institutional change has also been explored in advanced capitalist countries. Multilayered institutional hybridity has been a particularly rich theme in studies of the institutional change in the European Union (Ansell 2000; Hooghe and Marks 2001; Ansell and Di Palma 2004; Ansell and Gash 2008; Jabko 2012). This unbundling of territory, space, agency, and power approximates scholarship in critical geography, interrogating the nature of place and by implication the "situatedness" of action (Massey, Allen, and Sarre 1999).

The idea that practical authority is constructed on the ground has also been explored in entirely different institutional contexts from those we have examined here. Lund (2006, 686) analyzes the adoption and adaptation of different manifestations of state authority in African villages, describing public authority as the "amalgamated result of the exercise of power by a variety of local institutions and the imposition of external units, conjugated with the idea of a state. Hence the practice of governing varies from place to place and even from field to field." State units are also constantly in the process of being formed. They are what Lund calls "twilight institutions" that continuously recombine parts of state and society, public and private. The shape-shifting nature of instantiations of the state challenges the notion that there is a bright line between successful and failed institutional projects. In Lund's experience, as in ours, local actors build practical authority after they translate projects into their own political idiom and make creative use of whatever resources they find. Albert O. Hirschman made the same discoveries decades ago, when he insisted that economic development was associated not with grandiose plans, but with the capacity to solve problems (1973; 1984).

Authors from a variety of perspectives have also tried to explain the process through which actors transform institutions. Exploring experiences as different as national state building in the United States and property institutions in Senegal and Kenya, Berk and Galvan (2009, 544) make a leap into a phenomenological view of structure and change. They argue for seeing structure as a skill and "institutions as always-decomposable resources, rearranged and redeployed as a result of action itself." They draw heavily on John Dewey in their call for creative syncretism in the study of institutions. Like us, they do not advocate an abandonment of institutions as a focus of study but rather a shift from a structural to an experiential approach that sees institutions "not prior to, exogenous from, or determinative of action, but as the raw materials for action" (Berk and Galvan 2009, 575).

Looking at the inner life of organizations, a Scandinavian school of organizational sociology has investigated the "institutional work" required to create and maintain institutions (Lawrence and Suddaby 2006; Delbridge and Edwards 2008). Working at the interinstitutional and field levels, these authors (like us) draw on the account of agency proposed by Emirbayer and Mische (1998), which pays attention to habit, imagination, and judgment as different agentic orientations. In a rare examination of failed institution building, Edwards and Jones (2008) look at how the effort to rework an organization's goals—a process we have discussed at length in this book— can fail. In that case, the effort to define a mission that would bring together actors with different long-term preferences ended up reinforcing conflicts instead of mitigating them, thus ending the experiment and leaving the status quo intact (Edwards and Jones (2008), 50–53).

Scholars in the applied social sciences seem to have been particularly interested in practice-based approaches (Sabel and Zeitlin 2012). Many of the organizational sociologists exploring institutional work are employed by (mainly British or Scandinavian) business schools, following a trend begun by students of practice, learning, and change (see, e.g., Lave and Wenger 1991; Wenger 1998; Suchman 2011). A similar move toward practice and agency has occurred in critical public policy scholarship; these scholars focus on the layered topography of politics and governance and embrace an interpretive approach to a practice-oriented policy analysis (Hajer and Wagenaar 2003). Planning theorists, such as Forester (1999) and Friedmann (1987), have also explored the intricacies of action in the public domain.

All of these studies address the well-known deficits in the institutionalist literature with regard to understanding change, conventionally perceived as unusual and hard to bring about. We all suggest that change is constant, even if steering it in any particular direction may be hard. Nelson (2003, 52) argues that these approaches "see the world as continually in creation, with a balanced ontological importance given to stability, order, habit and the past on the one hand, and flux, chaos, novelty, and the future on the other." From all of these perspectives, creative human action—invisible from the standpoint of conventional institutionalism—comes into view, challenging our understanding of the dynamics of change. We hope that the conceptual vocabulary developed here for explaining how actors build the ingredients of practical authority can contribute to this extremely rich and diverse emerging literature.

IMPROVISATION, EXPLANATION, AND CLOSURE

Our look at the role of agency in complex environments reveals a world of unpredictability. Readers may have noticed that we have not explored the question of human motivation. Some actors seem to devote themselves to the construction of new river basin organizations for the sake of promoting environmental protection or flood control, while others are more interested in defending their economic interests. We do not try to explain why they do so. Our presumption is that motivation is complex—people usually combine self-interest with group identity and other-regarding concerns, leavened with passions and beliefs (Hirschman, 1977; 1982). We do not need to know what leads different actors to take on certain commitments to try to explain what kinds of actions make the most difference. Yet it is perhaps this question—answered, we believe, in a different way for each person—that might explain why some actors dedicate themselves to river basin committees and others do not. The dotted lines in the figure we presented in chapter 1 convey the idea of possibility, not determinacy. They are dotted because people do not always follow the arrows we have drawn. Sometimes they have other things to do.

Thinking about theory as the study of possibility rather than of strict causality has implications for how students of agency can understand the status of their concepts. We have tried to generate tools that can help to identify some of the processes we have studied, but we do not pretend to make strong causal statements. We would endorse the affirmation that Henry Farrell and Martha Finnemore (2009, 67) made in a recent article:

> Pragmatist accounts of how politics works are thus more modest in their scientific ambitions than many forms of positivism, but also are explicitly committed to the refining, testing, and re-testing of empirical knowledge. They are notably more ambitious than positivist accounts in that they aspire to explanation.

By emphasizing agency, a practice approach avoids the determinism of much structural thinking. By focusing on how agents engage with their contexts, it also avoids a methodologically individualist conception that may overestimate (and homogenize) individual choice.[6] In our approach, situated people and groups draw creatively from a diverse range of repertoires and experiences (Hajer and Wagenaar 2003). Actions are difficult to systematize beyond the contexts in which they are so deeply imbued.

The problem of this approach from a methodological perspective is that in presupposing creativity, or at least the possibility that actors may at any moment act creatively, we add a factor of profound unpredictability

---

6. This is similar to the point that Hay (2006) makes about the virtue of constructivist individualism, which avoids a kind of determinism present both in structuralist and rational-choice individualist approaches (which base analysis on predefined expectations of how individuals act).

into our analysis: our human subjects. The result may be that the study of practices resists scientific method as it is commonly understood. As Bevir (2006, 287) notes (referring to agency as "the will"), "No doubt human scientists are unable to say much about the way the will operates . . . but that they are unable to do so is not a failing so much as a necessary consequence of the nature of the will: The will is a creative faculty."

By affirming that experimenting and engaging can produce capabilities and recognition, by identifying common "routes through entanglement," or by defining analogous tasks that organization builders engage in, we are nonetheless trying to think systematically about the *qualities* of improvisational action. This kind of systematization is entirely different from predicting what actors will do under particular circumstances and is better understood in the tradition of typology construction of interpretative sociology than as specific causal theories or mechanisms that can explain multiple cases. These categories are descriptive classifications rather than causal explanations in themselves. The causality is to be found in the particular stories, where, equipped with our concepts, we can show *how* actors creatively interacted with their context, all too often in unexpected ways. Indeed, doing the unexpected with the ideas, resources, and relationships at hand seems to be the most important task for those building institutions under complexity.

What might be the purpose of categorizing practices in this way? In our experience, doing so has been quite useful for helping us know what to look for in case analysis. Studies of complex institutional reform are bedeviled by the elusiveness of units of analysis, precisely because actors in the field often fail to respect the frontiers of action that researchers define. This means that one of the most difficult tasks of studying institutional reform is to figure out what to look for. Identifying key characteristics of activities (engagement, experimentation), strategies for dealing with entanglement (hedging, bricolage, scale shifting, small-scale action), or the tasks that institution builders must undertake (reworking missions, building organizations, creating organizational niches) helps us guide that search.

Such a way of thinking may also be helpful to practitioners themselves. Beate Frank, one of our research colleagues and research subjects, organizes workshops with struggling river basin committees in which she tries to help them find practical frames to guide actions. This task involves examining the problems, resources, and potentials of a particular group and place and trying to come up with short and medium-term goals on which the group has the power to act. To help local actors thus pragmatically rethink their missions, Frank used her own creative skills and tried to teach those skills to those she was working with—but she did not start each session from scratch. She reflected and abstracted on what occurred in her own experience (see chapter 7), building general categories of action that are in many ways similar to our classifications of practices (Frank and Pereira 2010). In addition to inspiring our own work, hers makes us believe that thinking systematically about how practices work might be useful, in practice.

As this book approaches its final pages, the processes we have examined continue on. Having studied water management for more than 10 years, we are sure of one thing: the moment of institutional creation is far from over. Comparing processes rather than outcomes has this as its corollary: there is no good reason to think that one moment in time is better than another for rendering judgments. We have seen processes ebb and flow, enjoying periods of high energy and others of comparative stasis. The fact that we have finished our book says nothing at all about the state of river basin committees or even of the broader legal framework in which they operate. The committees to which we attributed progress might next week lose their main activists to some other activity and take years to recover. Laws can be redesigned. We can make provisional assessments on the basis of comparisons of particular practices and trajectories. But we must insist that these remain provisional; the processes we are studying may become quite different from what they are now.

Is it possible to imagine a social science without closure? Only by accepting that things are not always as they seem and that people (we ourselves) always act on assumptions about our physical and relational settings that are subject to change. The capacity to learn from experience is at the basis of human agency. A "bias for hope" (Hirschman 1985) requires keeping our options open and allowing for the possibility that things may be becoming something entirely different.

Methodological Narrative

OUR RESEARCH PROCESS

When we first met in 1999, as a result of Keck's review of Abers's first book manuscript for a publisher, we could not have imagined the long, rewarding, sometimes painful, and sometimes exhilarating collaboration that would ensue. We decided to organize and raise money for the Watermark Project, working with several Brazilian colleagues who were also interested in the prospect. We visualized a longitudinal project from the beginning and proposed a five-year research period. That seemed like a long time back then, which we thought would give our study greater explanatory power than most comparative research on institutional reforms.

Five years later, however, the process we were studying had not progressed in the way we expected, and much of the conceptual apparatus we had begun with had collapsed or at least was listing precariously. We spent many of the first five years designing a study of a process whose parameters we thought we could identify. We ended up spending a second five years trying to figure out exactly what it was that we were studying. The longer this went on, the more complex and entwined the institutional changes we were examining became and the more evident it was that wherever we located the beginning and end points of our study, that choice would have much less to do with the timing of the process itself than with our own. Finally, as we tried to pull our ideas together into a book, the challenge was to find a conceptual vocabulary with which to pry open the world of actors and actions involved in institutional becoming. In this narrative, we hope to share with the reader not only our methodological choices and techniques but also some of the dilemmas we faced over the course of this somewhat unorthodox research experience and how we dealt with them.

River basins differ dramatically from each other: in the problems people living in them experience (droughts, urban pollution, floods, combinations of those), their predominant economic activities (industrial, urban, agricultural, tourism, or combinations), their populations (level and distribution of income, age, education levels, etc.), and their institutional contexts (some states have well-developed water management structures, and others do not; in some places international agencies or the federal government are active, and in others they are not). Rivers themselves are inevitably dynamic. They dry up or overflow or turn putrid with the sludge humans deposit in them. They present us not just with a set of characteristics but also with a reminder that those characteristics are neither fixed nor fully responsive to human interventions—at least, not in the ways that we expect them to be.

In the early stages of our research, we understood our project as a comparison of river basin institutions, created according to a similar model under diverse conditions. We thought of our task as to identify which of those conditions could be associated with positive and negative outcomes. We needed to do case studies because these conditions had unique configurations (Ragin 2000) and because we wanted to know how river basin committees worked within their specific contexts to solve problems (Yin 1984). But just a few cases would not do justice to the diversity of those contexts. We therefore decided to devise a medium N sample that would include substantial variation but also would allow for an in-depth study of the relationships between new organizations and their contexts.

From the start, we worked with practitioners involved in creating river basin committees who were interested in the social and political side of water policy. At a first meeting on the proposal, in 2000, we talked about it with two specialists, Gerôncio Rocha, who was closely involved in water reform in São Paulo, and Rosa Formiga Johnsson, who worked at a research institute for water management engineering and had recently finished a doctorate in planning under a noted French water expert, Bernard Barraqué, with a dissertation comparing water resources management in Brazil and France. We gave our proposal a name: "The Watermark Project" ("Projeto Marca d'Água" in Portuguese) and succeeded in raising seed money from the John D. and Catherine T. MacArthur Foundation and from the Johns Hopkins University Center for Livable Future. With the help of a National Science Foundation postdoctoral fellowship, Abers was able to dedicate most of her time to coordinating the project.

The research began in earnest after 2001. With a growing group of academic researchers, including our students and other scholars, along with practitioners with knowledge of the field, we made an initial list of river basins that had very different characteristics. The list included cases from various states—some of which were much more advanced than others in the reform process—with varying levels of urbanization, territorial, and population size and different combinations of water uses and problems. Then we set out to find people to conduct baseline studies. In many cases, we were able to involve researchers already studying the basins we chose. We managed to persuade our graduate students and colleagues to take on the rest. In some cases, practitioners themselves did the research, some studying the basins in which they worked and others investigating ones where they did not have prior experience. Abers and Keck each conducted two case studies (later taking over a fifth). We dropped cases when we could not find anyone to study them and added other cases accordingly. It was what might be called a convenience sample, imbued with a substantial effort to guarantee diversity.

The group—by then nearly 40 people—met several times between 2001 and 2004. Abers and Keck wrote the documents guiding the meetings, but the group discussed them in depth to produce common research questions, methods of key informant selection and document collection, lists of questions to be answered, and the structure of each final report. In 2001, 23 individuals or research groups conducted case studies on that many basins, following a research protocol that Abers had drawn up. In August of that year, the group held a meeting at a rudimentary civil servants' vacation hotel in Campos do Jordão, São Paulo, at which researchers hung posters and presented the preliminary results of their baseline studies. Several observers attended, including the Brazil representative of the Hewlett Foundation, who liked what he saw enough to fund the next phase of the project.

These studies gave rise to two products in Portuguese: a self-published volume of case study summaries, edited by Rosa Formiga Johnsson and Paula Duarte Lopes (2003), which was very widely distributed, and full reports of around 50 pages each on the river basins studied, along with detailed maps made for the purpose, posted on the group's website. As important as these initial studies was the network that they created—a group of academics and policy makers who identified with the project and helped to put together relevant information. It came to include several of the people who have appeared as protagonists in this book: Beate Frank (Itajái), Rosa Mancini (Litoral Norte), and Luis Firmino Pereira (Lagos São João).

In 2002 and 2003, project participants gathered information from key informants to fill out standard questionnaires, in an attempt to gain more comparable information about organizational history and structure for each case. By then, we had substantial resources and could pay researchers to collect information; grants from the Hewlett Foundation and from the Sectoral Fund for Water Resources (CTHIDRO) of Brazil's Science and Technology Agency the CNPq, had followed up on the MacArthur seed grant (see acknowledgments). However, it proved harder than we expected to obtain comparable information for all the cases. Much later, we realized that we were suffering from what Ragin (2000, 27) notes is a common problem in medium-N research—we were "confronted by what [seemed] like unmanageable diversity."

The first paper that the two of us wrote together was partly published as the introduction and conclusions of the self-published volume and was subsequently presented, along with several of the case studies, at the 2004 Latin American Studies Association meetings in Dallas. In that paper, we began to grapple with some inconvenient facts: the contextual factors we had expected would generate significant variation in the organization of basin committees appeared not to be very significant; internal organizational factors were proving much more important than we had expected. Many of the ideas that we develop in this book had their first exposure there—but we did not yet know what to do with them and wanted to test these new ideas on a broader terrain.

At the time, we thought the solution was to go quantitative. In 2003, we decided to conduct a sample survey and, with the help of sociologists[1] from the Federal University of Minas Gerais, designed a questionnaire that was administered to more than 600 members of river basin committees. We hoped that by collecting consistent, quantifiable information about committee members—their attributes, attitudes, and behaviors—we could compare the cases more systematically. Sampling was a key problem, the seriousness of which we would understand only much later (though we cannot say we weren't warned). Through our network, we conducted a sample frame study of the universe of committees in existence at the time. The quantitative sociologists we hired to help us wisely suggested that we use the sample frame to select a small number of members from as large and varied a number of basins as was feasible. Such a sample would allow us to make affirmations about the characteristics of committee members in general. We rejected that approach—we were interested in the committees as organizations, not so much in the individuals that participated in them. We also wanted to try to combine the quantitative work with the previous qualitative studies and had ambitions to do some network analysis as well. We devised a stratified sample that reflected the contextual conditions (detected in the sample frame) of the universe of committees but maximized the number of cases from our earlier studies (this was possible for 17 of 18 cases). The data resulted in a number of papers, an edited volume of academic articles (Abers 2010), and an interactive CD and book targeted

---

1. Led by Solange Simões of the Center for Quantitative Research in Social Sciences, Federal University of Minas Gerais.

to Brazilian technical and policy audiences (Frank 2008). But it turned out to be very hard to use the survey results for the study of institutional change presented in this book.

There were several reasons for this difficulty. We had interviewed more than 600 people, but comparing organizations required aggregating individual responses into 18 organizational indicators (one for each committee or consortium surveyed). When we correlated those variables, they almost never produced statistically significant results. The data revealed perceptions individual members had of how well their organizations were working, but not why they saw it that way, making the responses hard to compare. For example, we originally thought we might be able to build indicators of committees' effectiveness through questions on how members perceived the organization's influence on the behavior of other government agencies. We found, however, that member ratings were often lower precisely in committees we knew from fieldwork to be especially active and influential. Considering the nature of survey research—in which questions are predefined and answers are simplified and superficial—the study could not supply explanations for these anomalies. We concluded that the data were less a reflection of what committees had actually done than they were of levels of optimism, which were influenced by many other factors such as how long the organization had been trying and how well other institutions worked in the region. Moreover, it took a snapshot of a single moment in time, when increasingly it seemed that we needed to pay attention to longer and more complex—and erratic—processes. Since 2004, when the survey was conducted, many of the committees we studied have changed dramatically, with some losing energy and others finally getting projects and capabilities off the ground. The explanations range from changes in political context to a shift in organizing strategies, altering what the participants did with the resources at hand. The survey, to capture these changes, would have to be repeated, something we had a hard time justifying given how little it had produced in useful results the first time.

Although we do not use the survey formally in this book, conducting and analyzing it provided us with a huge amount of qualitative information. Devising the sample required numerous phone calls, e-mails, and conversations about how each committee worked. As we later interrogated the resulting data, we talked with key informants—often informally—to try to understand the variations that we observed. The survey data were also used to supplement case studies conducted by other researchers, especially graduate students in Brazil and the United States who carried out in-depth follow-up studies on the basis of the baseline studies and the survey data. A total of 13 master's theses and nine doctoral theses were ultimately written by members of the original Watermark Project or by their students, along with two studies that we know of that reproduced our research design and three unfinished graduate theses that resulted in preliminary papers and analyses. We cite these studies extensively throughout the book.

In 2008, the Watermark Project engaged in a particularly unorthodox action research activity that also grew out of the survey: participatory workshops with 15 of the river basin organizations that had been studied. These workshops—coordinated by Beate Frank, professor at the Regional University of Blumenau (FURB) in Santa Catarina and longtime leader of the Itajaí River Basin Committee—involved presenting committee members with reports on the 2004 survey data and then facilitating a daylong discussion on how the organization had changed since then and where the members wanted to take it in the future. These workshops—three of which Abers personally participated in—resulted in detailed reports on the issues and problems the committees faced. The workshops were particularly interesting arenas for thinking about how people devise and implement institution-building practices.

Although we draw on the wide array of research done in the context of this study, in five river basins (Alto Tietê, Litoral Norte, Paranoá, Velhas, and Itajaí) we did most of the fieldwork ourselves, including lengthy interviews and document collection, and subsequently hired research assistants to revisit previously visited sites. A total of 107 formal interviews were done in these five basins in 2001, 2003, 2007, and 2008, in addition to countless informal conversations. The more in-depth case studies helped us know what to look for in the cases where we relied more on the research of other members of the project. This was especially true when little seemed to be happening.

We also conducted 37 lengthy formal interviews with actors either from other river basins or involved in negotiating or attempting to implement the institutional design either in São Paulo, where it began, or nationally.[2] Several interviews that Keck had done in 1990 for a previous project turned out to contain material highly relevant to this one and had the advantage of capturing the accounts of important actors very early in the process. These formal interviews were complemented with hundreds of informal conversations with people involved in Brazilian water management as well as numerous instances of participant observation at a variety of events and meetings, where we discussed water management politics with practitioners from government and civil society organizations. Examples

---

2. In the text, we almost always refer to the interviewees by an anonymous code (see appendix 2). However, some interviews with public officials, especially those conducted by Keck in this earlier phase, were not anonymous, and the names are cited in the text.

were the well-attended annual conferences of national organizations such as the Brazilian Association of Water Resources or the National Forum of River Basin Committees, where we listened to accounts of experiences in different parts of the country and made presentations ourselves.

We have had access to an enormous amount of documentary material, which has greatly contributed to our understanding of the processes studied. Much of that material was posted on the Internet at some point in time, and although not all of it is still available online, a great deal can still be found on basin committee and government agency websites. On paper and through the Internet, we have had access to plenary meeting minutes (often transcripts), resolutions, declarations and statements, and reports. We and our research assistants obtained access to organizational file cabinets and personal archives, sometimes following particular reports or plans through many drafts. Also important have been papers presented at annual meetings, documentation from dozens of NGOs involved in the process, and magazines of professional associations. International funding agencies have also produced valuable research reports, program documents, and evaluations. Although we do not discuss many of these written materials in detail, the thousands and thousands of pages we have perused shaped the perspective we develop here.

By the time we began to write this book, we could assemble consistent comparative information about the political development of freshwater management in 13 river basins, combining our own fieldwork with others for which we had good case studies and other data to rely on as a result of multiple waves of Watermark Project research. The 13 cases were all river basins under state domain—that is, since the rivers in question flow only within a state's boundaries, they are governed under state laws and regulated primarily by state government institutions.

As we framed the book, however, we realized that we needed to include some other cases in our story, not so much to explore the implementation of the water reform model but rather to understand its construction. Three river basins, Paraíba do Sul (chapter 4), Piracicaba (chapter 6), and São Francisco (chapter 6), had become iconic among water policy makers. They were closely watched both as test cases for demonstrating the effectiveness of the model and as arenas for developing technical and legal changes to it. People active in river basin committees throughout Brazil studied those cases as examples and paid attention to the legislative changes provoked by experimentation that went on in them. Not by coincidence, these were interstate river basins, meaning that water management reform would be governed by both national water law (for federally owned waters, such as the main channel of rivers crossing state boundaries) and state laws (for tributaries that lay fully within a single state). Because they are well-studied cases, we could rely largely on excellent secondary sources in addition to, in two of them, Watermark Project research conducted in the first half of the 2000s and occasional consultation with knowledgeable individuals.

As discussed at length in chapter 5, we discovered that our original approach to the case study research, in which we expected to compare cases under different conditions to identify the factors producing variations in outcomes, was problematic, given the diversity of environmental characteristics, human settlement patterns, institutional dynamics, social organization, economic development, and so on. Evidently, as long as we attempted to think about our cases only in terms of such contextual conditions, the infinite array of what Ragin calls "configurations" of aspects would be quite daunting. Technically, it would have been possible to examine the cases systematically in terms of these conditions, giving them scores for size, problem, average income, or any other aspect, as proposed by authors of medium-N comparative method such as Ragin (1994, 2000) and Levitsky and Way (2010). But our early attempts to examine such conditions failed to provide convincing results.

Besides inconsistent variation in conditions, we found it was common for adjacent river basins with similar conditions and problem structures to experience wildly different institution-building processes. The main explanation for such variation appeared to lie in the practices people engaged in. Differences in action profiles resulted not automatically from conditions but rather from what actors did with the resources and possibilities their conditions provided. When we adopted this perspective, it became clear that we had to classify not so much the conditions but rather the stories, the processes in which actors and organizations engaged, leading some committees to paralysis and others to dynamism. This is what we tried to do in chapters 5, 6, and 7.

The long duration of this research project gave us time to see how initial evaluations could be misguided and made us aware of the danger of making assumptions about the causal effect of underlying or preexisting conditions that seem to coincide with different outcomes. If we had stopped our research after the first phase (2001–2003), we probably would have made some erroneous assessments. Two contrasting cases come to mind: the Paranoá and the Velhas basins. In the former, a coalition of civil society actors mobilized intensely, first to get the legislature to pass a new water law and then to create a river basin committee. At the end of 2001, leaders had cleverly negotiated with a government that was opposed to the initiative. The governor had approved the formal creation of the Paranoá committee, and his political appointees had even taken on a leadership role in the commission created to implement that decision. The organizers were energized. In the Velhas River Basin, the state government had created a committee in 1997 mainly to meet World Bank stipulations on institutional reforms. There was no civic mobilization, nor was there a discernible local demand for it. By 2001, the committee was paralyzed, with meetings constantly being canceled for lack of quorum. Had we stopped there, we certainly would have attributed what seemed like greater success in the first case to the existence of a demand within society. We might also have pointed to the difficulty in mobilizing in basins as large and socially diverse as that of the Velhas River. Such conclusions would have been entirely off-base. By 2010, the Velhas case had developed into one of the most effective river basin committees we studied, linked into a broad network of civil society and state actors throughout the huge basin (chapter 7). The Paranoá committee, on the other hand, had spent nine years in legal limbo, beginning to hold meetings only in 2010 (chapter 5).

The ability of many of the other organizations under study to influence state and private decision making also changed over time; this ability shifts not only with the capabilities of the water committees but also with the sometimes abrupt policy swings of new state and sometimes municipal administrations. Their fortunes continue to change even as we write this book. Our goal, therefore, is not to categorize *cases* as successes or failures but rather to understand the *processes* through which actors produce more or less effective organizations at different points in time. Understanding this fluctuating situation requires accepting that no conclusions concerning the cases themselves will likely hold true for very long. That notion coheres with our insistence that what explains the course of institutional reform are practices rather than preexisting conditions.

GETTING ENTANGLED

The Watermark Project provided us with a wealth of resources, connections, and interlocutors who helped us gain knowledge of the inner workings of multiple cases and the capacity to interpret our story. But the action research involved, and its long duration, also involved us in some parts of the story and created a number of methodological challenges.

Our initial proposal was to construct what we thought of as a "framework project"—a loose network of researchers and practitioners with different kinds of disciplinary training who could collaborate on a core project but would also communicate with one another around related ones. The original idea for the project evolved out of conversations with practitioners, some academically inclined and others simply reflective. Most of them were frustrated with the engineering focus of the vast majority of academic discussions of water management. They wanted to think about political and social aspects and particularly about how to make the new decision-making arenas contribute to democratization. Early project meetings were energizing; the practitioners had innumerable stories to tell (mostly not for publication); the scholars asked each other and the practitioners unexpected questions. But over time, the fact that reflective practitioners and full-time researchers had very different reasons for participating began to produce conflicts within the group. Some practitioners came to feel that they were being "used" by researchers as informants rather than as collaborators. Some researchers were frustrated with the practitioners' insistence on making decisions about research goals without committing their own time and resources to implement them.

After the first stage of qualitative studies, we concluded that our strategy of large-scale participatory action research—with as many as 40 people involved in establishing the agenda—was unmanageable for a research project. A smaller group of academics, including three who were deeply involved in river basin committees themselves, slowly took up the reins. But the early stage had produced a long-lasting network of researchers and practitioners throughout Brazil who referred to themselves as members of the Watermark Project for many years. If on the one hand we relied on our partners in this network to help understand the political process we were studying, on the other hand we found ourselves contributing, even if in a small way, to those processes. The summary volume produced out of the baseline studies was widely disseminated, and the project developed a (frequently exaggerated) reputation for high-quality research.

Abers, who lives in Brazil, was regularly asked to participate in professional meetings of water specialists or to speak to the members of some of the newly created decision-making arenas we were studying. Such occasions were opportunities to find out more about what different kinds of actors thought about the process. But they also meant that in some way, however small, we were changing it. Abers's work as a university professor often crossed over with that of observer of water politics, as professionals from the area took her courses, sought her advice, and so on. In perhaps the most complicated of such relationships, she became co-advisor to an engineering doctoral student who had been a key actor working for the National Water Agency in most of that agency's dealings with river basin committees. The student had extensive knowledge of some of the committees we were studying and about the National Water Agency. His other adviser had been director of that agency and a key actor in the national water policy since its inception.

The fact that the Watermark Project started disseminating results in the technical community long before the research ended also had strange feedback effects on our own work. This was demonstrated vividly in 2007, when a graduate student we hired interviewed the new president of one of the committees we had been following closely since 2001. The student asked the interviewee to describe the history of the committee. When she asked where he had heard a certain part of the story, he said he had read it in a Watermark Project report written by Abers. We realized that by studying them over time our subjects were influenced by the narratives we had constructed about their own organizations.

Perhaps more disconcertingly, several of our closest research colleagues from the project have been involved in policy making, lately in leadership positions in their states. We have been deeply influenced in our understanding of how Brazilian water management works by their interpretations. But if on the one hand we have pilfered many of their ideas and used them for our own purposes in this book, on the other hand their practices have certainly been influenced by our ongoing discussions. The construction of close relationships is probably the natural result of any long-term research on human interactions and contributes deeply to our interpretive capacity. But they also place us hopelessly outside of any conception of social scientists as neutral observers. We are also tangled up.

In a clear demonstration of our own entanglement, the project sponsored a two-day conference, August 18–20, 2008, in São Paulo called "Água da Gente: Um Olhar sobre os Comitês de Bacia Hidrográfica," or "The People's Water: An Assessment of River Basin Committees." The event was held in the auditorium of CETESB, the São Paulo state environmental agency, a space granted thanks to Rosa Maria Mancini, then director of water resources in the state's environmental secretariat. Mancini, who figures in the book as the executive secretary of the Litoral Norte basin committee, was also a member of the founding group of practitioners in the Watermark Project. The meeting was attended by several hundred people, including committee members, scholars, students, and activists from the north to the south of Brazil. There were three groups of speakers. One presented a set of papers that would later be published in 2010 as the edited volume *Água e Política* (Abers 2010). The second group included several well-known experts in Brazilian and Latin American water policy: one, Gilberto Canali, is a long-time participant in the Brazilian Water Resources Association; another, Axel Dourjeanni, is one of two water policy specialists at CEPAL/ECLA in Santiago. The third group included practitioners from most Brazilian states, who reported on the current situation of river basin committees and of state government approaches to water management where they were working. Some had long-standing connections to the project, and others did not.

A striking feature of many of the presentations and of the discussions that followed them was an assumption that the Watermark Project itself had become a functioning institution—indeed, that it had at least as much solidity and duration as many of the committees it was studying. It had become a thing—it had acquired a certain kind of practical authority. Participants in the meeting made suggestions about which river basins or topics the Watermark Project should study next. In general, these comments were guided not by academic curiosity but by the more pragmatic desire to discover the strategies people were using to deal with emerging problems. But by then, the project was already ending. At the present moment, it has no independent funding or plans for action. On the other hand, as we have shown in this study of river basin organizations, such initiatives rise and fall over time. New leaders revive and make use of dormant traces of structures or identities, enliven them with new practices, and engage publics they had not been reaching. If such an occurrence were to create a new generation of *marcadaguenses* (the word one participant coined to describe the people associated with the project), we could only applaud.

List of Interviews

1. Federal government official, Secretariat of the Environment (SEMA), Brasília, November 1, 1990, by Margaret Keck
2. Federal government official, DNAEE, Brasília, May 15, 1991, by Margaret Keck
3. Two state government officials, FUNDAP, São Paulo, May 25, 1999, by Margaret Keck
4. Ex-state government official, FUNDAP, São Paulo, May 18, 1999, e-mail conversation, with Margaret Keck
5. State government official, FUNDAP São Paulo, December 1990, by Cristina Saliba
6. Employee, state sanitation company, SABESP, São Paulo, May 26, 1999, by Margaret Keck
7. Government official, DAEE, São Paulo, May 13, 1999, by Margaret Keck
8. Former state government official, DAEE, São Paulo, May 26, 1999, by Margaret Keck
9. Two state government officials, Secretariat of Environment, May 1999, São Paulo, by Margaret Keck.
10. State government official, DAEE, São Paulo, July 20, 2000, by Margaret Keck
11. NGO leader, São Paulo, July 19, 2000, by Margaret Keck
12. State government official, CETESB, São Paulo, July 17, 2001, by Margaret Keck
13. Federal government official, National Water Agency, Brasília, May 10, 2002, by Rebecca Abers
14. Federal government official, National Water Agency, Brasília, May 22, 2002, by Rebecca Abers
15. Federal government official, National Secretariat of Water Resources, Brasília, May 15, 2002, by Rebecca Abers

16. International agency staffer, IICA, Brasília, May 15, 2002, by Rebecca Abers

17. Congressional staff member, national Chamber of Deputies, Brasília, May 16, 2002, by Rebecca Abers

18. Ex-state government official, DNAEE, Brasília, May 22, 2002, by Rebecca Abers

19. Federal government official, National Secretariat of Water Resources, Brasília, May 27, 2002, by Rebecca Abers

20. Federal government official, National Secretariat of Water Resources, Brasília, January 1, 2001, by Rebecca Abers

21. Ex-employee, national Chamber of Deputies, Brasília, June 26, 2002, by Rebecca Abers

22. Federal government official, National Water Agency, Brasília, 2003, by Margaret Keck and Rebecca Abers

23. Consultant, Minas Gerais State Association of Industries, Belo Horizonte, May 28, 2003, by Rebecca Abers

24. Federal government official, National Water Agency, telephone interview, Brasília, February 7, 2001, by Rebecca Abers

25. Federal government official, National Water Agency, Brasília, February 14, 2001, by Rebecca Abers

26. Federal government official, National Secretariat of Water Resources, Brasília, March 23, 2005, by Rebecca Abers

27. State government official, INEA, Rio de Janeiro, June 11, 2009, by Rebecca Abers

28. State government official, INEA, Brasília, June 30, 2011, by Rebecca Abers

29. Former federal government official, National Water Agency, e-mail correspondence, Brasília, September 20–21, 2010, by Rebecca Abers

30. Former federal government official, National Water Agency, e-mail correspondence, October 13–26, 2011, with Rebecca Abers

31. Former state government official, DAEE, Brasília, January 29, 2010, by Rebecca Abers

32. State government official, INEA, Rio de Janeiro, April 15, 2010, by Rebecca Abers

33. State government official, INEA, Rio de Janeiro, April 15, 2010, by Rebecca Abers

34. Former federal government official, National Water Agency, Brasília, December 14, 2010, by Rebecca Abers

35. Municipal government official (City of Belo Horizonte), Belo Horizonte, June 21, 2001, by Rebecca Abers

36. State government official, EMATER, Belo Horizonte, June 22, 2001, by Rebecca Abers

37. Community activist, Belo Horizonte, June 22, 2001, by Rebecca Abers
38. University professor, Manuelzão Project, Belo Horizonte, June 22, 2001, by Rebecca Abers
39. Businessperson (Tourism), Belo Horizonte, June 23, 2001, by Rebecca Abers
40. NGO staffer, Belo Horizonte, June 25, 2001, by Rebecca Abers
41. Corporate employee (Mining), Belo Horizonte, June 25, 2001, by Rebecca Abers
42. State government official, IGAM, Belo Horizonte, June 25, 2001, by Rebecca Abers
43. Municipal government official (Belo Horizonte), Belo Horizonte, June 26, 2001, by Rebecca Abers
44. NGO Staffer, Belo Horizonte, November 5, 2001, by Rebecca Abers
45. Researcher, Fundação João Pinheiro, Belo Horizonte, November 7, 11, 2001, by Rebecca Abers
46. Professor, Federal University of Minas Gerais, Belo Horizonte, November 8, 2001, by Rebecca Abers
47. State government official, IGAM, Belo Horizonte, November 5, 2001, by Rebecca Abers
48. Municipal government official (Raposas), Belo Horizonte, November 9, 2001, by Rebecca Abers
49. University professor/Manuelzão project, Belo Horizonte, November 9, 2001, by Rebecca Abers
50. Municipal government official (Varzea da Palma), telephone interview, November 9, 2001, by Rebecca Abers
51. Municipal government official (Rio Acima), Belo Horizonte, November 10, 2001, by Rebecca Abers
52. Employee of the Velhas Committee Technical Unit, Belo Horizonte, May 22, 2003, by Rebecca Abers
53. State government official, IGAM, Belo Horizonte, May 22, 2003, by Rebecca Abers
54. Former state government official, IGAM, telephone interview, April 4, 2002, by Rebecca Abers
55. Staff, Peixe Vivo Water Agency, Belo Horizonte, January 31, 2008, by Ana Karine Pereira
56. State sanitation company employee (COPASA), Belo Horizonte, January 29, 2008, by Ana Karine Pereira
57. Municipal sanitation agency employee (Itabirito), Belo Horizonte, January 30, 2008, by Ana Karine Pereira
58. Corporate employee (mining), Belo Horizonte, June 28, 2008, by Ana Karine Pereira

59. Community activist, Ouro Preto, January 30, 2008, by Ana Karine Pereira
60. Municipal government official (Belo Horizonte), Belo Horizonte, January 30, 2008, by Ana Karine Pereira
61. Municipal sanitation agency employee (Sete Lagoas), Belo Horizonte, January 29, 2008, by Ana Karine Pereira
62. Staffer, Manuelzão Project, Belo Horizonte, January 28, 2008, by Ana Karine Pereira
63. Farmer, Belo Horizonte, January 25, 2008, by Ana Karine Pereira
64. University professor (FURB), telephone interview, April 20, 2009, by Rebecca Abers
65. University employee (FURB), Foz de Iguaçu, October 26, 2007, by Ana Karine Pereira
66. State government official (SDS), Florianópolis, October 29, 2007, by Ana Karine Pereira
67. Three state government officials (DEINFRA), Florianópolis, October 29, 2007, by Ana Karine Pereira
68. NGO activist, Blumenau, October 31, 2007, by Ana Karine Pereira
69. Employee of the Itajaí Water Agency, Blumenau, November 1, 2007, by Ana Karine Pereira
70. Journalist involved in the Itajaí committee, Blumenau, November 1, 2007, by Ana Karine Pereira
71. Employee of the Piava Project, Blumenau, November 1, 2007, by Ana Karine Pereira
72. Federal government official (Caixa Economica Federal), Blumenau, November 5, 2007, by Ana Karine Pereira
73. State government official (EPAGRI), Itajaí, November 6, 2007, by Ana Karine Pereira
74. NGO staffer, Itajaí, November 6, 2007, by Ana Karine Pereira
75. Employee of agroindustrial cooperative, Rio do Sul, November 6, 2007, by Ana Karine Pereira
76. Businessperson, Itajaí, November 7, 2007, by Ana Karine Pereira
77. Employee of the Piava Project, Blumenau, November 7, 2007, by Ana Karine Pereira
78. Employee of the Japan International Cooperation Agency, Tokyo, June 22, 2010, interview by Jackson de Toni
79. University professor (FURB), telephone interview, June 3, 2011, by Rebecca Abers
80. State government official, former executive secretary of basin committee, Ubatuba, July 25, 2001, by Margaret Keck
81. Journalist, Ubatuba, July 25, 2001, by Margaret Keck

82. Employee of Chamber of Commerce and Industry, Ubatuba, July 25, 2001, by Margaret Keck

83. Civil engineer and government official, state health secretariat, Caraguatatuba, July 26, 2001, by Margaret Keck

84. Community activist, Ubatuba, July 26, 2001, by Margaret Keck

85. Municipal government official, Ubatuba, July 26, 2001, by Margaret Keck

86. Farmer, Ubatuba, July 27, 2001, by Margaret Keck

87. Municipal government official, Caraguatatuba, July 27, 2001, by Margaret Keck

88. Municipal government official, Caraguatatuba, June 2002, by Margaret Keck

89. Lawyer, Caraguatatuba, July 27, 2001, by Margaret Keck

90. Two municipal government officials, Ilha Bela, July 30, 2001, by Margaret Keck

91. Former municipal government official, Ilha Bela, July 30, 2001, by Margaret Keck

92. Municipal government official, São Sebastião, July 30, 2001, by Margaret Keck

93. State sanitation company (SABESP), Ubatuba, July 31, 2001, by Margaret Keck

94. State government official (CETESB), Ubatuba, June 10–11, 2002, by Margaret Keck

95. Prosecutor, Ministério Público, Caraguatatuba, June 2002, by Margaret Keck

96. Member of the municipal legislature, Caraguatatuba, June 2002, by Margaret Keck

97. Environmental engineer, Caraguatatuba, June 2002, by Margaret Keck

98. Municipal government official (São Sebastião), Caraguatatuba, June 2002, by Margaret Keck

99. Journalist, São Sebastião, June 2002, by Margaret Keck

100. Environmental activist, Ubatuba, June 2002, by Margaret Keck

101. Municipal government official (Ilha Bela), São Sebastião, June 2002, by Margaret Keck

102. Agronomist, state forest protected area, Ubatuba, June 2002, by Margaret Keck

103. State government official (CETESB), Ubatuba, December 14, 2007, by Ana Karine Pereira

104. NGO activist, Ubatuba, December 15, 2007, by Ana Karine Pereira

105. NGO activist, Ubatuba, December 15, 2007, by Ana Karine Pereira

106. NGO activist, Ubatuba, December 17, 2007, by Ana Karine Pereira

107. State government employee (CETESB), Ubatuba, December 17, 2007, by Ana Karine Pereira
108. State government official (Forestry Institute), Ubatuba December 17, 2007, by Ana Karine Pereira
109. State government official (Secretariat of Environment), Ubatuba, December 18, 2007, by Ana Karine Pereira
110. Engineer and NGO activist, Ubatuba, December 18, 2007, by Ana Karine Pereira
111. Employee, state sanitation company, Ubatuba, December 18, 2007, by Ana Karine Pereira
112. Two state government officials (Secretariat of Education), Ubatuba, December 19, 2007, by Ana Karine Pereira
113. Geologist, Ubatuba, December 19, 2007, by Ana Karine Pereira
114. State government official (CETESB), telephone interview, July 7, 2011, by Rebecca Abers
115. University professor, Brasília, April 19, 2001, by Rebecca Abers
116. Employee, Federal District legislature, Brasília, April 27, 2001, by Rebecca Abers.
117. Federal District government official (Secretariat of the Environment), Brasília, July 23, 2001, by Rebecca Abers
118. NGO activist, Brasília, July 25, 2001, by Rebecca Abers
119. Federal District government official (environment secretariat), Brasília, July 26, 2001, by Rebecca Abers
120. University professor, Brasília, July 31, 2001, by Rebecca Abers
121. Community activist, Brasília, September 9, 2001, by Rebecca Abers
122. Employee, Federal District sanitation company (CAESB), Brasília, September 9, 2001, by Rebecca Abers
123. Community activist, Brasília, September 4, 2001, by Rebecca Abers
124. Federal District government official (Secretariat of the Environment), Brasília, September 13, 2001, by Rebecca Abers
125. Federal District government official (EMATER), Brasília, September 14, 2001, by Rebecca Abers
126. Activist for a sports club, Brasília, September 15, 2001, by Rebecca Abers
127. State government official (DAEE), São Paulo, May 28–29, 1998, by Margaret Keck
128. State government official (DAEE), São Paulo, São Paulo, March 6, 2001, by Margaret Keck
129. Former state government official (Secretariat of Water Resources), São Paulo, March 19, 2001, by Margaret Keck
130. Former state government official (Secretariat of the Environment), São Paulo, May 1999, by Margaret Keck

131. Former federal deputy, São Paulo, May 28, 1999, by Margaret Keck
132. Environmental activist, Diadema, May 1999, by Margaret Keck
133. Two state government officials, CETESB, São Paulo, July 16, 2001, by Margaret Keck
134. NGO staffer, São Paulo, 2001, by Margaret Keck
135. NGO activist, Rio de Janeiro, telephone interview, July 7, 2011, by Rebecca Abers
136. State government official (FUNDAP), São Paulo, 2002, by Paula Lopes
137. Former state government official (IGAM), Belo Horizonte, May 23, 2003, by Rebecca Abers
138. State government officials (CETESB), Ubatuba, August 14, 2004, by Margaret Keck
139. State government official (DAEE), São Paulo, August 17, 2001, by Margaret Keck
140. University professor, Brasília, July 10, 2012, by Rebecca Abers
141. State government official (IGAM), telephone interview, Belo Horizonte, July 11, 2012, by Rebecca Abers
142. Consultant, telephone interview, Florianópolis, July 17, 2012, by Rebecca Abers
143. State government official, e-mail correspondence, Porto Alegre, January 2, 2011, with Rebecca Abers
144. University professor, Blumenau, November 19, 2009, by Rebecca Abers

REFERENCES

Abers, Rebecca Neaera. 1996. "The Workers' Party and Participatory Planning in Brazil: From Ideas to Practice in an Emerging Democracy." *Latin American Perspectives* 23 (4): 35–53.
———. 2000. *Inventing Local Democracy: Grassroots Politics in Brazil.* Boulder, Colo.: Lynne Reinner.
———, ed. 2010. *Água e política: Atores, instituições e poder nos organismos colegiados de bacia hidrográfica no Brasil.* São Paulo: Annablume.
Abers, Rebecca Neaera, and Karina Jorge Dino. 2005. "Descentralização da gestão da água: Por que os comitês de bacia estão sendo criados?" *Ambiente e Sociedade* 8 (2): 1–26.
Abers, Rebecca N., and Margaret E. Keck. 2008. "Representando a diversidade: Estado, sociedade e 'relações fecundas' nos conselhos gestores." *Caderno CRH 21* (52): 99–112.
———. 2009. "Mobilizing the State: The Erratic Partner in Brazil's Participatory Water Policy." *Politics & Society* 37 (2): 289–314.
Abers, Rebecca Neaera, Lizandra Serafim, and Luciana Tatagiba. 2011. "A participação na era Lula: Repertórios de interação em um estado heterogêneo." Paper presented at the 35th National Meeting of Anpocs, Caxambu/MG, October 24–28.
Abers, Rebecca Neaera, and Marisa von Bülow. 2011. "Movimentos sociais na teoria e na prática: Como estudar o ativismo através da fronteira entre estado e sociedade?" *Sociologias* 13 (28) (December): 52–84.
Abrucio, Fernando Luiz. 1994. "Os barões da federação." *Lua Nova: Revista de Cultura e Política* 33: 165–183.
———. 2005. "A coordenação federativa no Brasil: A experiência do período FHC e os desafios do governo Lula." *Revista de Sociologia e Política* 24: 41–67.
Agência Nacional de Águas. 2002. *A evolução da gestão dos recursos hídricos no Brasil.* Brasília: Agência Nacional de Água.
———. 2003. "Bacia hidrográfica do Rio Paraíba do Sul. Cobrança pelo uso da água. Resolução CNRH No. 19/2002. Balanço da Arrecadação—Por Usuários. Exercício de 2003." Available at http://www.ana.gov.br/GestaoRecHidricos/CobrancaUso/_docsArrecadacao/2003/PorUsuarioPBS_2003.pdf, accessed April 23, 2010.
———. 2007. *GEO Brasil recursos hídricos componente da série de relatórios sobre o estado e perspectivas do meio ambiente no Brasil—Resumo executivo* Brasília: Agência Nacional de Água. Available at http://www.ana.gov.br/bibliotecavirtual/arquivos/20070309135854_GEO%20Brasil%20Recursos%20H%C3%ADdricos%20-%20Resumo%20executivo.pdf, accessed April 23, 2010.
———. 2010a. *Cobrança pelo uso da água—Bacia hidrográfica do Rio Paraíba do Sul. Arrecadação por usuários—Exercício de 2010.* Brasília: Agência Nacional de Águas, Superintendência de Administração, Finanças e Gestão de Pessoas. Available at http://www.ana.gov.br/GestaoRecHidricos/CobrancaUso/_docsArrecadacao/2010/PorUsuarioPBS_2010.pdf, accessed April 23, 2010.

Agência Nacional de Águas. 2010b. *Cobrança pelo uso da água—Bacia hidrográfica do Rio Paraíba do Sul Balanço da arrecadação—Exercícios de 2003 a 2010.* Brasília: Agência Nacional de Águas, Superintendência de Administração, Finanças e Gestão de Pessoas. Available at http://www.ana.gov.br/GestaoRecHidricos/CobrancaUso/_docsArrecadacao/2010/AcumuladaPBS_2010.pdf, accessed April 23, 2010.

AGEVAP, Associação Pró-Gestão das Águas da Bacia Hidrográfica do Rio Paraíba do Sul. 2007. *Plano de recursos hídricos da Bacia do Rio Paraíba do Sul—Resumo. Relatório contratual— R-10—PSR-012-R1.* Rio de Janeiro: AGEVAP/Fundação COPPETEC/Laboratório de Hidrologia e Estudos de Meio Ambiente.

Akhmouch, Aziza. 2012. *Water Governance in Latin America and the Caribbean: A Multi-level Approach.* OECD Regional Development Working Papers. Paris: OECD. Available at http://www.oecd.org/gov/regional-policy/50064981.pdf, accessed April 2, 2013.

Alexander, Jeffrey C. 2004. "Cultural Pragmatics: Social Performance between Ritual and Strategy." *Sociological Theory* 22 (4): 527–573.

Allen, John. 2008. "Pragmatism and Power, or The Power to Make a Difference in a Radically Contingent World." *Geoforum* 39 (4): 1613–1624.

Almeida, Debora Cristina Rezende de. 2011. "Repensando representação política e legitimidade democrática: Entre a unidade e a pluralidade." Doctoral diss. (political science), Universidade Federal de Minas Gerais.

Alvim, Angélica Tanus Beatti. 2008. "Desafios à gestão integrada da bacia metropolitana de São Paulo a partir das ações do Comitê do Alto Tietê." Paper presented at the 4th National Meeting of the Associação Nacional de Pesquisa e Pós-Graduação em Ambiente e Sociedade, Brasília, June 4–6.

Amaral, Helena Kerr do. 1998. "Relatório parcial de tese: A política regulatória da água e a democratização do espaço público." Unpublished manuscript.

Ansell, Chris[topher K.] 2000. "The Networked Polity: Regional Development in Western Europe." *Governance* 13 (2): 279–291.

——. 2011. *Pragmatist Democracy: Evolutionary Learning as Public Philosophy.* New York: Oxford University Press.

Ansell, Christopher K., and Giuseppe Di Palma, eds. 2004. *Restructuring Territoriality: Europe and the United States Compared.* Cambridge, U.K.: Cambridge University Press.

Ansell, Chris[topher K.], and Alison Gash. 2008. "Collaborative Governance in Theory and Practice." *Journal of Public Administration Research and Theory* 18 (4): 543–571.

Antunes, Elton, Ana Carolina Silveira Fonseca, and Rennan Lanna Martins Mafra. 2007–2008. "Projeto Manuelzão e a extensão em comunicação, um constante aprendizado." *Revista Brasileira de Ensino de Jornalismo* 1 (3): 136–157. Available at http://www.fnpj.org.br/rebej/ojs/viewissue.php?id=7, accessed July 17, 2012.

Arantes, Rogério Bastos. 2002. *Ministério Público e política no Brasil.* São Paulo: Editora da PUC.

Arendt, Hannah. 1961. *Between Past and Future.* New York: Viking.

Arretche, Marta. 2000. *Estado federativo e políticas sociais: Determinantes da descentralização.* São Paulo: Editora Revan.

Associação dos Engenheiros e Arquitetos de Piracicaba, Divisão de Meio Ambiente. 1987. "Campanha Ano 2000 Redenção Ecológica da Bacia da Piracicaba: Carta de Reivindicações ao Governo Orestes Quércia." Unpublished document. May.

Avritzer, Leonardo. 2002. "Modelos de deliberação democrática: Uma análise do orçamento participativo no Brasil." In *Democratizar a democracia: Os Caminhos da democracia participativa,* ed. Boaventura da Souza Santos, 561–598. Rio de Janeiro: Civilização Brasileira.

——. 2003. "O orçamento participativo e a teoria democrática: Um balanço crítico." In *A inovação democrática no Brasil,* ed. Leonardo Avritzer and Zander Navarro, 14–57. São Paulo: Cortez.

——. 2009. *Participatory Institutions in Democratic Brazil*. Baltimore, Md.: Johns Hopkins University Press.

——, ed. 2010. *A dinâmica da participação local no Brasil*. São Paulo: Cortez.

Axelrod, Robert, and Michael D. Cohen. 2001. *Harnessing Complexity: Organizational Implications of a Scientific Frontier*. New York: Simon & Schuster.

Azevedo, Luiz Gabriel T. de, and Musa Asad. 2000. "Implementation of Bulk Water Pricing in Brazil." In *The Political Economy of Water Pricing Reform*, ed. Ariel Dinar, 321–338. Washington, D.C.: World Bank.

Baiocci, Gianpaolo. 2005. *Militants and Citizens: The Politics of Participatory Democracy in Porto Alegre*. Stanford, Calif.: Stanford University Press.

Bakker, Karen. 2010. *Privatizing Water: Governance Failure and the World's Urban Water Crisis*. Ithaca, N.Y.: Cornell University Press.

Ballestero, Andrea. 2004. "Institutional Adaptation and Water Reform in Ceará: Revisiting Structures for Social Participation at the Local Level." Master's thesis (natural resources and environment), University of Michigan.

Barbi, Fabiana. 2007. "Capital social e ação coletiva na gestão das bacias dos Rios Piracicaba, Capivari e Jundiaí: Os desafios da gestão compartilhada do sistema Cantareira—SP." Master's thesis (education), University of São Paulo.

Barraquê, Bernard. 2000. "Water Institutions and Management in France." In *Water Resources Management: Brazilian and European Trends and Approaches*, ed. Gilberto Canali, Francisco Nunes Correia, Francisco Lobato, and Enéas Machado, 77–92. Porto Alegre: Brazilian Water Resources Association, International Water Resources Association.

Barrow, Christopher J. 1998. "River Basin Development Planning and Management: A Critical Review." *World Development* 26 (1): 171–186.

Barth, Flávio Terra, n.d. "Cobrança como suporte financeiro á política estadual de recursos hídricos." Unpublished manuscript.

——. 1998. "Relatório sobre a sessão 'aspectos institucionais: Legislação e organização de siste-mas de recursos e entidades participantes: Natureza jurídica, composição, atribuições e formas de participação." Paper presented at the Simpósio Internacional sobre Gestão de Recursos Hídricos, Gramado, Rio Grande do Sul, October 5–8.

Barzelay, Michael. 2001. *The New Public Management: Improving Research and Policy Dialogue*. Berkeley: University of California Press.

Baumgartner, Frank R., and Brian D. Jones. 1993. *Agendas and Instability in American Politics*. Chicago: University of Chicago Press.

Berk, Gerald, and Dennis Galvan. 2009. "How People Experience and Change Institutions: a Field Guide to Creative Syncretism." *Theory and Society* 38 (6): 543–580.

Bevir, Mark. 2006. "How Narratives Explain." In *Interpretation and Method: Empirical Research Methods and the Interpretive Turn*, ed. Dvora Yanow and Peregrine Schwartz-Shea, 281–290. Armonk, N.Y.: M. E. Sharpe.

Bevir, Mark, and R. A. W. Rhodes. 2010. *The State as Cultural Practice*. New York: Oxford University Press.

Bevir, Mark, and David Richards. 2009. "Decentering Policy Networks: A Theoretical Agenda." *Public Administration* 87 (1): 3–14.

Blau, Peter M. 1963. "Critical Remarks on Weber's Theory of Authority." *American Political Science Review* 57 (2): 305–316.

Blyth, Mark. 2001. "The Transformation of the Swedish Model: Economic Ideas, Distributional Conflict and Institutional Change." *World Politics* 54 (1): 1–26.

——. 2002. *Great Transformations: The Rise and Decline of Embedded Liberalism*. Cambridge, U.K.: Cambridge University Press.

Borba, Julian, and Lígia Helena H. Lüchmann, ed. 2007. *Orçamento participativo: Análise das experiências desenvolvidas em Santa Catarina*. Florianópolis: Insular.

Börzel, Tanja A. 1998. "Organizing Babylon: On the Different Conceptions of Policy Networks." *Public Administration* 76, no. 2: 253–273.

Boschi, Renato. 2009. "Estado desenvolvimentista no Brasil: Continuidades e incertidumbres." Paper prepared for the colloquium The Brazilian State: Paths and Prospects of Dirigisme and Liberalization, Bildner Center for Western Hemisphere Studies, City University New York, November 9–10.

Bourdieu, Pierre. 1977. *Outline of a Theory of Practice.* Cambridge, U.K.: Cambridge University Press.

Breiger, Ronald L. 2000. "A Tool Kit for Practice Theory." *Poetics* 27 (2–3): 91–115.

Bresser-Pereira, Luiz Carlos. 2001. "Sociedade Civil: Sua democratização para a reforma do estado." In *Sociedade e estado em transformação*, ed. Luiz Carlos Bresser-Pereira, Jorge Wilheim, and Lourdes Sola, 67–118. São Paulo: Editora Unesp.

Bresser-Pereira, Luiz Carlos, and Eli Diniz. 2009. "Empresariado industrial, democracia e poder político." *Revista Novos Estudos* 84: 83–99.

Burt, Ronald S. 1995. *Structural Holes: The Social Structure of Competition.* Cambridge, Mass.: Harvard University Press.

Caldeira, Teresa, and James Holston. 2005. "State and Urban Space in Brazil: From Modernist Planning to Democratic Interventions." In *Global Assemblages: Technology, Politics and Ethics as Anthropological Problems*, ed. Aihwa Ong and Stephen J. Collier, 393–416. Malden, Mass.: Blackwell.

Callado, Antônio. 1960. *Os industriais da seca e os "galileus" de Pernambuco: Aspecto da luta pela reforma agrária no Brasil.* Rio de Janeiro: Civilização Brasileira.

Canepa, Eugenio Miguel, Jaildo Santos Pereira, and Antônio Eduardo Leão Lanna. 1999. "A política de recursos hídricos e o princípio usuário-pagador (PUP)." *Revista Brasileira de Recursos Hídricos* 4 (1): 103–117.

Cano, Wilson. 2000. "Celso Furtado e a questão regional no Brasil." In *Celso Furtado e o Brasil*, ed. Maria da Conceição Tavares, 93–120. São Paulo: Fundação Perseu Abramo.

Capoccia, Giovanni, and R. Daniel Kelemen. 2007. "The Study of Critical Junctures: Theory, Narrative, and Counterfactuals in Historical Institutionalism." *World Politics* 59 (3): 341–369.

Cardoso, Adalberto Moreira. 1999. *Sindicatos, trabalhadores e a coqueluche neoliberal: A era Vargas acabou?* Rio de Janeiro: Editora Fundação Getulio Vargas.

Cardoso, Fernando Henrique. 1970. "Aspectos politicos do planejamento." In *Planejamento no Brasil*, ed. Betty Mindlin Lafer, 161–184. São Paulo: Perspectiva.

Cardoso, Maria Lúcia de Macedo. 2003. "A Democracia das águas na sua prática: O caso dos comitês de bacias hidrográficas de Minas Gerais." Doctoral diss. (social anthropology), Rio de Janeiro, Museu Nacional.

Carmo, Roberto Luiz do, and Ana Claudia Chaves Teixeira. 2011. "Vinte anos de gestão participativa da água em São Paulo (Brasil): Uma avaliação." Paper presented at the 14th World Water Congress, September 25–29, Porto de Galinhas, Brazil.

Carpenter, Daniel P. 2000. "State Building through Reputation Building: Coalitions of Esteem and Program Innovation in the National Postal System, 1883–1913." *Studies in American Political Development* 14 (2): 121–155.

———. 2010. *Reputation and Power: Organizational Image and Pharmaceutical Regulation at the FDA.* Princeton, N.J.: Princeton University Press.

Castellano, Maria. 2007. "Relações entre poder público e sociedade na gestão dos recursos hídricos: O caso do Consórcio Intermunicipal das Bacias Hidrográficas dos Rios Piracicaba, Capivari e Jundiaí." Doctoral diss. (environmental science), University of São Paulo.

Castellano, Maria, and Fabiana Barbi. 2006. "Avanços na gestão compartilhada dos recursos hídricos nas bacias dos Rios Piracicaba, Capivari e Jundiaí." *Revista São Paulo em Perspectiva* 20 (2): 46–58.

Castiglione, Dario, and Mark Warren. 2006. "Rethinking Democratic Representation: Eight Theoretical Issues." Paper presented at the conference on Rethinking Democratic Representation, Centre for the Study of Democratic Institutions, University of British Columbia, May 18–19.

CBHSF, Comitê da Bacia Hidrográfica do São Francisco. 2003. "Deliberação 6," October 3. Available at http://www.saofrancisco.cbh.gov.br/_docs/deliberacoes/2003/DeliberacaoCBHSF_n_06.pdf, accessed October 18, 2011.

César, Julio Cerqueira, Rubens Born, and Malu Ribeiro. n.d. "O que é a cobrança da água." São Paulo, Rede das Águas. Available at http://www.rededasaguas.org.br/ferramentas/o_que_e.htm, accessed March 4, 2010.

Chisholm, Donald. 1995. "Problem Solving and Institutional Design." *Journal of Public Administration Research and Theory* 5 (4): 451–492.

Christofidis, Demétrios. 2001. "Olhares sobre a política de recursos hídricos no brasil: O caso da bacia do São Francisco." Doctoral diss. (sustainable development), University of Brasília.

Cleaver, Frances. 2002. "Reinventing Institutions: Bricolage and the Social Embeddedness of Natural Resource Management." *European Journal of Development Research* 14 (2): 11–30.

Clegg, Stewart. 2010. "The State, Power, and Agency: Missing in Action in Institutional Theory?" *Journal of Management Inquiry* 19 (1): 4–13.

Clemens, Elisabeth. S. 1993. "Organizational Repertoires and Institutional Change: Women's Groups and the Transformation of U.S. Politics, 1890–1920." *American Journal of Sociology* 98 (4): 755–798.

CNBB, Conferência Nacional dos Bispos do Brasil. 2004. "VERSAO 1, Texto base." Campanha da Fraternidade 2004: Agua fonte de vida. Available at http://www.cf.org.br, accessed July 15, 2010.

Coelho, Marco Antônio. 2005. *Os descaminhos do São Francisco.* São Paulo: Paz e Terra.

Collier, Ruth Berins, and David Collier. 2002. *Shaping the Political Arena: Critical Junctures, the Labor Movement, and Regime Dynamics in Latin America*, 2d ed. Notre Dame, Ind.: University of Notre Dame Press.

Conca, Ken. 2005. *Governing Water: Contentious Transnational Politics and Global Institution Building.* Cambridge Mass.: MIT Press.

Corrêa, Izabela Moreira. 2007. "Planejamento estratégico e gestão pública por resultados no processo de reforma administrativa do Estado de Minas Gerais." *Revista de Administração Pública* 41 (3): 487–504.

Cortês, Soraya M. V. 1998. "Conselhos municipais de saúde: A possibilidade dos usuários participarem e os determinantes da participação." *Ciência e Saúde Coletiva* 2 (1): 6–17.

Coslovsky, Salo, Roberto Pires, and Susan S. Silbey. 2012. "The Pragmatic Politics of Regulatory Enforcement." In *Handbook on the Politics of Regulation*, ed. David Levi-Faur, 322–334. Cheltenham, U.K.: Edward Elgar.

Costa, Maria Angelica. 2008. "Reflexões sobre a política participativa das águas: O caso CBH Velhas/MG." Master's thesis (geography), Universidade Federal de Minas Gerais.

Couto, Cláudio Gonçalves. 1998. "A longa constituinte: Reforma do estado e fluidez institucional no Brasil." *Dados* 41 (1). Available at http://www.scielo.br/scielo.php?script=sci_arttext&pid=S0011-52581998000100002, accessed April 2, 2013.

Cunha, Eleonora Schettini Martins. 2007. "A Efetividade deliberativa dos conselhos municipais de saúde e de criança e adolescente no Nordeste." In *A participação social no Nordeste*, ed. Leonardo Avritzer, 135–162. Belo Horizonte: Ed UFMG.

———. 2009. "Efetividade deliberativa: Estudo comparado de conselhos municipais de assistência social (1997–2006)." Doctoral diss. (political science), Universidade Federal de Minas Gerais.

Cury, Luana. 2002. "Comitê do rio Cipó: Esperança de maior preservação." *Jornal Manuelzão* 5 (20): 6.

Cunha, Fernando Monteiro da. 2004. "Desempenho institucional na gestão de recursos hídricos: O caso dos Subcomitês de Bacia Hidrográfica Cotia-Guarapiringa e Billings-Tamanduateí na Região Metropolitana de São Paulo." Master's thesis (environmental science), Universidade de São Paulo.

Silva, Simone Rosa da, Paula Kristhina Cordeiro Freire, Dayse Luna Barbosa, and Sandra Ferraz de Sá Wanderley. 2003. "A gestão de recursos hídricos no Estado de Pernambuco." Article by staff members at the Secretaria de Ciencia, Tecnologia, e Meio Ambiente, Unidade de Administração e Controle de Recursos Hidricos. Available at http://www.scribd.com/doc/95482771/A-Gestao-de-Recursos-Hidricos-Em-Pernambuco-Maio-2003, accessed August 24, 2012.

Dagnino, Evelina. 1998. "Culture Citizenship and Democracy: Changing Discourses and Practices of the Latin American Left." In *Cultures of Politics, Politics of Cultures: Revisioning Latin American Social Movements*, ed. Sonia Alvarez, Evelina Dagnino, and Artuto Escobar, 33–63. Boulder, Colo.: Westview Press.

———. 2002. "Sociedade civil, espaços públicos e a construção democrática no Brasil: Limites e possibilidades." In *Sociedade civil e espaços públicos no Brasil*, ed. Evelina Dagnino, 279–302. São Paulo: Paz e Terra.

Dagnino, Evelina, Alberto J. Olvera, and Aldo Panfichi. 2006. "Para uma outra leitura da disputa pela construção democrática na América Latina." In *A disputa pela construção democrática na América Latina*, ed. Evelina Dagnino, Alberto J Olvera, and Aldo Panfichi, 13–92. São Paulo: Paz e Terra.

Davis, Kenneth C. 1972. *Discretionary Justice*. Baton Rouge: Louisiana State University Press.

DCRH, Divisão de Controle de Recursos Hídricos. 1985. *Plano nacional de recursos hídricos: Documento preliminar, consolidando informações já disponíveis.* Brasília: MME/DNAEE/DCRH.

Defensoria da Água. 2004. *O estado real das águas no Brasil 2003–2004 (Sinopse).* Brasília: Defensoria da Água. Available at http://www.google.com.br/url?sa=t&source=web&ct=res&cd=2&ved=0CAoQFjAB&url=http%3A%2F%2Fwww.unifap.br%2Fppgdapp%2Fbiblioteca%2FEstado_aguas.doc&rct=j&q=defensoria+das+aguas&ei=tbl9S7-RFMK9lAf1_-WiBQ&usg=AFQjCNGMETkj0XmeHRHzJhdo55NYB95bg&sig2=iJffdJjm6-IObcazdBjsZg, accessed March 4, 2010.

Delbridge, Rick, and Tim Edwards. 2008. "Challenging Conventions: Roles and Processes during Non-isomorphic Institutional Change." *Human Relations* 61 (3): 299–325.

De Toni, Jackson. 2010. "Cooperação e conflito na construção da política industrial Brasileira: 1995 a 2010." Doctoral diss. proposal (political science), University of Brasília.

Dewey, John. 1927. *The Public and Its Problems*. Chicago: Swallow Press.

———. 1933. *How We Think*. Boston: D. C. Heath. Available at http://books.google.com.br/books?id=J-X9fDp0FpEC&printsec=frontcover&dq=dewey+how+we+think&source=bl&ots=oLcxR28Gl7&sig=eA6px9TateihXmgSADo3jKhI6uA&hl=en&sa=X&ei=r2pgUOa9CpCK9gS3w4DgDA&ved=0CCwQ6AEwAA#v=onepage&q&f=true, accessed September 24, 2012.

———. 1981. "The Need for a Recovery of Philosophy." In *The Philosophy of John Dewey*, ed. John J. McDermott, 58–97. Chicago: University of Chicago Press.

DiMaggio, Paul J., and Walter W. Powell. 1991. "The Iron Cage Revisited: Institutional Isomorphism and Collective Rationality in Organizational Fields." In *The New Institutionalism in Organizational Analysis*, ed. Walter Powell and Paul Dimaggio, 63–82. Chicago: University of Chicago Press.

Diniz, Eli, and Renato Boschi. 2000. "Globalização, herança corporativa e a representação dos interesses empresariais: Novas configurações no cenário pós-reformas." In *Elites políticas e econômicas no Brasil contemporâneo: A desconstrução da ordem corporativa e o papel do Legislativo no cenário pós-reformas*, ed. Renato Boschi, Eli Diniz, and Fabiano Santos, 15–90. São Paulo: Fundação Konrad Adenauer.

———. 2003. "Empresariado e estratégias de desenvolvimento." *Revista Brasileira de Ciências Sociais* 18 (52): 15–33.

DNAEE/SEMA, Departamento Nacional de Águas e Energia Elétrica/Secretaria de Meio Ambiente. 1983. *Anais do Seminário Internacional de Recursos Hídricos*. Brasília: DNAEE/SEMA.

Doimo, Ana Maria. 1995. *A vez e a voz do popular: Movimentos sociais e participação política no Brasil pós-70*. Rio de Janeiro: Relume Dumará.

Dooley, Kevin. 1997. "A Complex Adaptive Systems Model of Organizational Change." *Nonlinear Dynamics, Psychology, and Life Science* 1 (1): 69–97.

Douglas, Mary. 1986. *How Institutions Think*. Syracuse, N.Y.: Syracuse University Press.

Draibe, Sonia. 2003. "A política social no período FHC e o sistema de proteção social." *Tempo Social* 15 (2): 63–101.

Dulci, Otávio S. 1999. *Política e recuperação econômica em Minas Gerais*. Belo Horizonte: Editora UFMG.

Eça, Rodrigo Furtado, and Ana Paula Fracalanza. 2010. "Cobrança pelo uso da água em bacias de dupla dominialidade: Conflitos técnicos e de gestão nas Bacias Hidrográficas dos Rios Piracicaba, Capivari e Jundiaí." Paper presented at the 6th National Conference of the Associação Nacional de Pesquisa e Pós-Graduação em Ambiente e Sociedade, Florianópolis, October 4.

Edwards, Tim, and Ossie Jones. 2008. "Failed Institution Building: Understanding the Interplay between Agency, Social Skill and Context." *Scandinavian Journal of Management* 24 (1): 44–54.

Elmore, Richard F. 1979–1980. "Backward Mapping: Implementation Research and Policy Decisions." *Political Science Quarterly* 94: 601–616.

Emirbayer, Mustafa, and Jeff Goodwin. 1994. "Network Analysis, Culture and the Problem of Agency." *American Journal of Sociology* 99 (6): 1411–1454.

Emirbayer, Mustafa, and Ann Mische. 1998. "What Is Agency?" *American Journal of Sociology* 103 (4): 962–1023.

Empinotti, Vanessa Lucena. 2007. "Re-framing Participation: The Political Ecology of Water Management in the Lower São Francisco River Basin—Brazil." Doctoral diss. (geography), University of Colorado.

Evans, Peter B. 1995. *Embedded Autonomy: States and Industrial Transformation*. Princeton, N.J.: Princeton University Press.

———. 2002. "Introduction: Looking for Agents of Urban Livability in a Globalized Political Economy." In *Livable Cities? Urban Struggles for Livelihood and Sustainability*, ed. Peter B. Evans, 1–30. Berkeley: University of California Press.

Farrell, Henry, and Martha Finnemore. 2009. "Ontology, Methodology, and Causation in the American School of International Political Economy." *Review of International Political Economy* 16 (1): 58–71.

Feldmann, Fabio. 1994. "Projeto de Lei No 2.249, de 1991." Unpublished paper. Comissão de Defesa do Consumidor, Meio Ambiente e Minorias, Câmara dos Deputados, Brasília.

Fernandes, Rubem Cesar. 1994. *Privado porém público: o terceiro setor na América Latina*. Rio de Janeiro: Relume-Dumará.

Figueiredo, Argelina, and Fernando Limongi. 2006. "Poder de agenda na democracia Brasileira: Desempenho do governo no presidencialismo pluripartidário." In *Reforma política: Lições da história recente*, ed. Glaucio Soares and Lúcio Rennó, 249–280. Rio de Janeiro: Editora FGV.

Fligstein, Neil, and Doug McAdam. 2012. *A Theory of Fields.* New York: Oxford University Press.

Folha de São Paulo. 2003. "Só consenso total pode salvar projeto de cobrança." *Folha de São Paulo,* March 11. Available at http://www1.folha.uol.com.br/fsp/cotidian/ff0311200319.htm, accessed April 4, 2013.

Fontes, Aurélio Teodoro, and Marcelo Pereira Souza. 2004. "Modelo de cobrança para a gestão da escassez de água." *Revista Brasileira de Recursos Hídricos* 9 (2): 97–114.

Fontes, Luis Carlos. 2007. "Transposição: Água para todos ou água para poucos? Anatomia da maior fraude hídrica e o conflito federativo de uso da água no Brasil." *Revista do Comitê da Bacia Hidrográfica do Rio São Francisco* 1: 60–73.

Forester, John. 1999. *The Deliberative Practitioner: Encouraging Participatory Planning Processes.* Cambridge, Mass.: MIT Press.

Formiga Johnsson, Rosa Maria. 1998. "Les eaux brésiliennes: Analyse du passage à une gestion intégrée dans l´Etat de São Paulo". Doctoral diss. (environmental sciences and techniques), Université Paris XII, Val de Marne.

Formiga Johnsson, Rosa Maria, Jander Duarte Campos, Paulo Canedo de Magalhães, Paulo Roberto Ferreira Carneiro, Evaristo Samuel Villela Pedras, Patrick Thadeu Thomas, and Sergio Flavio Passos de Miranda. 2003. "A construção do pacto em torno da cobrança pelo uso da água na bacia do Rio Paraíba do Sul." Paper presented at the 15th Simpósio Brasileiro de Recursos Hídricos: Desafios à Gestão da Água no Limiar do Século XXI, Curitiba, Paraná, November 23–27.

Formiga Johnsson, Rosa Maria, and Karin Erika Kemper. 2005. "Institutional and Policy Analysis of River Basin Management: The Alto Tietê River Basin, São Paulo, Brazil." Working paper 3650, World Bank Policy, Washington, D.C.

———. 2008. "Institutional and Policy Analysis of Decentralization of Water Resources Management in Ceará State: The Case of the Jaguaribe River Basin." Paper presented at the 4th National Conference of the Associação Nacional de Pesquisa e Pós-Graduação em Ambiente e Sociedade, Brasília, June 4–6.

Formiga Johnsson, Rosa Maria, Lori Kumler, and Maria Carmen Lemos. 2007. "The Politics of Bulk Water Pricing in Brazil: Lessons from the Paraíba do Sul Basin." *Water Policy* 9: 87–104.

Formiga Johnsson, Rosa Maria, and Paula Duarte Lopes, eds. 2003. *Projeto Marca d´Água: Seguindo as mudanças na gestão das bacias hidrográficas do Brasil, Caderno 1, Retratos 3x4 das bacias pesquisadas.* Brasília: Finatec.

Fracalanza, Ana Paula. 2006. "Modelos de gestão das águas: O caso do sistema Cantareira (São Paulo—Brasil)." Paper presented at the 3rd National Conference of the Associação Nacional de Pesquisa e Pós-Graduação em Ambiente e Sociedade, Brasília, May 23–26.

Franco, Augusto de. 2001. "A reforma do estado e o terceiro setor." In *Sociedade e estado em transformação,* ed. Luiz Carlos Bresser-Pereira, Jorge Wilheim, and Lourdes Sola, 273–293. São Paulo: UNESP.

Frank, Beate. 2002. "Relatório da pesquisa efetuada na bacia da Lagoa da Conceição, Santa Catarina." Technical report, Projeto Marca d'Agua. Available at http://www.furb.br/ipa/marcadagua/biblioteca/relat/conceicao.pdf, accessed November 20, 2012.

———. 2003. "Uma historia das enchentes e seus ensinamentos." In *Enchentes na Bacia do Itajai: 20 anos de experiências,* ed. Beate Frank and Adilson Pinheiro, 15–62. Blumenau: IPA/ Edifurb.

———, ed. 2008. *Comitês de bacia sob o olhar dos seus membros*. Blumenau: FURB/Projeto Marca d'Agua.

Frank, Beate, and Noemia Bohn. 2003. "A formalização da gestão das cheias no âmbito da Bacia do Itajaí." In *Enchentes na Bacia do Itajaí: 20 anos de experiências*, ed. Beate Frank and Adilson Pinheiro, 223–236. Blumenau: IPA/Edifurb.

Frank, Beate, and Graciane Pereira. 2010. "Governing River Basins in Brazil: Analysis of Collaboration at River Basin Committees." Paper presented at the 6th National Conference of the Associação Nacional de Pesquisa e Pós-Graduação em Ambiente e Sociedade, Florianópolis, October 4.

Frank, Beate, and Lúcia Sevegnani. 2009. *Desastre de 2008 no vale do Itajaí: Agua, gente e política*. Blumenau: Comitê do Itajaí, FURB.

Friedmann, John. 1987. *Planning in the Public Domain: From Knowledge to Action*. Princeton, N.J.: Princeton University Press.

Fuks, Mario, Renato M. Perissinotto, and N. R. Souza, eds. 2004. *Democracia e participação: Os conselhos gestores do Paraná*. Curitiba: UFPR.

FUNDAP. 1989. *Sistema estadual de gestão de recursos hídricos. Vol. 2. Relatório base. Versão preliminar. Junho de 1989*. São Paulo: FUNDAP.

———. 1994. *Comitê das Bacias Hidrográficas dos Rios Piracicaba, Capivari e Jundaí: Relatório final. Outubro de 1994*. São Paulo: FUNDAP.

Fung, Archon, and Erik Olin Wright. 2003. "Countervailing Power in Empowered Participatory Governance." In *Deepening Democracy: Institutional Innovations in Empowered Participatory Governance*, ed. Archon Fung and Erik Olin Wright, 259–290. The Real Utopias Project IV. London: Verso.

Galvan, Dennis C. 2004. *The State Must Be Our Máster of Fire: How Peasants Craft Culturally Sustainable Development in Senegal*. Berkeley: University of California Press.

Gama, Ana Maria Cardoso de Freitas, ed. 2001. *Pirapama: Construindo o desenvolvimento sustentável local: Uma experiência que vale a pena conhecer e repetir*. Recife: CPRH/DFID.

———. 2002. "Comitê da Bacia Hidrográfica do Rio Pirapama no Estado de Pernambuco: Instrumento de gestão dos recursos hídricos." Technical report, Projeto Marca d'Agua. Available at http://www.furb.br/ipa/marcadagua/biblioteca/relat/pirapama.pdf, accessed November 20, 2012.

Garjulli, Rosana, João Lúcio Farias de Oliveira, Marcos André Lima da Cunha, and Edecarlos Rulim de Souza. 2003. "Jaguaribe." In *Projeto Marca d´Água: Seguindo as mudanças na gestão das bacias hidrográficas do Brasil, Caderno 1, Retratos 3x4 das bacias pesquisadas*, ed. Rosa Maria Formiga Johnsson and Paula Duarte Lopes, 42–46. Brasília: Finatec.

Garrido, Raymundo. 2000. "Considerações sobre a formação de preços para a cobrança pelo uso da água no Brasil." In *A cobrança pelo uso da Água*, ed. Antônio Carlos de Mendes Thame, 57–92. São Paulo: Instituto de Qualificação e Editoração (IQUAL).

Garrido, Alberto, and Javier Calatrava. 2010. "Agricultural Water Pricing—EU and Mexico." OECD. Available at http://www.oecd.org/eu/45015101.pdf, accessed November 20, 2012.

Gay, Robert. 1990. "Community Organization and Clientelist Politics in Contemporary Brazil: A Case Study from Suburban Rio de Janeiro." *International Journal of Urban and Regional Research* 14 (4): 648–666.

Geddes, Barbara. 1994. *Politician's Dilemma: Building State Capacity in Latin America*. Berkeley: University of California Press.

Giddens, Anthony. 1984. *The Constitution of Society: Outline of the Theory of Structuration*. Berkeley: University of California Press.

Goldemberg, José. 1978. "Brazil: Energy Options and Current Outlook." *Science* 200 (4338): 158–164.

Grindle, Merilee S. 2000. "The Social Agenda and the Politics of Reform in Latin America." In *Social Development in Latin America: The Politics of Reform*, ed. Joseph S. Tulchin and Allison M. Garland, 17–54. Boulder, Colo.: Lynne Rienner.

Grodzins, Morton. 1966. *The American System: A New View of Government in the United States.* New Brunswick, N.J.: Transaction.

Gruben, Anna, Paula Duarte Lopes, and Rosa Maria Formiga Johnsson. 2002. "Projeto Marca d'Água Fase I: Relatório da bacia do Rio Paraíba do Sul." Technical report, Projeto Marca d'Agua. Available at http://www.furb.br/ipa/marcadagua/biblioteca/relat/paraiba_sul. pdf, accessed November 20, 2012.

Grupo Técnico Científico. 2009. *Plano integrado de prevenção e mitigação de desastres naturais na bacia hidrográfica do Rio Itajaí.* Santa Catarina: Secretaria de Estado do Desenvolvimento Econômico Sustentável/FAPESC.

Gutiérrez, Ricardo A. 2006a. "Between Knowledge and Politics: State Water Management Reform In Brazil." Doctoral diss. (political science), Johns Hopkins University.

——. 2006b. "Comitê Gravataí: Gestão participativa da água no Rio Grande do Sul." *Lua Nova* 69: 79–121.

——. 2009. "When Experts Do Politics: Introducing Water Policy Reform in Brazil." *Governance* 23 (1): 59–88.

Haas, Peter M. 1992. "Introduction: Epistemic Communities and International Policy Coordination." *International Organization* 46 (1): 1–35.

Hajer, Maarten A. 2005. "Coalitions, Practices, and Meaning in Environmental Politics: From Acid Rain to BSE." In *Discourse Theory in European Politics: Identity, Policy, and Governance*, ed. David R. Howarth and Jacob Torfing, 297–315. New York: Palgrave Macmillan.

Hajer, Maarten A., and Hendrik Wagenaar. 2003. *Deliberative Policy Analysis: Understanding Governance in the Network Society.* Cambridge, U.K.: Cambridge University Press.

Hamaguchi, Nobuaki. 2002. "Will the Market Keep Brazil Lit Up? Ownership and Market Structural Changes in the Electric Power Sector." *Developing Economies* 40 (4): 522–552.

Haugaard, Mark. 2003. "Reflections on Seven Ways of Creating Power." *European Journal of Social Theory* 6 (1): 87–113.

Hay, Colin. 2006. "Constructivist Institutionalism." In *The Oxford Handbook of Political Institutions*, ed. R. A. W. Rhodes, Sahah A. Binder, and Bert A. Rockman, 56–74. Oxford, U.K.: Oxford University Press.

Helmke, Gretchen, and Steven Levitsky. 2004. "Informal Institutions and Comparative Politics: A Research Agenda." *Perspectives on Politics* 2 (4): 725–740.

Hill, Michael James. 2009. *The Public Policy Process*, 5th ed. Harlow, U.K.: Pearson Education.

Hirschman, Albert O. 1970. *Exit, Voice, and Loyalty: Responses to Decline in Firms, Organizations, and States.* Cambridge Mass.: Harvard University Press.

——.1973. *Journeys Towards Progress: Studies of Economic Policy-Making in Latin America.* New York: W. W. Norton.

——.1977. *The Passions and the Interests: Political Arguments for Capitalism before its Triumph.* Princeton: Princeton University Press.

——.1982. *Shifting Involvements: Private Interest and Public Action.* Princeton: Princeton University Press.

——.1984. *Getting Ahead Collectively: Grassroots Experiments in Latin America.* New York: Pergamon Press.

——. 1985. *A Bias for Hope: Essays on Development and Latin America.* Boulder, Colo.: Westview.

Hochstetler, Kathryn, and Margaret E. Keck. 2007. *Greening Brazil: Environmental Activism in State and Society.* Durham, N.C.: Duke University Press.

Hodgson, Stephen. 2004. *Land and Water: The Rights Interface.* Rome: United Nations Food and Agriculture Organization.

Holston, James. 2008. *Insurgent Citizenship: Disjunctions of Democracy and Modernity in Brazil.* Princeton, N.J.: Princeton University Press.

Hooghe, Liesbet, and Gary Marks. 2001. *Multi-level Governance and European Integration.* Oxford, U.K.: Rowman & Littlefield.

Huitema, Dave, and Sander Meijerink, eds. 2009. *Water Policy Entrepreneurs: A Research Companion to Water Transitions around the Globe.* Cheltenham, U.K.: Edward Elgar.

IBGE, Instituto Brasileiro de Geografia e Estatística. 2009. "Pesquisa de informações básicas municipais." Brasília. Available at http://www.ibge.gov.br/home/estatistica/economia/perfilmunic/2009/default.sht, accessed January 29, 2012.

Ingram, Helen. 1977. "Policy Implementation through Bargaining: The Case of Federal Grants-in-Aid." *Public Policy* 25 (4): 499–526.

International Conference on Water and the Environment. 1992. The Dublin Statement. Dublin, Ireland. Available at http://www.inpim.org/files/Documents/DublinStatmt.pdf, accessed January 19, 2010.

Ioris, Antonio A. R. 2008. "Os limites políticos de uma reforma incompleta: A implementação da lei dos recursos hídricos na bacia do Paraíba do Sul." *Revista Brasileira de Estudos Urbanos e Regionais* 10 (1): 61–85.

———. 2009. "Water Reforms in Brazil: Opportunities and Constraints." *Journal of Environmental Planning and Management* 52 (6): 813–832.

IPEA, Instituto de Pesquisa Econômica Aplicada. 2005. *Brasil: O estado de uma nação.* Brasília: Ministério de Planejamento, Orçamento e Gestão/IPEA.

———. 2010. *Estado, instituições e democracia: Republica.* Fortalecimento do estado, das instituições e da democracia (book 9, vol. 1). Brasília: IPEA.

ISA, Instituto Sócioambiental. 2005. "Uma lei em conta-gotas." São Paulo: ISA. Available at http://www.socioambiental.org/esp/agua/pgn/otrechosulemananciais.html, accessed March 3, 2010.

Jabko, Nicolas. 2012. *Playing the Market: A Political Strategy for Uniting Europe, 1985–2005.* Ithaca, N.Y.: Cornell University Press.

Jenkins-Smith, Hank C., and Paul A. Sabatier. 2003. "The Study of Public Policy Processes." In *The Nation's Health,* ed. Philip Randolph Lee, Carroll L. Estes, and Fátima M. Rodríguez, 135–144. London: Jones & Bartlett Learning.

Joas, Hans. 1996. *The Creativity of Action.* Chicago: University of Chicago Press.

Johnson, Nancy, Helle Munk Ravnborg, Olaf Westermann, and Kirsten Probst. 2002. "User Participation in Watershed Management and Research." *Water Policy* 3 (6): 507–520.

Jones, Charles O. 1975. *Clean Air: The Policies and Politics of Pollution Control.* Pittsburgh, Pa.: University of Pittsburgh Press.

Jordan, Andrew, Rüdiger K. W. Wurzel, and Anthony Zito. 2005. "The Rise of 'New' Policy Instruments in Comparative Perspective: Has Governance Eclipsed Government?" *Political Studies* 53 (3): 477–496.

Jornal Manuelzão. 2004. "Em 2010, vou navegar, pescar e nadar no Rio das Velhas." *Jornal Manuelzão,* supp., November.

Keck, Margaret E. 1989. "The New Unionism in the Brazilian Transition." In *Democratizing Brazil,* ed. Alfred Stepan, 252–296. New York: Oxford University Press.

———. 1992. *The Workers' Party and Democratization in Brazil.* New Haven, Conn.: Yale University Press.

———. 2002. "'Water, Water, Everywhere, nor Any Drop to Drink': Land Use and Water Policy in São Paulo, Brazil." In *Livable Cities? Urban Struggles for Livelihood and Sustainability,* ed. Peter B. Evans, 162–194. Berkeley: University of California Press.

Keck, Margaret E., and Kathryn Sikkink. 1998. *Activists beyond Borders: Advocacy Networks in International Politics.* Ithaca, N.Y.: Cornell University Press.

Kelman, Jerson. 2000. "Outorga e cobrança de recursos hídricos." In *A cobrança pelo uso da água*, ed. Antonio Carlos de Mendes Thame, 93–114. São Paulo: Instituto de Qualificação e Editoração (IQUAL).

Kleemans, Ineke J. M. 2008. "Shifting Governance in River Basin Management: Water Allocation in the São Francisco Basin and the Role of River Basin Committees in Brazil." Master's thesis (international land and water management and water management in rural development), Wageningen University and Institut des Région Chaudes.

Kolko, Gabriel. 1965. *Railroads and Regulation, 1877–1916*. Princeton, N.J.: Princeton University Press.

Lalonde, Jennifer. 2005. "Sustaining Collective Management of Environmental Resources: A Case Study of the Pirapama Basin Committee in Pernambuco, Brazil." Unpublished paper, Johns Hopkins University.

Landim, Leilah. 1993. "A invenção das ONGs: Do serviço invisível à profissão impossível." Doctoral diss. (social anthropology), Museu Nacional and Universidade Federal do Rio de Janeiro.

Lane, David, and Robert Maxfield. 1996. "Strategy under Complexity: Fostering Generative Relationships." *Long Range Planning* 29 (2): 215–231.

Latour, Bruno. 1986. "The Powers of Association." In *Power, Action and Belief: A New Sociology of Knowledge?* ed. John Law, 264–280. London: Routledge & Kegan Paul.

———. 1996. *ARAMIS or the Love of Technology*. Cambridge, Mass.: Harvard University Press.

Latour, Bruno, and Jean-Pierre Le Bourhis. 1995. " 'Donnez-moi de la bonne politique et je vous donnerai de la bonne eau…' : Rapport provisoire sur la mise en place des CLE pour le compte de la direction de l'eau du Ministère de l'Environnement." Paris: Centre de Sociologie de l'Innovation, Ecole Nationale Supérieure des Mines.

Lave, Jean, and Etienne Wenger. 1991. *Situated Learning: Legitimate Peripheral Participation*. Cambridge, U.K.: Cambridge University Press.

Lawrence, Thomas B., and Roy Suddaby. 2006. "1.6 Institutions and Institutional Work." In *The Sage Handbook of Organization Studies*, ed. Stewart R. Clegg, Cynthia Hardy, Tom Lawrence, and Walter R. Nord, 215–254. London: Sage.

Lawrence, Thomas B., Roy Suddaby, and Bernard Leca. 2009. "Introduction: Theorizing and Studying Institutional Work." In *Institutional Work: Actors and Agency in Institutional Studies of Organization*, ed. Thomas B Lawrence, Roy Suddaby, and Bernard Leca, 1–27. Cambridge, U.K.: Cambridge University Press.

Leach, William D., and Neil W. Pelkey. 2001. "Making Watershed Partnerships Work: A Review of the Empirical Literature." *Journal of Water Resources Planning and Management* 127 (6): 378–385.

Leal, Ione Oliveira Jatobá. 2004. "Avaliação do processo de gestão participativa de recursos hídricos na bacia do Rio Itapicuru: O caso da microrregião de Jacobina." Master's thesis (sustainable development), Universidade de Brasília.

Lemos, Maria Carmen, and João Lúcio Farias Oliveira. 2004. "Can Water Reform Survive Politics? Institutional Change and River Basin Management in Ceará, Northeast Brazil." *World Development* 32 (12): 2121–2137.

Levitsky, Steven, and María Victoria Murillo. 2005. "Conclusion: Theorizing about Weak Institutions: Lessons from the Argentine Case." In *Argentine Democracy: The Politics of Institutional Weakness*, ed. Steven Levitsky and María Victoria Murillo, 269–290. University Park: Pennsylvania State University Press.

Levitsky, Steven, and Lucan Way. 2010. *Competitive Authoritarianism: Hybrid Regimes after the Cold War*. New York: Cambridge University Press.

Liberato Júnior, Guarim. 2004. "O caminho das águas: Das sociedades de vala ao comitê da bacia: O estudo sobre os modos de apropriação da água no meio rural do Vale do Itajaí." Master's thesis (political sociology), Universidade Federal de Santa Catarina.

Limongi, Fernando, and Argelina Figueiredo. 1998. "Bases Institucionais do Presidencialismo de Coalizão." *Lua Nova* 44: 82–105.

Lin, Nan. 2001. *Social Capital: A Theory of Social Structure and Action.* Cambridge, U.K.: Cambridge University Press.

Lisboa, Apolo Heringer. 2010. "Projeto Manuelzão/UFMG: As bases conceituais da Meta 2010 e 2014 para o Rio das Velhas." *Revista Manuelzão* 18 (August). Available at http://www. manuelzao.ufmg.br/comunicacao/noticias/projeto-manuelz%C3%A3oufmg-as-bases-conceituais-da-meta-2010-e-2014-para-o-rio-das-velhas?searched=meta+2010&advse arch=allwords&highlight=ajaxSearch_highlight+ajaxSearch_highlight1+ajaxSearch_ highlight2, accessed January 14, 2011.

Lopes, Paula Duarte. 2003. "Bacias dos Rios Piracicaba, Capivari e Jundiaí." In *Projeto Marca d´Água: Seguindo as mudanças na gestão das bacias hidrográficas do Brasil, Caderno 1, Retratos 3x4 das bacias pesquisadas,* ed. Rosa Maria Formiga Johnsson and Paula Duarte Lopes, 123–128. Brasília: FINATEC.

Loureiro, Maria Rita. 1997. *Os economistas no governo: Gestão econômica e democracia.* Rio de Janeiro: Fundação Getúlio Vargas.

Lubell, Mark, Paul A. Sabatier, Arnold Vedlitz, Will Focht, Zev Trachtenberg, and Marty Matlock. 2005. "Conclusions and Recommendations." In *Swimming Upstream: Collaborative Approaches to Watershed Management,* ed. Paul A. Sabatier, Will Focht, Mark Lubell, Zev Trachtenberg, Arnold Vedlitz, and Marty Matlock, 261–296. Cambridge, Mass.: MIT Press.

Lüchmann, Ligia Helena Hahn. 2002. "Possibilidades e limites da democracia delibera-tiva: A experiência do orçamento participativo de Porto Alegre." Doctoral diss. (social sciences), Universidade Estadual de Campinas.

Lukes, Steven. 2005. *Power: A Radical View,* 2d ed. New York: Palgrave MacMillan.

Lund, Christian. 2006. "Twilight Institutions: Public Authority and Local Politics in Africa." *Development and Change* 37 (4): 685–705.

Mafra, Rennan. 2011. "Relações públicas e mobilização social: A construção estratégica de dimensões comunicativas." Paper presented at the 5th Conferencia da Associação Brasileira de Pesquisadores de Comunicação Organizacional e Relações Públicas (Abrapcorp), São Paulo, May 5–8.

Mahoney, James. 2001. *The Legacies of Liberalism: Path Dependence and Political Regimes in Central America.* Baltimore, Md.: Johns Hopkins University Press.

Mahoney, James, and Kathleen Ann Thelen. 2010. "A Theory of Gradual Institutional Change." In *Explaining Institutional Change: Ambiguity, Agency, and Power,* ed. James Mahoney and Kathleen Ann Thelen, 1–37. New York: Cambridge University Press.

Mairinque, Carolina de Souza Scott. 2010. "Informação, redes sociais e a construção de políticas públicas para o meio ambiente em Minas Gerais: A (re)configuração discursiva da Meta 2010." Master's thesis (information sciences), Universidade Federal de Minas Gerais.

Mais, Ivanir. 2001. "Projeto Marca d'Água: Relatórios preliminares 2001: A bacia do Rio Itajaí, Santa Catarina—2001." Available at http://www.furb.br/ipa/marcadagua/biblioteca/ relat/itajai.pdf, accessed November 20, 2012.

Mann, Michael. 1993. *The Sources of Social Power: The Rise of Classes and Nation-States, 1760–1914,* vol. 2. New York: Cambridge University Press.

March, James G., and Johan P. Olsen. 1989. *Rediscovering Institutions: The Organizational Basis of Politics.* New York: Simon & Schuster.

MARE, Ministério da Administração Federal e Reforma do Estado. 1995. *Plano diretor da reforma do aparelho estado.* Brasília: Presidência da República/Imprensa Oficial.

Marques, Eduardo Cesar. 2000. *Estado e redes sociais: Permeabilidade e coesão nas políticas urbanas no Rio de Janeiro.* São Paulo: Revan.

Martinez, Francisco, Jr., and Francisco Carlos Castro Lahoz. 2007. "A Cobrança pelo uso da água nas bacias hidrográficas do Piracicaba, Capivari e Jundiaí: Aplicação e perspectivas."

Paper presented at the 17th Simpósio Brasileiro de Recursos Hídricos, São Paulo, November 25–29.

Martins, Carlos Estevam. 1987. "Uma estratégia para a polítização da questão dos recursos hídricos." *Revista Águas e Energia Elétrica* 4 (12): 48–51.

Martins, Luciano. 1997. "Reforma da Administração Pública e Cultura Política no Brasil: Uma Visão Geral." *Cadernos ENAP* 8: 1–57.

Mascarenhas, Ana Cristina Monteiro. 2008. "Conflitos e gestão de águas: O caso da bacia hidrográfica do Rio São Francisco." Master's thesis (sustainable development), University of Brasília.

Massey, Doreen, John Allen, and Philip Sarre, eds. 1999. *Human Geography Today*. Cambridge, U.K.: Polity Press.

Mazmanian, Daniel A., and Paul A. Sabatier. 1981. *Effective Policy Implementation*. Lexington, Mass.: Lexington Books.

McAdam, Doug, John D. McCarthy, and Mayer N. Zald. 1996. *Comparative Perspectives on Social Movements: Political Opportunities, Mobilizing Structures, and Cultural Framings*. New York: Cambridge University Press.

McAdam, Doug, Sidney G. Tarrow, and Charles Tilly. 2001. *Dynamics of Contention*. Cambridge, U.K.: Cambridge University Press.

McAllister, Lesley. 2008. *Making Law Matter: Environmental Protection and Legal Institutions in Brazil*. Stanford, Calif.: Stanford University Press.

Medeiros, Yvonilde. 2007. "Processo de construção do plano da bacia do Rio São Francisco." *Revista do Comitê da Bacia Hidrográfica do Rio São Francisco* 1 (September): 15–22.

Meijerink, Sander, and Dave Huitema. 2010. "Policy Entrepreneurs and Change Strategies: Lessons from Sixteen Case Studies of Water Transitions around the Globe." *Ecology and Society* 15: 2. Available at http://www.ecologyandsociety.org/vol15/iss2/art21/, accessed April 3, 2013.

Melo, Marcus André. 2002. *Reformas Constitucionais no Brasil: Instituições políticas e processo decisório*. Rio de Janeiro: Editora Revan.

Menand, Louis, ed. 1997. *Pragmatism: A Reader*. New York: Vintage.

Meyer, John W., and Brian Rowan. 1977. "Institutionalized Organizations: Formal Structure as Myth and Ceremony." *American Journal of Sociology* 83 (2): 340–363.

Migdal, Joel S. 2001. *State in Society: Studying How States and Societies Transform and Constitute One Another*. New York: Cambridge University Press.

Ministério do Meio Ambiente, Secretaria de Recursos Hídricos. 2000. "PROÁGUA SEMI-ARIDO, Oficina temática. Gestão participativa dos recursos hídricos, estado da arte" (versão preliminar). December.

Mische, Ann. 2009. *Partisan Publics: Communication and Contention across Brazilian Youth Activist Networks*. Princeton, N.J.: Princeton University Press.

Mody, Jyothsna. 2004. "Achieving Accountability through Decentralization: Lessons for Integrated River Basin Management." Policy Research Working Paper 3346, Washington, D.C., World Bank, Agricultural and Rural Development Department.

Molle, François. 2007. "Scales and Power in River Basin Management: The Chao Phraya River in Thailand." *Geographical Journal* 173 (4): 358–373.

——. 2008. "Nirvana Concepts, Narratives and Policy Models: Insights from the Water Sector." *Water Alternatives* 1 (1): 131–156.

Molle, François, and J. Berkoff, eds. 2007. *Irrigation Water Pricing Policy: The Gap between Theory and Practice*. Wallingford, U.K.: CAB International. Available at http://www.iwmi.cgiar.org/Publications/CABI_Publications/CA_CABI_Series/Water_Pricing/protected/, accessed on April 3, 2013.

Molle, François, and Philippus Wester. 2009. "River Basin Trajectories: An Inquiry into Changing Waterscapes." In *River Basin Trajectories: Societies, Environments and Development*, ed.

François Molle and Philippus Wester, 1–19. Comprehensive Assessment of Water Management in Agriculture, vol. 8. Wallingford, U.K.: CAB International.

Montpetit, Éric. 2002. "Policy Networks, Federal Arrangements, and the Development of Environental Regulations: A Comparison of the Canadian and American Agricultural Sectors." *Governance: An International Journal of Policy, Administration and Institutions* 15 (1): 1–20.

Morais, Lecio A. M. de. 2004. "*O processo de escolha da política monetária em 1999: Idéias econômicas e a tendência à homogeneização em políticas monetárias*" Master's thesis (political science), Universidade de Brasília.

Moreira, Maria Manuela M. A. 2010. "A atuação dos governos estaduais nos comitês de bacia." In *Água e política: Atores, instituições e poder nos organismos colegiados de bacia hidrográfica no Brasil*, ed. Rebecca Abers, 137–158. São Paulo: Annablume.

Moretti, Luiz Roberto, and Wilde Cardoso Gontijo. 2005. "Conciliação de conflito dentro da política brasileira de recursos hídricos: O caso do sistema Cantareira." Paper presented at the 16th Simpósio Brasileiro de Recursos Hídricos, João Pessoa, November 20–24.

Moroni, J. A., and Alexandre Ciconello. 2005. "Participação social no governo Lula: Avançamos?" In *A Abong nas conferências 2005—Criança e adolescente—Assistência social*, ed. Alexandre Ciconello, José Antônio Morni, José Fernando da Silva, and Rosângela Paz, 31–54. Brasília: Abong, 2005.

Mortatti, Jefferson, Milton José Bortoletto Júnior, Luiz Carlos Eduardo Milde, and Jean-Luc Probs. 2004. "Hidrologia dos Rios Tietê e Piracicaba: Séries temporais de vazão e hidrogramas de cheia." *Revista de Ciência & Tecnologia* 12 (23): 55–67.

Needleman, Martin L., and Carolyn Emerson Needleman. 1974. *Guerrillas in the Bureaucracy: The Community Planning Experiment in the United States*. New York: Wiley.

Nelson, Julie A. 2003. "Confronting the Science/Value Split: Notes on Feminist Economics, Institutionalism, Pragmatism and Process Thought." *Cambridge Journal of Economics* 27 (1): 49–64.

Neri, Marcelo Cortes. 2010. *A nova classe média: O lado brilhante dos pobres*. Rio de Janeiro: Fundação Getúlio Vargas. Available at http://www.fgv.br/cps/ncm/, accessed January 9, 2012.

Neves, Marcelo J. M. 2004. "Efetividade dos planos de recursos hídricos: Uma análise dos casos no Brasil após 1990." Master's thesis (environmental technology and water resources), Universidade de Brasília.

Nicolini, Davide. 2009. "Zooming In and Zooming Out: A Package of Method and Theory to Study Work Practices." In *Organizational Ethnography: Studying the Complexities of Everyday Life*, ed. Sierk Ybema, Dvora Yanow, Harry Wels, and Frans Kamsteeg, 120–138. London: Sage.

Nunes Leal, Vitor. 1948. *Coronelismo, enxada e voto: O municipio e o regime representativo no Brasil*. Rio de Janeiro: Forense.

O'Donnell, Guillermo A. 1973. *Modernization and Bureaucratic-Authoritarianism: Studies in South American Politics*. Berkeley: Institute of International Studies, University of California.

———. 1993. "On the State, Democratization, and Some Conceptual Problems: A Latin American View with Some Postcommunist Countries." *World Development* 21 (8): 1355–1369.

———. 1999. "Polyarchies and the (Un)rule of Law in Latin America: A Partial Conclusion." In *The (Un)rule of Law and the Underprivileged in Latin America*, ed. Juan E. Mendez, Guillermo A. O'Donnell, and Paulo Sérgio Pinheiro, 303–337. Notre Dame, Ind.: University of Notre Dame Press.

Ohira, Aline. 2010. "Uma trajetória de mudança: Idéias, instituições e a reforma da política de gestão de recursos hídricos no Paraná." Master's thesis (political science), Universidade de Brasília.

Oliver, Pamela E., and Daniel J. Myers. 2002. "The Coevolution of Social Movements." *Mobilization* 8 (1): 1–24.

O'Neill, Kate, Jorg Balsiger, and Stacy VanDeveer. 2004. "Actors, Norms and Impact: International Cooperation Theory and the Influence of the Agent-Structure Debate." *Annual Review of Political Science* 7: 149–175.

Ostrom, Elinor. 1990. *Governing the Commons: The Evolution of Institutions for Collective Action.* Cambridge, U.K.: Cambridge University Press.

Ostrom, Vincent, Robert Bish, and Elinor Ostrom. 1988. *Local Government in the United States.* San Francisco, Calif.: ICS Press.

Owen-Smith, Jason, and Walter W. Powell. 2008. "Networks and Institutions." In *The Sage Handbook of Organizational Institutionalism,* ed. Royston Greenwood, Christine Oliver, Roy Suddaby, and Kerstin Sahlin-Andersson, 594–621. London: Sage.

Padgett, John F., and Christopher K. Ansell. 1993. "Robust Action and the Rise of the Medici, 1400–1434." *American Journal of Sociology* 98 (6): 1259–1319.

Pagnoccheschi, Bruno. 2000. "A politica de recursos hídricos no Brasil na década de 90 e a fragmentação do estado." Doctoral diss. proposal (sustainable development), University of Brasília.

Parkinson, John, and Jane Mansbridge, eds. 2012. *Deliberative Systems: Deliberative Democracy at the Large Scale.* New York: Cambridge University Press.

Pereira, Carlos, Timothy Power, and Lucio R. Rennó. 2008. "Agenda Power, Executive Decree Authority, and the Mixed Results of Reform in the Brazilian Congress." *Legislative Studies Quarterly* 33 (1): 5–33.

Pereira, Dilma Seli Pena, and Rosa Maria Formiga Johnsson. 2003. *Governabilidade dos recursos hídricos no Brasil: A implementação dos instrumentos de gestão na bacia do Rio Paraíba do Sul.* Brasília: Agência Nacional de Águas.

Pereira, Graciane Regina, Inez Zatz, and Beate Frank. 2008. *Relatório da oficina "refletindo o comitê do Gravataí" (22/4/2008).* Blumenau: Watermark Project.

Pereira, José de Sena. 1997. *Vetos presidenciais à lei no 9.433, de 08 de janeiro de 1997: Política nacional de recursos hídricos.* Brasília: Câmara dos Deputados.

Pereira, Luiz Firmino Martins. 2007. "As territorialidades que emergem na gestão das águas: Um caminho para a agenda 21." Doctoral diss. (geography), Universidade Federal Fluminense.

Pereira, Luiz Firmino Martins, and Samuel Barreto. 2009. "Recovery with Social Participation— The Experience of Lagos São João Consortium, RJ, Brazil." *IOP Conference Series: Earth and Environmental Science* 6. Available at http://iopscience.iop.org/1755-1315/6/40/402007/pdf/ees9_6_402007.pdf, accessed November 17, 2012.

Pierson, Paul. 2000. "Increasing Returns, Path Dependence, and the Study of Politics." *American Political Science Review* 94 (2): 251–267.

———. 2004. *Politics in Time: History, Institutions, and Social Analysis.* Princeton, N.J.: Princeton University Press.

Pinheiro, Armando C. 2000. "The Brazilian Privatization Experience: What's Next?" Working Paper 87, Rio de Janeiro, BNDES. Available at http://www.bndes.gov.br/SiteBNDES/export/sites/default/bndes_en/Galerias/Download/studies/td87i.pdf, accessed April 3, 2013.

Podolny, Joel M., and Karen L. Page. 1998. "Network Forms of Organization." *Annual Review of Sociology* 24: 57–76.

Pontifical Council for Justice and Peace. 2004. *Compendium of the Social Doctrine of the Church.* Vatican City: USCCB Publishing.

Power, Timothy J. 2010. "Optimism, Pessimism, and Coalitional Presidentialism: Debating the Institutional Design of Brazilian Democracy." *Bulletin of Latin American Research* 29 (1): 18–33.

Pressman, Jeffrey L., and Aaron Wildavsky. 1984. *Implementation: How Great Expectations in Washington Are Dashed in Oakland; Or, Why It's Amazing That Federal Programs Work at All, This Being a Saga of the Economic Development Administration as Told by Two Sympathetic Observers Who Seek to Build Morals on a Foundation.* Berkeley: University of California Press.

Putnam, Robert D., Robert Leonardi, and Raffaella Y. Nanetti. 1993. *Making Democracy Work: Civic Traditions in Modern Italy.* Princeton, N.J.: Princeton University Press.

Queiroz, Bernardo L., and André B. Golgher, 2008. "Human Capital Differentials across Municipalities and States in Brazil." *Population Review* 47 (2): 25–49.

Ragin, Charles C. 1994. "An Introduction to Qualitative Comparative Analysis." In *The Comparative Political Economy of the Welfare State,* ed. Thomas Janoski and Alexander M. Hicks, 299–319. Cambridge, U.K.: Cambridge University Press.

——. 2000. *Fuzzy-Set Social Science.* Chicago: University of Chicago Press.

Rahaman, Muhammad Mizanur, and Olli Varis. 2005. "Integrated Water Resources Management: Evolution, Prospects and Future Challenges." *Sustainability: Science, Practice, & Policy* 1 (1). Available at http://ejournal.nbii.org/archives/vol1iss1/0407-03.rahaman.pdf, accessed January 19, 2010.

Ramos, Marilene. 2007. "Gestão de recursos hídricos e cobrança pelo uso da água." Available at http://www.eclac.cl/dmaah/noticias/paginas/9/28579/Cobrancapelousoda.pdf, accessed September 20, 2011.

Raustiala, Kai, and David G. Victor. 2004. "The Regime Complex for Plant Genetic Resources." *International Organization* 58 (2): 277–309.

Rhodes, R. A. W. 1997. *Understanding Governance: Policy Networks, Governance, Reflexivity, and Accountability.* Buckingham, U.K.: Open University Press.

——. 2006. "Policy Network Analysis." In *The Oxford Handbook of Public Policy,* ed. Michael Moran, Martin Rein, and Robert E. Goodin, 425–447. Oxford, U.K.: Oxford University Press.

Ribeiro, César Augusto Oliveira. 2006. "Participação social e a gestão de recursos hídricos na Bahia: Estudo de caso da bacia hidrográfica do Rio Itapicuru." Master's thesis (administration), Universidade Federal da Bahia.

Ridenti, Marcelo. 2008. "Desenvolvimentismo: O retorno." Paper presented at the 36th Encontro Nacional de Economia da Associação Nacional de Centros de Pós-Graduação em Economia (ANPEC), Salvador, December 9–12.

Rigotti, José Irineu Rangel. 2001. "A transição da escolaridade no Brasil e as desigualdades regionais." *Revista Brasileira de Estudos da População* 18 (1–2): 59–73.

Risse-Kappen, Thomas. 1996. "Ideas Do Not Float Freely: Transnational Coalitions, Domestic Structures, and the End of the Cold War." In *International Relations Theory and the End of the Cold War,* ed. Ned Lebow and Thomas Risse-Kappen, 187–222. New York: Columbia University Press.

Rodrigues, Leôncio Martins. 1990. *Partidos e sindicatos: Escritos de sociologia política.* São Paulo: Ática.

Rose, Nikolas, and Peter Miller. 1992. "Political Power beyond the State: Problematics of Government." *American Journal of Sociology* 43 (2): 173–205.

Sabatier, Paul A. 1986. "Top-Down and Bottom-Up Approaches to Implementation Research: A Critical Analysis and Suggested Synthesis." *Journal of Public Policy* 6 (1): 21–48.

——. 1987. "Knowledge, Policy-Oriented Learning, and Policy Change." *Science Communication* 8 (4): 649–692.

——. 1999. "The Need for Better Theories." In *Theories of the Policy Process,* ed. Paul A. Sabatier, 3–17. Boulder, Colo.: Westview.

Sabatier, Paul A., Will Focht, Mark Lubell, Zev Trachtenberg, Arnold Vedlitz, and Marty Matlock, eds. 2005. *Swimming Upstream: Collaborative Approaches to Watershed Management.* Cambridge, Mass.: MIT Press.

Sabatier, Paul A., and Hank C. Jenkins-Smith, eds. 1993. *Policy Change and Learning: An Advocacy Coalition Approach.* Boulder, Colo.: Westview.

Sabel, Charles, and Jonathan Zeitlin. 2012. "Experimentalist Governance." In *The Oxford Handbook of Governance,* ed. David Levi-Faur, 169–184. Oxford, U.K.: Oxford University Press.

Santoro, Wayne A., and Gail M. McGuire. 1997. "Social Movement Insiders: The Impact of Institutional Activists on Affirmative Action and Comparable Worth Policies." *Social Problems* 44: 503–519.

Santos, Boaventura de Sousa. 1998. "Participatory Budgeting in Porto Alegre: Toward a Redistributive Democracy." *Politics and Society* 26 (4): 461–510.

Santos, Wanderley Guilherme dos. 2006. *O Ex-leviatã brasileiro: Do voto disperso ao clientelismo concentrado.* São Paulo: Civilização Brasileira.

Santos Júnior, Orlando Alves dos, Sergio Azevedo, and Luiz Cesar de Queiroz Ribeiro. 2004. "Democracia e gestão local: A experiência dos conselhos municipais no brasil." In *Governança Democrática e Poder Local: A Experiência Dos Conselhos Municipais No Brasil,* ed. Orlando Alves dos Santos Júnior, Luis Cesar de Queiroz Ribeiro, and Sergio Azevedo, 11–56. Rio de Janeiro: Revan.

Saward, Michael. 2006. "The Representative Claim." *Contemporary Political Theory* 5: 297–318.

Scherer-Warren, Ilse. 1993. *Redes de Movimentos Sociais.* Florianópolis: Edições Loyola.

Schmidt, Vivian. 2008. "Discursive Institutionalism: The Explanatory Power of Ideas and Discourse." *Annual Review of Political Science* 11 (1): 303–326.

Schneider, Ben Ross. 1992. *Politics within the State: Elite Bureaucrats and Industrial Policy in Authoritarian Brazil.* Pittsburgh, Pa.: University of Pittsburgh Press.

Schwartzman, Simon. 2010. "Benchmarking Secondary Education in Brazil." Paper presented at the International Seminar on Best Practices of Secondary Education (IDB/OCED/ Ministry of Education), Brasília, May 3–4. Available at http://www.drclas.harvard.edu/ files/benchmarkin2010.pdf, accessed January 29, 2012.

Scott, W. Richard, Martin Reuf, Peter J. Mendel, and Carol Caronna. 2000. *Institutional Change and Health Care Organizations.* Chicago: University of Chicago Press.

Sebastianes, Juan A. M. 1992. "Histórico das campanhas e lutas pela despoluição do Rio Piracicaba." *Consórcio Intermunicipal* 8. Piracicaba: Consórcio Intermunicipal das Bacias dos Rios Piracicaba e Capivari/DAEE/FUNDAP.

Selznick, Philip. 1957. *Leadership in Administration: A Sociological Interpretation.* New York: Harper & Row.

Seminário Técnico. 1992. *Sistema nacional de gerenciamento de recursos hídricos.* Brasília: Comissão de Defesa do Consumidor, Meio Ambiente e Minorias da Câmara de Deputados, ABRH, DAEE, Secretaria de Administração e Modernização do Serviço Público do Estado de São Paulo, FUNDAP. Transcripts.

Sepulveda, Rogério de Oliveira. 2006. "Subcomitês como proposta de descentralização da gestão das águas na bacia do rio das Velhas: O Projeto Manuelzão como fomentador." *Cadernos Manuelzão* 1 (2): 4–10.

Sewell, William H., Jr. 1992. "A Theory of Structure: Duality, Agency, and Transformation." *American Journal of Sociology* 98 (1): 1–29.

——. 2005. *Logics of History: Social Theory and Social Transformation.* Chicago: University of Chicago Press.

Sikkink, Kathryn. 1991. *Ideas and Institutions: Developmentalism in Brazil and Argentina.* Ithaca, N.Y.: Cornell University Press.

Silbey, Susan S. 1984. "The Consequences of Responsive Regulation." In *Enforcing Regulation*, ed. K. Hawkins and J. M. Thomas, 147–170. Boston, Mass.: Kluwer-Nijhoff.

Silva, Enid R. A. da. 2009. *Participação social e as conferências nacionais de políticas públicas: Reflexões sobre os avanços e desafios no período de 2003–2006*. Brasília: IPEA.

Silva, Luciano Meneses Cardoso da. 2007. "Cobrança pelo uso de recursos hídricos para diluição de efluentes." Paper presented at the 17th Simpósio Brasileiro de Recursos Hídricos, São Paulo, November 25–29.

Skidmore, Thomas. 1967. *Politics in Brazil, 1930–1964: An Experiment in Democracy*. New York: Oxford University Press.

Snowiss, Sylvia. 2003. "The Marbury of 1803 and the Modern Marbury." *Constitutional Commentary* 20: 231–254.

Sousa Júnior, Wilson Cabral. 2004. *Gestão de águas no Brasil: Reflexões, diagnósticos e desafios*. Brasília: Instituto Internacional de Educação do Brasil, Embaixada do Reino dos Países.

Souza, Celina. 2001. "Federalismo e gasto social no Brasil: Tensões e tendências." *Lua Nova* 52: 5–28.

Stark, David. 1999. "Heterarchy: Distributing Authority and Organizing Diversity." In *The Biology of Business: Decoding the Natural Laws of Enterprise*, ed. John Clippinger, 153–180. San Francisco, Calif.: Jossey-Bass.

Steinberg, Paul F. 2001. *Environmental Leadership in Developing Countries: Transnational Relations and Biodiversity Policy in Costa Rica and Bolivia*. Cambridge, Mass.: MIT Press.

Steinmo, Sven, Kathleen Thelen, and Frank Longstreth, eds. 1992. *Structuring Politics: Historical Institutionalism in Comparative Analysis*. New York: Cambridge University Press.

Stepan, Alfred. 1971. *The Military in Politics: Changing Patterns in Brazil*. Princeton, N.J.: Princeton University Press.

——. 2000. "Brazil's Decentralized Federalism: Bringing Government Closer to the Citizens?" *Daedalus* 129 (2): 145–169.

Streek, Wolfgang, and Kathleen Thelen. 2005. "Introduction: Institutional Change in Advanced Political Economies." In *Beyond Continuity: Institutional Change in Advanced Political Economies*, ed. Wolfgang Streek and Kathleen Thelen, 1–39. Oxford, U.K.: Oxford University Press.

Suchman, Lucy. 2011. "Anthropological Relocations and the Limits of Design." *Annual Review of Anthropology* 40: 1–18.

Swidler, Ann. 1986. "Culture in Action: Symbols and Strategies." *American Sociological Review* 51 (2): 273–286.

Taddei, Renzo. 2011. "Watered-Down Democratization: Modernization versus Social Participation in Water Management in Northeast Brazil." *Agriculture and Human Values* 28 (1): 109–121.

Tarrow, Sidney G. 2005. *The New Transnational Activism*. Cambridge, U.K.: Cambridge University Press.

——. 2011. *Power in Movement: Social Movements and Contentious Politics*, 3rd ed. Cambridge, U.K.: Cambridge University Press.

Tatagiba, Luciana. 2002. "Os conselhos gestores e a democratização das políticas públicas no Brasil." In *Sociedade Civil e Espaços Públicos no Brasil*, ed. Evelina Dagnino, 47–104. São Paulo: Paz e Terra.

Thelen, Kathleen. 1999. "Historical Institutionalism in Comparative Politics." *Annual Review of Political Science* 2: 369–404.

Thelen, Kathleen, and Sven Steinmo. 1992. "Historical Institutionalism in Comparative Politics." In *Structuring Politics: Historical Institutionalism in Comparative Analysis*, ed. Sven Steinmo, Kathleen Thelen, and Frank Longstreth, 1–32. New York: Cambridge University Press.

Theodoro, Hildelano Delanusse. 2011. "Planejamento e gestão participativos: A metodologia para o início da aplicação dos recursos." Available at http://www.administradores.com.br/

informe-se/artigos/planejamento-e-gestao-participativos-a-metodologia-para-inicio-da-aplicacao-dos-recursos/58901/, accessed July 3, 2012.

Thomas, J. W., and Merilee S. Grindle. 1990. "After the Decision: Implementing Policy Reforms in Developing Countries." *World Development* 18 (8): 1163–1181.

Tilly, Charles. 1984. *Big Structures, Large Processes, Huge Comparisons.* London: Russell Sage Foundation.

Tsebelis, George. 1990. *Nested Games: Rational Choice in Comparative Politics.* Berkeley: University of California Press.

———. 2002. *Veto Players: How Political Institutions Work.* Princeton, N.J.: Princeton University Press.

Viana, Luna Bouzada Flores. 2011. "Entre o abstrato e o concreto: Legados do embate sobre o projeto de integração do São Francisco ou da transposição." Master's thesis (political science), Universidade de Brasília.

Viola, Eduardo, and Mirian Goldenberg. 1992. "O movimento ambientalista no Brasil 1971–1991: Da denúncia e conscientização para a institucionalização e desenvolvimento sustentável." In *Ecologia, Ciência e Política*, ed. Eduardo Viola and Mirian Goldenberg, 49–75. Rio de Janeiro: Revan.

Viveiros, Mariana. 2003. "Sem taxa, SP deixa de receber R$ 440 mi." *Folha de São Paulo*, Cotidiano, March 11, 2003. Available at http://www1.folha.uol.com.br/fsp/cotidian/ff0311200317.htm, accessed March 12, 2010.

von Bülow, Marisa. 2010. *Building Transnational Networks: Civil Society and the Politics of Trade in the Americas.* Cambridge, U.K.: Cambridge University Press.

von Bülow, Marisa, and Rebecca Neaera Abers. 2000. "Civic Associations and the State in Brazil: Some Recent Changes in the Legal Framework and an Agenda for Research." Paper presented at the meeting of the Latin American Studies Association, Miami, March 16–18.

Wagenaar, Henrik, and Noam S. D. Cook. 2003. "Understanding Policy Practices: Action, Dialectic and Deliberation in Policy Analysis." In *Deliberative Policy Analysis: Understanding Governance in the Networks Society*, ed. Maarten A. Hajer and Hendrik Wagenaar, 139–171. Cambridge, U.K.: Cambridge University Press.

Wampler, Brian. 2007. *Participatory Budgeting in Brazil: Contestation, Cooperation, and Accountability.* University Park: Pennsyvania State University Press.

Ward, Michael D., Katherine Stovel, and Audrey Sachs. 2011. "Network Analysis and Political Science." *Annual Review of Political Science* 14: 245–264.

Warner, Jeroen, Philippus Wester, and Alex Bolding. 2008. "Going with the Flow: River Basins as the Natural Units for Water Management?" *Water Policy* 10 (S2): 121–138.

Watermark Project. 2002. *Formação dos comitês de bacia e acompanhamento das ações em 2001* [Database on river basin committee formation and activities]. Brasília: Projeto Marca d'Agua.

Watts, Duncan J. 2004. "The 'New' Science of Networks." *Annual Review of Sociology* 30: 243–270.

Weber, Max. 1968. *Economy and Society.* Edited by Guenther Roth, Claus Wittich. New York: Bedminster Press.

Wedeen, Lisa. 2002. "Conceptualizing Culture: Possibilities for Political Science." *American Political Science Review.* 96(4): 713-728.

Weffort, Francisco C. 1984. *Por quê democracia?* São Paulo: Brasiliense.

Weil, Cristiana Andrade Renato. 2007. "Rio das Velhas ganha vida." *Estado de Minas*, March 22.

Wenger, Etienne. 1998. *Communities of Practice: Learning, Meaning and Identity.* Cambridge, U.K.: Cambridge University Press.

Werner, Jann, and Kai Wegrich. 2006. "Theories of the Policy Cycle." In *Handbook of Public Policy Analysis: Theory, Politics, and Methods*, ed. Frank Fischer, Gerald J. Miller, and Mara S. Sidney, 43–62. New York: Taylor & Francis.

Weyland, Kurt G. 2002a. "Limitations of Rational-Choice Institutionalism for the Study of Latin American Politics." *Studies in Comparative International Development* 37 (1): 57–85.

———. 2002b. *The Politics of Market Reform in Fragile Democracies: Argentina, Brazil, Peru, and Venezuela*. Princeton, N.J.: Princeton University Press.

White, Harrison. 1992. *Identity and Control*. Princeton, N.J.: Princeton University Press.

Wood, Donna. J., and Barbara Gray. 1991. "Toward a Comprehensive Theory of Collaboration." *Journal of Applied Behavioral Science* 27 (2): 139–162.

World Bank. 1993. *Loan Agreement (Minas Gerais Water Quality and Pollution Control Project) between International Bank for Reconstruction and Development and State of Minas Gerais, February 1, 1993*. Washington, D.C.: World Bank.

Xavier, André Luis do Santos. 2006. "A contribuição dos comitês de bacia estadual e federal à gestão das bacias hidrográficas dos Rios Piracicaba, Capivari e Jundiaí em São Paulo: Ações mais relevantes, perspectivas e desafios (1993–2006)." Master's thesis (architecture and urbanism), Universidade de São Paulo.

Yassuda, Eduardo Riomey. 1983. "*Transcript of speech*," Seminário Internacional de Recursos Hídricos, Brasília, DNAEE/SEMA.

Yin, Robert K. 1984. *Case Study Research: Design and Methods*. London: Sage.

CPSIA information can be obtained at www.ICGtesting.com
Printed in the USA
BVOW02s0028010515

398385BV00001B/1/P

9 780199 985272